PATRICK PEARSE AND THE LOST REPUBLICAN IDEAL

Patrick Pearse, at the age of 16

PATRICK PEARSE
and the
LOST REPUBLICAN IDEAL

To John in memory of Grandma's 'Grand Tour' of Ireland — 12 . VII . 92
Paddy.

BRIAN P. MURPHY

Every good wish.

Brian Murphy osb.

Dublin
JAMES DUFFY
1991

PUBLISHED IN 1991 BY JAMES DUFFY AND COMPANY LTD.
4 LEINSTER ST., DUBLIN 2, IRELAND.

Cataloging-in-Publication Data

Murphy, Brian P.
Patrick Pearse and the Lost Republican Ideal
1. Ireland, Republicanism, History
I. Title
321.8609415

Printed in Great Britain by
Billing and Sons Ltd., Worcester

For my mother
and in memory of my father,
Dr. John Murphy

Contents

THE FOOL

——AN EXTRACT

Since the wise men have not spoken, I speak that am only
    a fool;
A fool that hath loved his folly,
Yea, more than the wise men their books or their counting
    houses, or their quiet homes,
Or their fame in men's mouths;
A fool that in all his days hath done never a prudent thing,
Never hath counted the cost, nor recked if another reaped
The fruit of his mighty sowing, content to scatter the seed;
A fool that is unrepentant, and that soon at the end of all
Shall laugh in his lonely heart as the ripe ears fall to the
    reaping-hooks
And the poor are filled that were empty,
Tho' he go hungry.

I have squandered the splendid years that the Lord God
    gave to my youth
In attempting impossible things, deeming them alone worth
    the toil.
Was it folly or grace? Not men shall judge me, but God. . . .

—— PATRICK PEARCE, 1916

Acknowledgements

Many people have helped me during the five years of my research. Ten libraries and records offices are listed in the bibliography and the staff of all those institutions was always unfailingly courteous and helpful. To the library staff of the Mary Immaculate Teacher Training College in Limerick, under the direction of John Power and John Eustace, special gratitude is due for allowing me to use their microfilm collection of Irish newspapers, and for assisting my research in so many other ways well beyond the call of duty. The names of those who have helped me in a specifically historical capacity are listed as part of the bibliography. Some of those whom I interviewed are now dead. Of these it is fitting to pay tribute to Abbot Sylvester Mooney of Douai Abbey in Berkshire who provided me with much background information on the English mission to the Vatican during the First World War; and to Fr John MacMahon SJ who told me many things of interest concerning his father, the Rt Hon. James MacMahon, the Under-Secretary at Dublin Castle in the years before the Treaty. The former was 102 when he died; the latter 96. One other person of that generation whom I interviewed still lives on: General Thomas Maguire, born in 1892, recalled for me his military operations against the British in the War of Independence, his election to Dáil Eireann in 1921, and his reasons for voting against the Treaty in 1922. It was my privilege and good fortune to meet such a fine old gentleman — the last survivor of an earlier era. It goes without saying that my contact with the Modern Irish History Department of University College, Dublin, especially with Professor Dónal McCartney, Dr Michael Laffan and James Maguire, was both agreeable and of immense benefit. Special thanks are also due to Dr Leon Ó Broin whose wise guidance and direction

9

were of inestimable value. He has a rare knowledge of the location of source material and of the people living who might recall, at first or second hand, further details of information which would add colour and substance to the primary sources. His sharing of that knowledge with me was deeply appreciated. A similar debt of gratitude is due to Dr Brian P. Kennedy whose constructive criticism at all stages of my work served to stimulate and to sustain further study. During my stay at Glenstal I have been greatly helped by Frs Mark Tierney and Henry O'Shea: the former allowed me to use his valuable collection of source material and to benefit from his own knowledge of the period; the latter assisted with his advice at certain stages of my work.

Special thanks are also given to Nóirín Connolly who encouraged me in my endeavours in the very early stages, and to John and Ellen McKean, Noel and Deirdre Kelly and Mary FitzPatrick whose kindness at many and various times made it possible to carry out research in Dublin. Two other people were of great assistance: Gerry Cronin spent countless hours with me translating Irish manuscripts and books, thus making it possible for me to benefit fully from the original material which I discovered, and Walter McCann, a student at Glenstal School, generously gave of his time to instruct me in the art of word processing. Many others deserve particular mention and I can only hope that they will forgive the frailty of my memory. Above all my thanks must go to the Abbot and Community of Glenstal and to Mortimer O'Kelly for without their assistance it would not have been possible to produce either a doctoral thesis or a publishable manuscript. Their part in the production of the book is explained more fully in the Introduction. Sadly Mortimer O'Kelly died suddenly in June of this year, 1989. My debt to him was great beyond all telling. Not only did he allow me free use of his manuscript material, but also he left me free to write as I wished. I can only hope that he would have been happy to accept this book as a token of thanks.

For permission to publish, I thank the authorities responsible for the Dublin Diocesan Archives, the House of Lords Records Office, the Limerick Diocesan Archives, the National Library of Ireland, the Public Records Office (England), the Public Records Office (Ireland), the State Paper Office (Dublin Castle), the Trinity College Dublin Archives, the University College Dublin, Folklore Department, and the University College Dublin Archives. In the last named archives grateful acknowledgement is tendered to the trustees of the Mulcahy collection, and to the families donating the MacNeill and MacSwiney collections.

Needless to say the opinions expressed in the book are my own. As I am told that some of the interpretations are controversial it needs to be stressed, possibly more than in most other such works, that the professional historical advice manifested itself in assistance regarding research methods and in critical dialogue concerning events of the period. It did not extend to shared agreement on matters of interpretation. Having said that, I leave it to the reader to decide if the book is, indeed, controversial.

Brian P. Murphy
September 1989

Postscript and Errata.

An unforeseen delay in publication provides the opportunity to record with sadness the death of Dr. Leon Ó Broin on 26 February 1990. The delay also makes it possible for the author to point out some errors in the captions to the photographs. Facing p.129 is a photograph of General Thomas Maguire. Having outlined his anti-Treaty stance in the caption, the final comment associated him with the pre-Treaty Republican Dáil. Most regrettably a typographical error has resulted in describing him as belonging to the 'pro-Treaty Republican Dáil Eireann.' This is, of course, incorrect: the caption should read, 'last survivor of the pre-Treaty Republican Dáil Eireann.' On the preceeding pages of photographs Mgr. John Hagan is incorrectly described as 'Horgan;' and the assembly of the Republican Second Dáil took place in 1929, not in 1928 as stated in the caption.

Introduction

As I read the full report of the New Ireland Forum in the *Irish Times* of 3 May 1984, I was immediately disturbed by the tone and content of the historical introduction. It was so facile and so superficial, avoiding and evading many real issues, that it could not possibly serve as the basis for a critical appraisal of the factors affecting the unity of Ireland and the relationship between England and Ireland. Having sat at the feet of A. J. P. Taylor at Oxford in the early 1960s, I was puzzled as to why the views of the most celebrated English historian of the modern period had not found any expression, however oblique, in the historical analysis. Taylor has always been critical of the imperial nature of English rule in Ireland and believes that no solution can be found until the British leave Ireland. Reviewing the life of Sir Roger Casement by Brian Inglis in 1973, Taylor wrote:

> Here is Casement's message for the present day. There is no Irish problem beyond solution. The problem that has marked Ireland for centuries is the British presence in Ireland. That problem can be solved only by British withdrawal.[1]

In his assessment of the peace following the First World War Taylor was prepared to admit that the only small nation seeking self-determination and to be refused its request was Ireland. What circumstances, I wondered, had contrived to neglect such significant comments and to produce a report so bland and banal? If history were to be used to decipher the possible constitutional options for a resolution of the Irish problem, it was important that it be sound history. I recalled that Robert Kee called his television programme on the Irish question 'Prisoners of History', a title derived from a remark made by Eddie McAteer, the Northern nationalist. McAteer so described the attitude of his supporters and added, 'I'm glad too.'[2] The same purblind acceptance of their historical roots might, not unfairly, also be ascribed to the followers of the Unionist tradition. It is important, however, that, if we are to be prisoners of history, it should be good history. With that thought in mind I gave up my teaching job, and enrolled to study for a further degree in modern Irish history in UCD under the direction of Professor Dónal McCartney. Here the quest for historical truth overlaps to a certain extent with my own personal plans and movements. These will be narrated briefly.

It was arranged, thanks to the kindness of the Abbot of Glenstal, that I should do some teaching in the school attached to the Abbey, while spending most of my time engaged in research. Aware, in the words of F. X. Martin, that a tremendous amount of work had been carried out 'to transfer the rising of 1916 from the realm of mythology to the sphere of history',[3] I was keen to direct my research towards the many recent cultural interpretations of modern Ireland. My eventual choice of subject was determined, to some extent, by a process of what might be called serendipity — of making happy discoveries by accident. Having talked of my proposed project to Fr Mark Tierney, author of the life of Archbishop Croke and of numerous school text books, he suggested that I should look at the copies of the *Catholic Bulletin* in the Glenstal monastic library. Complete sets of the *Bulletin* are hard to come by and I was grateful for the opportunity to peruse at leisure a journal which I knew figured prominently in recent cultural studies. On checking references it became immediately apparent that, for the most part, extracts from the *Bulletin* had been taken out of context and did not reflect accurately either the article they were taken from or the tone of the journal itself. Indeed the *Bulletin* presented a view of Irish life at marked variance with the interpretations put upon it by many historians. It was, therefore, worthy of detailed study.

Having decided to focus my attention and my efforts on the *Catholic Bulletin*, my first requirement was to identify the editor. In this matter, and for other matters throughout my research, I endeavoured to follow the example of A. J. Symons, as exemplified in his masterly biographical study, *The Quest for Corvo*. Detective work was to be the rule of the game. Basic questions had to be asked; leads had to be followed up; and any clues that appeared had to be unravelled. Motivated by these principles I wrote to Fr Denis Costello, the parish priest of Valentia, Co Kerry, where one of the possible candidates for the editorship, J. J. O'Kelly, was reputedly born. Fr Costello confirmed that O'Kelly was born on Valentia on 7 July 1872. (The family, it should be noted, observe 4 July as his birthday). He also mentioned that Mrs Clare Ring and Brother Peadar Ó Loinsigh could give me further information about his family. Although I was unaware of it at the time, the contact with Mrs Ring put me into close association with the events of 1916. Her father-in-law, Tim Ring, transmitted a cable on Easter Monday, the day of the Rising, to John Devoy's housekeeper reading: 'Mother operated on successfully today'. Secretly dispatched from the Valentia Cable Station, this coded news of the Rising reached America as soon as it became known in England. Both Mrs Ring and Br Lynch gave me invaluable assistance by putting me in touch with Mortimer, the son of J. J. O'Kelly. It is said that to produce a good historical thesis you need to find valuable unpublished material. My meeting with Mortimer O'Kelly led to such a find – a veritable gold mine of precious records and personal letters. It also led to a warm friendly relationship with the O'Kelly family, for which I am grateful.

The main documentary records in the O'Kelly collection are as follows: the original minute books, four in all, of the Society for the Preservation of the Irish Language which date from 1876 to 1941; the original minute book of the Gaelic League for the years 1906-1912; the minute book of the Republican Second Dáil Eireann for the years 1923-1926; and four volumes of letters containing J. J. O'Kelly's official correspondence as Republican envoy in the United States for the year 1924. These documents are complemented by other smaller items of a documentary nature and a vast collection of personal letters. The effect of this find was to change the dimension of my research: I found, at one end of the scale, that I had original material concerning the early days of the language movement with particular references to Douglas Hyde and to Patrick Pearse which could not be ignored; at the other end of the scale I also found myself with original material which shed sensational new light on Michael Collins and Eamon de Valera.

These finds changed the orientation of my study. I resolved to check the original material that I had uncovered with existing sources in recognised collections and with official publications. Having come to the task unwittingly, I basically reproduce here the story which was dictated by the new evidence that I encountered. The first two chapters are concerned with Patrick Pearse: in part they offer a critique of some recent cultural interpretations on the theme of revolutionary nationalism; in part they offer new information on the character of the Gaelic League. The next two chapters recount in historical narrative the emergence of republican Sinn Féin after

1916. The final chapters examine specific charges made against Michael Collins and Eamon de Valera by their republican opponents. On reading the story the relevance of the title, *Patrick Pearse and the Lost Republican Ideal*, will become apparent.

1

Pearse the Reformer

PEARSE: REFORMER OR REVOLUTIONARY

The story is commonly told of a visitor to Ireland who, having sought direction to a further destination, was advised that, all things considered, it would be better to begin the journey from another place. I am not sure whether the story is intended to illustrate the ingenuity or the perverseness of the Irish mind, but the importance of beginning from the right starting point cannot be denied – whether one is simply traversing a country, or attempting the somewhat more difficult task of unravelling the causes that have shaped that country's history. The evidence indicates that many recent commentators on the origins of the 1916 Rising have made a false start. Almost without exception they place the origins of Irish revolutionary nationalism in the early 1890s: the fall of Parnell (1891) and the foundation of the Gaelic League (1893) are seen as seminal steps on the path towards the Easter Rising.

Patrick O'Farrell, writing in 1971 in *Ireland's English Question*, proposed a revolutionary dynamism emanating from the 1890s. His work is of special moment as it exercised a major influence on *Culture and Anarchy in Ireland 1890-1939* by F. S. L. Lyons. O'Farrell maintained that, as early as 1890, Roman Catholic priests and the language revival were united in 'a linkage which swung religious attitudes into sympathetic alignment not only with the contemporary cultural revival, but with major elements in the Irish revolutionary tradition'.[1]

Lyons also was happy to begin his cultural survey from this vantage point in time, and selected a quotation from Yeats to set the tone of his study.

> The Modern literature of Ireland and indeed all that stir of thought which prepared for the Anglo-Irish war, began when Parnell fell from power in 1891. A disillusioned and embittered Ireland turned from parliamentary politics, an event was conceived and the race began, as I think, to be troubled by that event's long gestation.[2]

The fall of Parnell was also seen by Oliver MacDonagh as causing a 'revulsion from conventional parliamentary agitation and mere constitutional aims.'[3] MacDonagh also felt that the Gaelic aspirations for freedom in Pearse's celebrated speech in 1915 at O'Donovan Rossa's funeral proved 'the absolute parity in importance, between revolutionary and cultural nationalism'.[4]

The revolutionary nature of the Gaelic League is a central premise on which the revolutionary character of Irish nationalism is based. 'The League,' MacDonagh declared, 'inevitably manufactured separatists'.[5] This opinion is echoed by Terence Brown who describes the League as 'a nursery for active members of Sinn Féin and the Irish Volunteers of 1916.'[6] Tom Garvin, a more recent cultural commentator, subscribes uncritically to the pattern of interpretation already well established: writing of the IRB he states that, 'the final phase, one of romantic revolutionism, ran from 1891 to 1923'; and, in regard to the Gaelic League, he maintains that it 'was in many ways the central institution in the development of the Irish revolutionary elite'.[7] Both Garvin and Lyons emphasise the significance of Pearse's declaration, 'The Coming Revolution', which was made in November 1913, after the formation of the Irish Volunteers, to confirm the revolutionary nature of the Gaelic League.[8] At first glance there can be no arguing with the revolutionary quality of Pearse's profession:

> I had and I hope that you all had an ulterior motive in joining the Gaelic League. We never meant to be Gaelic Leaguers and nothing more than Gaelic Leaguers. We meant to do something for Ireland.[9]

On the face of it there can be no gainsaying the words of Pearse. The date, however, is important. The statement of Pearse was a direct response to the formation of Carson's Ulster Volunteers in September 1913. Pearse had undergone a dramatic conversion. The year previously he had appeared on a Home Rule platform at a massive demonstration in O'Connell Street and had spoken in support of the constitutional policy of Redmond. It is inexplicable that not one of the cultural critics under scrutiny records this fact. The omission is comparable to analysing the origins of the First World War without reference to the assassination at Sarajevo, or of assessing the causes of the Reformation without reference to the ninety-five

theses that Luther nailed to the church door at Wittenberg. Ruth
Dudley Edwards, the biographer of Pearse, pays full and fitting
regard to his conversion. Having examined Pearse's early life in
detail, she was in no doubt that his claims, in 'The Coming Revolution', to have been a revolutionary from his earliest days in the
Gaelic League were ill-founded.

> Parts of the article were disingenuous: Pearse disliked being accused of
> inconsistency, and here claimed that his League career had been a con-
> scious and deliberate apprenticeship for the vital work of political nation-
> alism. His writings in the *Claidheamh* belie this, as do his admissions to
> friends that in his youth he had been a harmless cultural nationalist.[10]

This judgement of Edwards has not been given the attention it
deserves. It is sufficient, of itself, to suggest that the projection by
historians of revolutionary tendencies on Pearse and on the Gaelic
League is misleading. One is prompted to question the starting
point for their journey of investigation. The opinion of Edwards is,
moreover, corroborated in considerable detail by an examination
of the relationship between Pearse and J. J. O'Kelly. Both men were
active in the League in Dublin from 1898. They did not see eye to
eye with each other. Their relationship was marked by discord and
recrimination, and it is precisely this lack of accord that confers on
the record of their relationship a special relevance. O'Kelly had no
wish to please Pearse; no wish to indulge in idle praise or fulsome
flattery. He wrote the simple truth as he saw it. And as he saw it,
Pearse was open to criticism because he was failing, in the early
days of the League, to uphold a proper ideal of Irish nationality.
Ironically, it was O'Kelly and not Pearse who held an advanced
nationalist position, and this was the root cause of the problem
between them. The conflict between them has often been adverted
to, most recently by Garvin who makes no attempt to explain the
basis of their differences, and it has regularly been presumed that
Pearse must be in the right. The Keating branch, of which O'Kelly
was a founder member in 1901, and in which he expressed his views,
has been derided as the group which opposed Pearse, Hyde and
Fr O'Hickey. Garvin again embodies this condemnation by uncritically accepting the verdict of Fr O'Hickey that the branch were
'footpads'; he also cites uncritically, as several others have done,
the opinion of Hyde that *Banba*, the journal of the branch which
was edited by O'Kelly, was 'the narrowest, meanest, and most bitter
of Irish publications'.[11] Neither Garvin, nor any of the other critics,
has attempted to assess the objectivity of Fr O'Hickey and of Hyde.
By failing to do so they have treated the Keating Branch unfairly.

They have also failed to detect a strange, but very real, connection between the taunt of 'footpads and South Sea islanders' and the expansion of the IRB before 1916. Before elucidating that connection and before examining the charges of Fr O'Hickey and Hyde, it is fitting to consider the first manifestation of difference between Pearse and O'Kelly which occurred in 1899.

PEARSE AND FR YORKE

On 6 September 1899 Fr Peter Yorke of San Francisco delivered the inaugural address to the Central Branch of the Gaelic League, in the Antient Concert Rooms, Dublin. It was anticipated, by those aware of his personal background and public record, that he would make a strong statement in support of Irish nationality. Born in Galway in 1864 of a seafaring family, Fr Yorke was sympathetic to Gaelic values and was deeply aware of the hardship of life on the west coast of Ireland. On entering Maynooth he had become friendly with Fr Eoghan O'Growney, one of the founders of the Gaelic League, and together they visited the Aran Islands to improve their Irish. After his ordination Fr Yorke left for America in 1886 but retained his interest in Ireland and Irish affairs. While acting as a priest in San Francisco he had edited two newspapers which made him a leading, if controversial, figure in California and in many states of America. Before leaving America on his Irish visit in 1899, he travelled over 1,000 miles to see Fr O'Growney who was close to death in Arizona.[12] The challenging address that Fr Yorke delivered may well have derived inspiration from the wish that his friend should not die in vain. His close association with Fr O'Growney certainly added to his own standing among Gaelic Leaguers and to the authenticity of his appeal. He was a fine orator and with forceful words he told the members of the League that,

> they should not stand by with folded hands and look on helplessly while their nationality was being taken from them. They should learn to think Irish thoughts, and to utter them in an Irish press, and in an Irish tongue ... Was the programme of the Gaelic League possible? [he asked and gave the reply] Nothing was impossible if the Irish people really set their hand to it. They must trust themselves, they must follow the motto of the Gaelic League 'Sinn Féin, Sinn Féin amháin!'[13]

The speech of Fr Yorke made a great impression. The spirit of renewal and the change of heart it engendered led to its being described as 'The Turning of the Tide'. Rarely is it adverted to that the original motto of the Gaelic League was 'Sinn Féin'. It is tempting to assume that, as the motto of the League embraced the nationalist position of Sinn Féin, the League itself was inevitably marked by revolutionary aspirations. Such was not the case, however. Quite the contrary. The League Executive was at pains to distance itself from Fr Yorke and his vision of nationality.

Lord Emly, despite some disquiet at his appointment, acted as chairman of Fr Yorke's meeting. Pearse, as a young member of the Executive, did attend Fr Yorke's address, but not all of the senior members of the Executive put in an appearance. Douglas Hyde, the League's president did not attend. It is clear from his later writing on the address that it made an impact on him. Fr Yorke, he said,

> spoke sharply, angrily, fiercely. He attacked clergy, nuns, politicians, newspapers, schoolmasters and school managers, fathers and mothers, and spared none of them. He said the things we badly needed to have said, the things I myself would have liked to say but that I was afraid to do it.[14]

Despite Hyde's frank admission that much good was produced by Fr Yorke's words, he calculated that it was best to stay away because of the controversy that was bound to result from his strong language. He particularly had no wish to see the League become identified with the national and political connotations connected with the term Sinn Féin. It may have been the League's motto; but it was not now to be the League's policy. It should be noted, however, that a study of Hyde's own political leanings reveals an unexpected complexity and a surprising ambivalence. As a young man of twenty he had written of a mythical Gaelic speaking grandfather who had fought bravely against the English in 1798:

> In ninety-eight when a rebel fate
> Drove men unarmed to arms,
> My grandsire then raised many men
> To avenge their burning farms
>
> They spoke in the Gaelic language old,
> The language of the land,
> And many a curse that is best untold
> They gave the English band.[15]

As late as 1897 Hyde had written a poem extolling the virtues of Sinn Féin. 'There is no watchcry,' he professed, 'worth any heed but one – Sinn Féin amháin – Ourselves Alone!'[16] Hyde's role as president of the Gaelic League, however, had made him aware of the need to be diplomatic; to make friends with the influential; to court the press; and to avoid controversy. Under his influence the

League concentrated on a policy of 'de-Anglicisation' in cultural terms rather than in political terms. This emphasis inevitably tempered the nationalist side of the movement. In 1898 Hyde and the League Executive abandoned his 'grandsire' as it resolved to take no part in the centenary celebrations of 1798 — an action which set the League apart from nationalist elements in Ireland — and in 1899 Hyde and the Executive played down their Sinn Féin pedigree by isolating themselves from Fr Yorke. The executive, however, was acutely aware of the importance of Fr Yorke's address. Eoin MacNeill, who also did not attend the talk, owing to ill health, later was to link it with the Dundalk Ard Fheis of 1915 when the League organisation was won over to the nationalist principles of the IRB. 'As far back as 1899,' MacNeill recorded in his memoirs, 'these principles had been clearly enunciated by Fr Yorke.'[17] The lesson from Fr Yorke's incursion into the affairs of the Gaelic League is clear: neither in 1899, nor in 1915 did the League Executive advocate any expression of advanced nationalism. It is equally clear that Pearse, a member of the executive, was happy to abide by the policy of his colleagues in 1899. The opinion of Edwards that Pearse in his youth was 'a harmless cultural nationalist' is endorsed and the question mark placed on the assumptions of the cultural commentators is seen to be fully justified.

Some members of the League, however, were in sympathy with the sentiments of Fr Yorke. J. J. O'Kelly, although never a member of the IRB, was greatly impressed by Fr Yorke's speech. Years afterwards, in May 1919, he traced a direct line from Fr Yorke's address to the Rising of 1916. Welcoming the members of the American peace delegation to the Dáil, he recalled how,

Twenty years ago one of the greatest champions of human liberty our race has produced — the Rev. Dr. Peter Yorke of San Francisco — came to Ireland, and by a memorable address entitled the 'Turn of the Tide,' placed the Young Irish Ireland movement of that time on a plane from which it has never receded. To-day, not only have we reached the turn of the tide — the flowing tide is with us, thanks to the martyrs whose blood and ashes sanctify the clay and hallow the quick-lime of Kilmainham.[18]

In 1899, however, O'Kelly and others like him were faced with a dilemma: there seemed to be no place for them in the League in which to cultivate the ideals of the language movement as espoused by Fr Yorke. Almost certainly the founding of the Keating branch of the League in 1901 was an attempt to resolve this problem. Although no direct causal connection can be provided, it is evident that the aims and aspirations of the Keating branch were at one with those of Fr Yorke. The very name Keating had a special significance: it referred to Geoffrey Keating, the Irish writer of the seventeenth century who, labouring on the Continent, challenged the misrepresentations of English historians writing about Ireland. His tone was aggressive. Giraldus Cambrensis was compared, as were other English historians, to a beetle which 'keeps bustling about until it meets with dung of horse or cow, and proceeds to roll itself therein.'[19] The Keating branch adopted a poem of Keating as its motto, 'Awaken your spirits, O Ireland'; and adopted his attitude as their own — aggressive, yes; but also marked by a commitment to the highest standards in the Irish language and to scholarly research. It is this branch which has been derided by Garvin and countless others. The charges of Fr O'Hickey and of Hyde which have been produced in order to condemn the branch will be considered later. Sufficient to note here the names and qualities of the founder members. Apart from O'Kelly himself, the other founding members were John O'Keeffe, Tadhg O'Donoghue, and Richard Foley. All four men enjoyed a distinguished literary and academic record: O'Kelly won countless Oireachtas prizes and composed over twenty Irish books of note; O'Keeffe wrote regularly for the *Freeman's Journal* and the *Irish Independent* before becoming head of the Government Information Service in the 1930s; O'Donoghue was professor of Irish at St Patrick's Teacher Training College, Drumcondra, before becoming professor of Irish at Cork University in 1916 — a post he retained until 1944, producing a vast corpus of scholarly work; Foley wrote many learned articles before becoming Director of the Place Names Commission (1946) and producing the Dictionary of Irish Place Names. The first president of the branch was Timothy Harrington, MP; the second was Fr Patrick Dinneen, famous for his dictionary, which was published in 1904, and for a tremendous amount of written work in various forms — prose, plays and poetry. The vice president of the branch from a very early date was Dr Denis Coffey. He was a man of wide European experience. Having attended the Catholic University in Dublin, he studied in Louvain, Leipzig and Madrid. He became the first president of University College Dublin in 1908 and retained his position until 1940. Simply to name the men and to reflect on their career records is to become aware immediately that there is something wrong with the blanket condemnation of these men with Munster origins. Before dealing explicitly with the charges of Fr O'Hickey and Hyde against these men it is instructive to measure the nationalist character of Pearse and the Gaelic League Executive against other men who responded positively to Fr Yorke's call to be true to the principle of Sinn Féin.

PEARSE, THE GAELIC LEAGUE AND SINN FÉIN

Arthur Griffith publicly welcomed Fr Yorke's address in the pages of the *United Irishman* and it was seen by contemporaries to stimulate the nationalist fervour which had been aroused by the 1898 centenary celebrations. Leon Ó Broin has most ably and readably charted the manner in which these celebrations of the 1798 rebellion served to revive the IRB and to give a more radical dimension to the Celtic Literary Society, the Transvaal Club, the Major MacBride Club and myriad other advanced nationalist organisations.[20] As indicated by their names, these societies received a further stimulus when popular indignation increased on hearing details of the British war against the Boers in South Africa. The pro-Boer resolution of the Celtic Literary Society, made in October 1899 with Maud Gonne acting as president, 'that we heartily approve of the action of the Irishmen who have taken up arms to assist the country of their adoption', reflects accurately the militant spirit of the more advanced nationalists.[21] It was a spirit that was not widely shared by either the public at large or by the Gaelic League Executive in particular. In 1900 when Griffith and William Rooney put forward their colleague Major John MacBride as a candidate for the South Mayo constituency he was easily defeated. Although this election took place before the formal constitution of Sinn Féin as a party, the campaign of Griffith and his supporters was considered to be in defence of the Sinn Féin ideal. The attitude of Hyde to the election further serves to illustrate the moderate stance of the Gaelic League. In his memoir, he records that he was opposed to the activities of Griffith and Rooney because they were damaging the Gaelic League by attacking the Parliamentary Party.[22] O'Kelly and Keating branch members, on the other hand, tended to support the Sinn Féin election policy. The same difference of approach to Sinn Féin was discernible after Griffith gave Sinn Féin organisational form at the Rotunda Convention in 1905. Even though the Sinn Féin constitution, adopted in 1908, was far from revolutionary — it allowed the King of England a place in the proposed new Irish constitution — the Gaelic League Executive and the majority of League members retained their sympathies for the Irish Parliamentary Party. Pearse, at this time, exemplified the option for moderation. He never joined Sinn Féin. His example was in marked contrast to that of J. J. O'Kelly who was a fellow member with Arthur Griffith in both the Celtic Literary Society and in Sinn Féin. A small incident, involving both Pearse and O'Kelly, provides further indication of the moderate stance of Pearse. In 1905 O'Kelly won a prize at the

Oireachtas for 'a patriotic song with chorus' — the title of his song
was 'Sinn Féin Amháin' (Ourselves Alone). The song, written in
Irish, was critical of 'the craven ways of John Bull', and called for
a return to the Irish language and to Irish traditions. The chorus,
in English translation, read:

> Let us remain in Ireland.
> Let us practise our Irish,
> And let us keep our customs
> as used to be done once;
> And we will free old Ireland,
> through 'Sinn Féin Amháin.'[23]

It is probably significant that Pearse as editor of *An Claidheamh
Soluis* did not publish the 'patriotic song' in 1905, while Griffith
printed it in the *United Irishman* of March 1906. Ironically, but
appropriately, the song was published in *An Claidheamh Soluis* in
December 1917 after Pearse had died for the republican cause and
Sinn Féin had been transformed along republican lines.[24] There
can be no doubt, however, that thoughts of a republic were far from
the mind of Pearse, the League Executive and the vast majority of
ordinary League members in the early years of the century. Their
actions in rejecting the Sinn Féin ideal proposed by Fr Yorke and
implemented by Arthur Griffith leave no doubt on that score. Moreover, the respect for the English King in the Sinn Féin constitution
casts further doubts on the cultural commentators who portray it
as a revolutionary organisation. For that reason a further word is
apposite on both the nature and the strength of Sinn Féin in 1916.

Reflection is required because central to the view of those who
project a revolutionary dynamism in Irish life from c. 1890 to 1916
is the contention that Sinn Féin was revolutionary and expanding
during those years, and that Gaelic League members were the main
source of Sinn Féin membership. Gaelic Leaguers were undoubtedly
members of Sinn Féin — perhaps they formed a majority of its
membership — but the organisation was radical rather than revolutionary. Judge Kingsmill Moore, having listened to the evidence in
the Sinn Féin Funds Case, delivered the opinion that the first phase
of Sinn Féin from 1905 to 1917, which was marked by the undisputed guidance of Arthur Griffith might fittingly be styled 'the
monarchical period.'[25] This judicial opinion reflects the popular
conception of Griffith and his movement — he was commonly
referred to as 'Kings, Lords and Commons' — and there seems no
good reason to disagree with it. Moreover, not only was the movement less revolutionary than some historians would have us believe,

but also it was not expanding. It was, in fact, dying. The secretary of Sinn Féin in the years before 1916, Patrick O'Keeffe, revealed that there were only five or six clubs outside Dublin in 1914, and 'that the only way being made by the movement was leeway.'[26] This opinion is substantiated by the findings of Richard Davis in his major study of Sinn Féin in which he found 'a deplorable situation' to exist as early as 1909.[27] The judgement of Kingsmill Moore is again instructive. Having listened to many witnesses, he concluded that,

> Sinn Féin, if not very successful, managed to avoid extinction and survived as a somewhat languishing and enfeebled organisation, familiar to few and kept alive only by the rugged courage and resource of Arthur Griffith.[28]

Moribund in 1916; resurrected as a term of abuse to describe, first, the Irish Volunteers, and, second, the participants in the Easter Rising – such was the level to which the Sinn Féin ideal had sunk. Where, it is reasonable to ask, is to be found the revolutionary dynamic so confidently identified by recent historians? Not, certainly, in Sinn Féin; nor, with equal certainty, may we say, with the Gaelic League Executive and the vast majority of its members. Any doubts on the attitude of the League in the years immediately before 1916 are dispelled by a speech of Douglas Hyde in Cork in December 1914, made, it should be noted, after the formation of the Irish Volunteers. In it he maintained,

> The great bulk of Gaelic Leaguers through the country are pretty much of the ordinary type of politics current in their respective counties. I may call them the moderate men.[29]

So, 'the moderate men', was how the President of the League described his members. No clearer reply to current interpretation of the character of the League could be found. It was endorsed at the time by the *National Volunteer* – a Redmondite journal – which claimed that these 'moderate men' were, in political terms, Home Rulers:

> The overwhelming majority of the rank and file of the Gaelic League organisation are sincere Nationalists, and Home Rulers, and loyal adherents of the party and policy with which John Redmond is identified.[30]

Where then were the advanced nationalists to be found – the men who masterminded the Easter Rising? They were IRB men, that fact is recognised by all; but in which more open societies did they express themselves and exert their influence? Which society did they use as a front for their secret planning sessions? The answer is simple and significant: they were concentrated almost exclusively in the Keating branch, the branch derided by recent commentators and regarded by the League Executive with distrust and antipathy. In the League, certainly; but not of it, in terms of national aspirations. The origins of the branch have been outlined: the steps by which the branch became the centre of IRB activity need now to be considered. In tracing those steps, a prominent part is played by the strange connection between the taunt of 'footpads and South Sea islanders' and the growth of the IRB.

'FOOTPADS, SOUTH SEA ISLANDERS' AND THE IRB

On 25 May 1903, in a letter to the *Freeman's Journal*, Fr Michael O'Hickey publicly accused some of the Keating branch members of behaving like 'footpads or South Sea islanders.'[36] He wrote in the aftermath of the appointment of Pearse as editor of *An Claidheamh Soluis*, as a result of which he had resigned his post as Vice-President of the League. It is this remark which has been taken as gospel by Garvin and many commentators before him. Hyde would appear to have initiated its use as it figures prominently in his memoirs, and served the purpose then of justifying the League Executive at the expense of the Keating branch.[32] It has been used in similar fashion ever since. In order to put the record straight it is as well to give a fuller quotation from Fr O'Hickey's letter in which he exonerates the Keating branch of any responsibility for his resignation.

> The Keating branch is in no way whatever responsible for my withdrawal from the vice-presidency of the Gaelic League. It is quite unfair to the branch to say so, and at the same time wholly misleading and mischievous .... [He resigned, he continued, because] I found myself opposed radically, fundamentally, vitally to the Cóiste Gnótha on some important matters, both of policy and method. I felt convinced that the decisions arrived at in certain cases were wrong in principle and insane in policy.[33]

Fr O'Hickey may have been annoyed with some members of the Keating branch but his main complaint over policy was with the League Executive. Hyde, understandably, had no wish to dwell on the charge that a policy decision which he had stood over – the appointment of Pearse as editor of the *Claidheamh* – was 'insane'.

As a result it is only Fr O'Hickey's slur on the Keating branch which has passed into history. It was immediately contested by the Keating branch in 1903 and an apology was requested from Fr O'Hickey. No explanation or apology was received. Fr O'Hickey retired to the remoteness of Maynooth and his withdrawal from

League activities appeared to bring the unsavoury episode to a close. It re-emerged, however, in 1909, with startling implications. Fr O'Hickey returned to a central position in the language movement with his defence of compulsory, sometimes called essential, Irish as an entrance requirement for the new National University. His return to the public scene was marked by the same extreme language that he had used in 1903. He saw the issue as 'a war between Ireland and West Britain', and added, in a letter read to a meeting of the Gaelic League conference in the Rotunda Rooms on 7 December 1908, that,

> If we tolerate this thing we are still a race of helots . . . our difficulties are of our own making. More particularly I regret to say, they are the making of the class to which I belong, the Irish clergy. Let us face our difficulties like men and not run away from them like whipped hounds.[34]

As the Bishops moved against the imposition of 'essential' Irish, Fr O'Hickey publicly criticised them and urged the Maynooth students to pray for the Clerical Senators of the new University — one of them, Dr Mannix, was the president of Maynooth! All of Irish-Ireland moved to support Fr O'Hickey in a great wave of popular enthusiasm. An enthusiasm encapsulated by Seán O'Casey in his dedication to *Drums under the Windows*, which reads:

> Forgotten, unhonoured, unsung in Eire, here's a Gael left who continues to say honour and Peace to your brave and honest soul, Michael O'Hickey, till a braver Ireland comes to lay a garland on your lonely grave.[35]

Such was the sympathetic mood manifested towards O'Hickey. County councils passed resolutions in support of his stand; 100,000 people attended a rally in Dublin in September 1909 to proclaim their solidarity; and all prominent Gaelic Leaguers conducted a campaign to uphold the principles which he embodied. What was the Keating branch to do? They fully supported Fr O'Hickey's campaign, and, as moves were made to dismiss him from his professorship at Maynooth, it was felt by some members of the branch, that they should formally express their sympathy with his plight. It was at this stage that their past differences became an obstacle. When, on 17 July 1909, a motion of support was placed on the agenda, John O'Keeffe left the chair.[36] J. J. O'Kelly took his place and later explained that, as well as being out of order,

> There was another factor in the matter and it should be mentioned. Fr. Michael never liked the work of the Keating branch. A little while before, he wrote a letter to the newspapers and he said without reason that some of us were the same as savages from the South Sea Islands. He never

apologised to us, although we asked him publicly to substantiate that
opinion, and although we agreed with him on Irish in the University,
some of us did not wish to interfere in his own dispute.[37]

O'Kelly concluded by praising O'Hickey's dedication to the language, but it is evident that the old taunt of 'footpads and South
Sea islanders' was a crucial issue in the resolution of sympathy to
Fr O'Hickey. By the time the annual general meeting of the Keating
branch was held, on 30 October 1909, Fr O'Hickey had been dismissed from his post at Maynooth, and the balance of feeling in the
branch had come down in favour of sending a message of sympathy.
A letter was sent and acknowledged. Some of the leading members
of the branch were unhappy with the decision and, as a result,
Richard Foley and Fr Dinneen resigned.[38] The resignation of Fr Dinneen as President had momentous consequences. He was succeeded
by Cathal Brugha, a member of the branch since its inception, a
supporter of the O'Hickey letter of sympathy but, more importantly,
a member of the IRB. The Keating branch had always expressed a
more advanced nationalism than the rest of the Gaelic League. Now,
with Cathal Brugha as president, it became the focus point of IRB
activity. In this process of development that made the Keating
branch an IRB stronghold it is evident that Fr O'Hickey's taunt of
'footpads and South Sea islanders' played no small part. Compelling
evidence exists, moreover, to indicate that the derogatory references
of both Fr O'Hickey and of Hyde were the product of subjective
prejudice rather than of objective judgement. This evidence will
now be considered.

Ever since Fr O'Hickey had succeeded Fr O'Growney to the
chair of Irish at Maynooth and had become vice-president of the
League, he had enjoyed a dominant position in the shaping of the
language movement. He had his own vision of the nationalist dimension of that movement, and he had his own ideas about the best
way of promoting the League's interests. The emergence of the
talented young men of the Keating branch was a threat to his
dominance. With Hyde often absent from Executive meetings owing
to his residence in Roscommon, Fr O'Hickey regularly took the
chair and the initiative in formulating League policy. In May 1902
he acted decisively and deviously to prevent a new constitution
proposed by the Keating branch from being accepted by the Gaelic
League.[39] Not only did he lead the criticism of the proposal at the
Executive meeting, but also, his biographer admits, secretly consulted with Hyde, Peadar MacGinley and many Maynooth trained
priests to marshal opposition at the Representative Congress.[40] He

was successful in his clandestine conspiracies. Other, smaller issues, occurred between Fr O'Hickey and the Keating branch, but his record over this major issue of reform in 1902 is alone sufficient to indicate that he was most unlikely to view the branch impartially.

It was the secret negotiations of Fr O'Hickey in particular that led O'Kelly to discuss, openly and critically, the affairs of the League in the pages of *Banba*. The strictures of Hyde that *Banba* was 'the narrowest, meanest, and most bitter' of all Irish publications should be judged in the light of the realisation that O'Kelly did have some reason to speak out. In April 1903 he was particularly critical of the manner in which the League Executive had made recent appointments to the editorship of *An Claidheamh Soluis*: firstly, he revealed the undue influence that Eoin MacNeill had exercised to secure the selection of Owen Naughton, rather than Tadhg O'Donoghue, as editor; and, secondly, he exposed the irregularities of the Executive's actions in the selection of Pearse in 1903.[41] Although he himself was a candidate for the post in 1903, and consequently his remarks may have been coloured by a certain bias, his comments, while cutting, appear to be borne out by other evidence. Pearse's biographer admits that he put up a 'brutally efficient fight' for seven weeks in order to secure the position as editor: O'Kelly stressed the fact that the position was advertised publicly only one week before the appointment.[42] In other words Pearse, a member of the Executive, had ample time to consult with the Executive and to plan his campaign. The majority of the Executive encouraged his ambitions. O'Kelly, having referred to the conduct of the Executive as the 'machinations' of a 'clique', concluded his April article with the damning observation that,

> This makes the fourth member of the Executive Committee appointed to its own salaried positions since last Congress. We hope the best thing has in all cases been done, though we would prefer this special line of development were less noticeable.[43]

His article was not designed to win friends. However, his strong words should not blind one to the fact that a substantial basis would appear to exist for his claim that a certain irregular influence had been used to secure the editorial appointment of Pearse. O'Kelly wrote as he did because he believed that the workings of the League should be opened up to a wider representation. It is in this context that the articles of O'Kelly in *Banba* should be judged. Garvin, typifying the usage of most authors, simply repeats Hyde's vicious verdict without examining the grounds for Hyde's judgement — without placing his comments in context. Confidence in Garvin's own judgement is diminished by his portrayal of *Banba* as being 'vitriolic in its criticism of many Cork Leaguers'.[44] In fact the fifteen copies of *Banba* produced between 1901 and 1906 were unreservedly sympathetic to League members from Cork, and Munster writers made up the majority of the contributors. Many of them were authors of note, such as Frs O'Leary and Dinneen, O'Donoghue, Foley and Osborn Bergin. In relation to the widely accepted criticism by Hyde it is significant that among the other contributors were to be found such men as Frederick O'Connell (Conall Cearnach), a Church of Ireland minister from Connemara, who later became assistant-director of Radio Eireann; Earnest Joynt (An Buachaillín Buide), a Methodist from Co Mayo, who became for many years headmaster of Bolton Street Technical College; and Michael Walsh of Connaught, a distinguished figure in the language movement, whose poem O'Kelly published and praised in March 1903 with the wish that more Connaught writers would send in contributions. The composition of the magazine bears out O'Kelly's claim that it was open to all dialects and to all religions. The articles were, in the main, written by men of calibre and of standing in language circles. Why then the bitter denunciation by Hyde? He was bound to be upset by O'Kelly's editorial articles about the Executive — articles which we have seen it is possible to justify — but the real answer for Hyde's antipathy may well lie in a review of his book of Irish poetry in the June 1903 number of *Banba*. Osborn Bergin bluntly began his review of Hyde's book with the words, 'This is rubbish.'[45] In the next issue of the magazine O'Kelly calmly justified the salutary effects of having such a stern, but scholarly, reviewer as Bergin in the service of Irish literature. He also made it clear that Hyde held a revered place in the language movement. Hyde, he wrote,

> has moved in a sphere — in various spheres, indeed, — which the nobodies can just glance at by standing on tip-toe; and there is little danger of his ever losing the warm place he occupies in the affections of the Irish people.[46]

One cannot but feel a certain sympathy for Hyde as his reputation was sacrificed on the altar of academic detachment; but, granted that the reviewer was Bergin — the first Professor of Early and Medieval Irish at UCD — it would appear that it was academic criteria which motivated his criticism. Naturally Hyde objected strongly to a journal which criticised both his own published work and the Executive of which he was President. However, as with the judgement of Fr O'Hickey, the indications are that subjective considerations obscured true objectivity on Hyde's part. The Keating branch emerges as a more respectable and responsible body than it has been given credit for. A consideration of other charges against the branch further enhances its reputation and sheds more light on the character of Pearse.

PEARSE AND THE KEATING BRANCH

Having considered the contents of *Banba* and the distinguished reputations of the leading Keating branch members, it is apparent that they deserve to be rescued from the taunt of Fr O'Hickey and the slur of Hyde. Two other incidents merit brief consideration in order to complete the rehabilitation of the branch. The authors who have wrongly accepted the opinions of Fr O'Hickey and Hyde concerning events in 1903 have also accepted uncritically the views of Hyde and Pearse concerning events in 1908 with the same harmful consequences to the Keating branch. There were two events central to the dispute between the Keating branch and the Gaelic League Executive in 1908: firstly, the dismissal of J.J. O'Kelly as the writer of the daily Irish column in the *Freeman's Journal*; and, secondly, the issue over the payment of fees to teachers for the teaching of Irish. Although O'Kelly's dismissal occurred in 1905, it only became a matter of public debate in 1908. In fact the two issues merged into one open conflict between the Keating branch and the League Executive which found public expression particularly in the pages of *An Claidheamh Soluis*. Writers of general histories, and the biographers of Pearse — Edwards and O'Sullivan — combine to condemn the Keating branch and to praise Pearse and the League Executive. The case for the Keating branch needs to be stated. The dismissal of O'Kelly from his post at the *Freeman's Journal* occurred as a result of a visit made by Hyde and three other members of the Executive — Agnes O'Farrelly, Edward Martyn and Fr Brian Crehan — to the offices of the editor of the *Freeman*. The visit was made at night after the conclusion of an Executive meeting. Following the visit, at which the deputation asked for more Connaught Irish in the *Freeman*, O'Kelly was dismissed from his job.[47] Hyde protested his innocence in 1907 of any direct responsibility for the sacking of O'Kelly, but the evidence clearly indicates that the visit occasioned the dismissal. At the very least, Hyde was extremely gullible. He, himself, admitted as much in his memoir when he recorded that 'unfortunately' a visit to the editor did take place.[48] Many contemporaries expressed sympathy with O'Kelly and much play was made of the fact that he, as a young recently married man, had lost his only means of livelihood. Even W. P. Ryan a member of the Executive and a friend of Pearse, remarked of the incident, 'the deputation was unfortunate. It was more; it was a mistake.'[49] The effect on the public image of Hyde may well be imagined. Any usage of the Hyde memoir in reference to O'Kelly and the Keating branch should be tempered by the knowledge that Hyde, however generous by nature, could not but view them with a jaundiced eye. Pearse, in his position as editor of *An Claidheamh Soluis*, refused to countenance any possibility that Hyde could be in the wrong. His aggressive intervention in the debate fuelled the fires of controversy; his intervention in the matter of teachers' salaries was even more forceful and damaging. It is common to condemn the Keating branch for its protests over this issue and to praise Pearse, the peace-maker. The reality is far other. Fr Dinneen, president of the Keating branch, did publicly attack Pearse in *The Leader* of 22 February 1908. Far from initiating a conflict, however, he was responding to a declaration by Pearse in *An Claidheamh Soluis* of 15 February. In this statement Pearse attempted to change a policy decision of the League Executive which directed that teachers should be paid extra for teaching Irish as an ordinary subject within school hours. This decision, taken on 14 January 1908, was based on proposals initiated by the Keating branch. Fr Dinneen simply pointed out the terms of the Executive decision, and the further directive that the editor of *An Claidheamh Soluis* should publicise the decisions and encourage League members to rally in support of it. The minute of the Executive meeting is quite clear and bears out Fr Dinneen's contention.

> We direct [it states] the editor of *An Claidheamh Soluis* to explain the situation correctly to the public, and to assist in urging the people towards such an agitation.[50]

Fr Dinneen only criticised Pearse when it became apparent on 15 February that not only was he refusing to implement the resolution of the Executive, but also that he was trying to subvert the original decision. Cathal Brugha and Piaras Béaslaí both wrote long letters to *An Claidheamh Soluis* in support of Fr Dinneen. Their letters appeared on 4 April — the same day as J. J. O'Kelly's letter appeared defending himself over the issue of his dismissal from the *Freeman*. Fierce controversy raged in the pages of *An Claidheamh Soluis*. In the course of a few weeks Pearse accused the Keating branch of being 'moral thugs', 'cranks', 'traitors', and 'the wrecker party'.[51] False charges, which have been repeated down to the present day, were made against the branch. The main scare tactic adopted by Pearse and by W. P. Ryan in the *Peasant and Irish Ireland* was the allegation that the Keating branch was trying to oust Hyde from the presidency of the League and to replace him with Fr Dinneen. On 30 May 1908, the very day that this charge hit the headlines, the Keating branch met and not only denied the allegation, but also declared its allegiance to Hyde.

> We also oppose [the branch statement read] the thing our President was accused of, without reason, in another place and which is being broadcast earnestly, i.e., that he wants to take the leadership of the League from Hyde. And we make known to Hyde how well we like his work and how suitable he is to be President of the League.[52]

Fr Dinneen, O'Kelly, Brugha, Béaslaí and Foley were amongst those present when the motion favourable to Hyde was passed. As the Keating branch moved to endorse Hyde's presidency, Pearse, however, made conciliation even more difficult by delivering his most savage attack on Fr Dinneen. He declared, also on 30 May, that,

> If this man [Fr Dinneen] is not deliberately seeking to bring the leaders of the language movement into bad odour before their fellow countrymen, then his words are the mere meaningless ravings of a diseased imagination.[53]

Faced by the facts of the case and the inherent justice of the Keating branch complaint — faced also by the intemperate nature of Pearse's response — it is impossible to justify the role of Pearse as peacemaker. Edwards may write of Pearse acting in 'his self-imposed duties as peacemaker,' and O'Suilleabháin may conclude of the issue that, 'as was his custom he [Pearse] attempts to take the poison out of it at the end'; but their conclusions, and those of Garvin based on the assumption that the Keating branch must be at fault, are not borne out by the evidence.[54] Contrary to almost all current interpretations, with the notable exception of O'Conluain, the biographer of Fr Dinneen, it has to be accepted that Pearse played a major part in inducing a warlike atmosphere into the League in 1908. His responsibility for the crisis was recognised by the League Executive. Soon after an extraordinary Ard Fheis had successfully resolved the points at issue on 9 June 1908, Hyde suggested that someone else be appointed to do the 'hard' work of editor of An Claidheamh Soluis; but it was agreed that Pearse should continue for a time as editor and pay for his own assistants.[55] The same adverse opinion of Pearse was communicated by John Sweetman, an experienced man of affairs, in a letter to Eoin MacNeill. He wrote,

> For years I have thought that Mr. Pierce [sic] as editor of An Claidheamh Soluis would bring the Gaelic League into difficulties. With the best intentions he has no prudence.[56]

This evaluation would certainly appear justified over the fees controversy, as, for all Pearse's efforts and endeavours, his style of editorial control cannot have been beneficial to the unity and progress of the League. Indeed his role and that of the Executive over the fees issue and the events surrounding it, including O'Kelly's dismissal from the *Freeman*, served only to further the conviction that the unquestioning acceptance of the judgements of the Executive against the Keating branch is less than fair to the latter. Both Pearse and the Keating branch are seen in a new light as a result of examining the major events that troubled the League in 1908. Some reflection is required on the changed perspectives provided by this new evidence.

Pearse appears, above all, as a young man desperately trying to make his mark in the language movement. A young man of ability, vision and ambition who was prepared to exploit to the full his personal contacts in the League to further his objectives. His ambitions related purely to the language movement and the renewal of an Irish identity which was associated with it. Revolutionary thoughts were not to be found in his mind or in the pages of *An Claidheamh Soluis*. He yearned deeply to master the Irish language and to write some works which would establish his literary reputation in the present and for posterity; he desired, and obtained, a position of importance on the League Executive; he longed to create a new system of education and his initiatives in that domain were considerable; and, finding his aims and objectives to be broadly in sympathy with the League Executive, he defended them as editor of *An Claidheamh Soluis* with aggressive impetuosity. In regard to Pearse's role as editor of *An Claidheamh Soluis*, it is difficult to detect any of the benign tolerance which Richard Kearney has attributed to him. Kearney writes of Pearse's belief in a 'high minded equation of a nation "Gaelic" and "free" ' in which all shades of opinion would be welcome.[57] From the evidence of Pearse's disputes with the Keating branch it is apparent that not all voices were to have the same say in the shaping of the nation. Kearney's study is, moreover, flawed by projecting on Pearse, as other commentators have done, the role of a permanent revolutionary. He writes of *An Claidheamh Soluis* as being 'unashamedly nationalist' with the design of furthering 'national self-determination.' The impression is given that Pearse and *An Claidheamh Soluis* were advocating revolutionary nationalism. In fact, while Pearse was editor, the journal was encouraging a policy of constitutional Home Rule. Kearney's error of interpretation is caused by an error, a serious error, of historical fact. In delineating the character of *An Claidheamh Soluis* he mentions that Pearse, MacNeill and The O'Rahilly, 'central figures in the founding of the Irish Republican Brotherhood,' were amongst its contributors.[58] MacNeill was never a member of the IRB; Pearse only joined the IRB in 1913 after he had given up the editorship of *An Claidheamh Soluis*; and The O'Rahilly, like MacNeill, was also never a member of the IRB – he was not even in Ireland for most of the time of Pearse's activities as editor. None of the three men was, of course, involved in founding the IRB. Errors like these have, sad to relate, characterised Kearney's treatment of historical material. These failings, together with the failure to recognise that Pearse was originally a Home Ruler, have led to a misrepresentation of both Pearse and *An Claidheamh Soluis*. In fact the examination of Pearse's dealings with the Keating branch provides full and final confirmation that the starting point for an interpretation of Pearse should focus on his conversion rather than on a lineal pedigree of revolutionary intent. If Pearse deserves to be treated in another light, so too does the Keating branch. It is fitting, and necessary, to distance considerations of it from the acrimonious circumstances that have perpetually surrounded treatment of the branch by historians. The branch had many positive qualities. These now merit consideration.

The names associated with the founding of the Keating branch and with *Banba*, as has already been indicated, are sufficient of themselves to raise considerable question marks over the universal condemnation of the group. Indeed, the names of O'Kelly, O'Donoghue, Foley, O'Keeffe, Dinneen, Coffey, O'Leary and Bergin – to list but a few – are a guarantee of professional integrity and of high academic attainment. They achieved much. Most enduring of their achievements was the founding of Ballingeary Teachers' Training College in West Cork in 1904.[59] A need was correctly identified – the need for good teachers of Irish – and a plan was rapidly put into practice that would meet all requirements. The college still operates successfully and immediately became a centre for cultural renewal as well as a teachers' college. Comparisons are odious, but simply to glance at Pearse's abortive efforts to establish his own school at St Enda's on a sound footing is revealing. There can be no doubt as to which enterprise was better planned. Most daring of their enterprises was the founding of the Keating players – a touring dramatic society composed of men and women – which was designed to encourage the use of Irish through the medium of plays. Pearse, incidentally, was highly critical of this initiative, although he later came to adopt it himself. The plays were an instant success both in Dublin and in other parts of Ireland. W. G. Fay directed their first play and he acknowledged its importance as a vital step that led him into contact with W. B. Yeats and the eventual founding of the Abbey Theatre. Fay recalled that he,

> had the honour of directing the first public performance of a play in Gaelic. It was *Tobar Draoídheachta* [The Magic Well] by Fr. Dinneen. This experience was the means of bringing me into intimate contact with the Literary Theatre.[60]

This connection with Fay illustrates the positive contribution that the Keating branch was making to the language movement and should alone guarantee that in future it be viewed in a fresh perspective. The leading members of the branch, it should be noted, men such as O'Kelly, O'Donoghue, Foley, O'Keeffe and Coffey, all participated in the plays – a cultural involvement for which none of their critics has given them credit.

In general it may be said that the efforts of the branch to spread the language were more practical and more successful than those of the League Executive. To a large extent they were more down to earth because they themselves were more earthy. They drank together in 'An Stad', a famous meeting place for all Irish-Irelanders in North Frederick Street;[61] they met together in the Phoenix Park and played Gaelic games – sometimes with the ageing Michael Cusack, founder of the GAA; and they quickly organised themselves in the Keating branch Gaelic teams as well as the Keating branch players. Pearse and the vast majority of the League Executive were not at home in the company of the Guinness drinkers of 'An Stad' or with the mud-stained companions of the Phoenix Park. These social differences accentuated their other differences, both academic and administrative, and, although demarcation lines between the two groups were not absolute, they contributed to the formation of two disparate bodies working within the same organisation. On top of these forces making for distinction, many of the Keating branch were happy to embrace the Sinn Féin ideal of Fr Yorke. They believed that a national policy – the call for an independent Ireland – was not a political policy, and this was another crucial reason for parting company with the League Executive. It was to be expected that the IRB, especially after Brugha's election to the presidency of the branch, should be at home in the Keating branch. All the evidence indicates, moreover, that the men they were joining were not the 'wreckers' they have been branded. Rather they were able academically, efficient in practical and business matters, and men of vision. The fusion between the Keating branch and the IRB contributed greatly to the 1916 Rising. This connection will now be considered.

THE KEATING BRANCH AND THE 1916 RISING

The popular impetus given to the IRB by the 1898 centenary celebrations, Fr Yorke's 'Turn of the Tide' speech and by the Boer
War had culminated in a romantic, rather than a truly revolutionary,
movement. In the early years of the century, it must be remembered, W. B. Yeats was enrolled as an IRB member. His infatuation
with Maud Gonne and his fascination with the fine featured old
Fenian, John O'Leary, had brought him to this pass. Arthur Griffith
also remained in the IRB for some years after the founding of Sinn
Féin — some say he never left it — and his case may be taken as
typical. For him and for many others membership of the IRB was
simply an involvement with an advanced form of nationalism: it
did not mean that one was ready 'to strike a blow for Ireland.' The
return of Tom Clarke to Dublin in 1907 changed all that. He returned
to Ireland from America with the blessing of John Devoy and Clan
na Gael, and with the declared intention of putting the IRB back on
its revolutionary Fenian lines. From his tobacco shop at 75a Great
Britain Street (Parnell Street), he began to fashion the new IRB
organisation. Cathal Brugha was totally in accord with the aims of
Clarke. Born in Fairview, Dublin, in 1874 and educated at Belvedere
College, he committed himself to the language movement from an
early age and became a fluent Irish speaker. He also joined the IRB
as a young man. As a travelling salesman for church furnishings he
journeyed throughout Ireland and used the opportunity to swear
people in to the IRB. Among those he enrolled were Austin Stack
and Piaras Béaslaí.

Even before Brugha became president of the Keating branch,
young men with advanced nationalist sentiments were attracted to
the branch. Richard Mulcahy, Chief of Staff of the Irish Volunteers
after the Rising, recalled that the whole of Parnell Square, and its
immediate precincts, was the centre of resistance to English rule in
Ireland. He said of it,

> I came to Dublin in 1907 and I entered Parnell Square through two
> doors; I entered through the door of the Keating branch of the Gaelic
> League.[62]

The other door, he added, was provided by IRB membership. No. 2
North Frederick Street provided the actual 'door' of the Keating
branch headquarters, until a move was made to 46 Parnell Square.
Mulcahy wondered wistfully why the British had not simply bombed
Parnell Square and eliminated their main opposition in Ireland.
Going over these recollections of Mulcahy with Leon Ó Broin, who

was engaged in Parnell Square activities from 1919 on, he agreed that Mulcahy was right about the bomb! Once Brugha became president of the Keating branch it was natural that even more young men would find their way to the door of that branch. One who did so was Seán Ó Muirthile, a Gaelic League organiser, who was sworn into the IRB by Brugha in 1912. After the Rising he was involved in the restoration of the IRB and became secretary of the Supreme Council of the organisation. His opinion, expressed in his memoir, is of special value because of his wide knowledge of both the Gaelic League and of the IRB. Writing of the League and of Cathal Brugha before the Rising, he expressed the view that,

> There were two sections in the Gaelic League from the beginning — those who wanted an independent Gaelic Ireland, and those who simply wanted a Gaelic speaking nation, and I knew Cathal as belonging to the former school.[63]

The distinction admirably clarifies the different approaches within the League: the Keating branch stood for 'an independent Gaelic Ireland' — for de-Anglicisation in political as well as cultural terms; the League Executive and the vast majority of ordinary members stood for 'a Gaelic speaking nation' — for de-Anglicisation in cultural terms alone. In political terms the former tended to be either separatist or even revolutionary in their aspirations; the latter were Home Rulers and accepted all the connections with England that were part of such a constitutional policy. Some Keating branch members exercised a predominant role in the Rising of 1916; others in its aftermath. Among its members were Tom Clarke, Seán Mac-Dermott, Thomas MacDonagh, Con Colbert, Thomas Ashe, Michael Collins, Fionan Lynch, Seán Tracey, Kevin Barry, Gearóid O'Sullivan, Diarmuid O'Hegarty, Eamon Ceannt and, of course, Cathal Brugha and Richard Mulcahy.[64] Some of these men had shaped their nationalist attitudes by long term membership of the branch; others, like Clarke and MacDermott, joined to secure a safe meeting place for their IRB activities. The final meeting of the special IRB military council took place at the Keating branch headquarters before action commenced on Easter Monday 1916. On the eve of the Rising it was estimated that IRB membership numbered about 2,000: some 700 being located in Dublin, and a large proportion of the organisation being resident in Britain.[65] After the Rising members of the branch, especially Brugha and J. J. O'Kelly, played a leading part in the creation of republican Sinn Féin and contributed to the republican character of Dáil Eireann.

Some cultural commentators may say that, despite this analysis,

the Keating branch was part of the Gaelic League and that, therefore, their generalisations concerning the revolutionary nature of
the League are correct. The examination of the branch, however,
has revealed not only that they were to a high degree unqiue in their
IRB commitment but also that their views were rejected by the
League as a body. The branch's contribution to the Easter Rising was
exceptional and exceptions do not contribute to universal rules or
generalisations. No, the argument of the cultural commentators
cannot be sustained. Neither on logical, nor on historical grounds
can it be shown that the Gaelic League was revolutionary or that
a revolutionary dynamism operated in Ireland from the early 1890s.
Some few genuine revolutionaries of the old Fenian tradition did
exist, but, as the large mass of the Irish-Ireland movement responded
to the Home Rule crisis and the World War, most put their trust in
England's promises. The IRB was strengthened by the few who did
not believe England's promises. Pearse was one of the few. Having
rejected the Sinn Féin ideal of Fr Yorke and having stood apart
from the advanced nationalist ideals of the Keating branch, he finally
decided in December 1913 to join the IRB. The story of Pearse the
revolutionary begins from that point. The events which impelled
him on a revolutionary course have implications not only for an
assessment of Pearse and his heritage, but also for an interpretation
of the Rising with all its long term consequences. These events will
now be considered.

2

Pearse the Revolutionary

PEARSE, THE IRB AND CARSON

It has become fashionable among some socio-psychological inter-
preters of the Easter Rising to say that Pearse was prompted to strike
out in 1916 owing to his own personal frustration – frustration
with his failing school enterprise, frustration at his failure to secure
a satisfactory heterosexual relationship, frustration at his inability
to come to terms with his own inherent homosexual tendencies.
Personality problems, it is argued, finally combined with his long
held revolutionary principles to provoke action – to provoke the
1916 Rising. There is no evidence for these suppositions. Some of
them, indeed, were squarely faced by Pearse and answered. Garvin,
for example, discusses 'the significance of unsuccessful business
careers' as a possible factor in the Rising, and notes that Pearse,
whom he depicts as having 'exaggerated postures of self-sacrifice,'
'had chronic financial difficulties.'[1] This argument by inuendo and
insinuation was directly rebutted by Pearse in a letter to Joe McGarrity in 1915. Faced by the demand for rent for St Enda's, Pearse
wrote,

> We are all convinced that it is part of a move to discredit me in the eyes
> of the public. It is their way of hitting at me. They will represent me as
> a bankrupt and discredited man who takes refuge in 'advanced' politics
> and hides his failure to meet his creditors by preaching sedition.[2]

The integrity of Pearse's revolutionary motivation is manifest, but
he was fearful that the authorities would lay a false charge against
him, if his school failed. The charge was scurrilous then and is
equally baseless today. In large part, Garvin and others have become

41

entangled in a mesh of hypothesis and supposition because they have treated both Pearse and the Gaelic League as being motivated by revolutionary principles. Once it is recognised that Pearse underwent a process of conversion, the starting point for an interpretation of his motivation is radically changed. All the evidence indicates that Pearse moved to a revolutionary position, in precise response to actions by Carson, Redmond and the English government. Although these actions are clearly identifiable, it is significant that they play no part in the interpretation of the Rising by Garvin, Lyons, MacDonagh and O'Farrell.

Carson's mobilisation of Ulster in resistance to the Home Rule Bill was the main factor in the formation of Pearse the revolutionary. The Irish Volunteers were formed in November 1913 in direct response to the signing of the Ulster Covenant (28 September 1912) and the setting up of a Provisional Government in Belfast (24 September 1913). Carson's actions, taken with the co-operation of the Tory party, were accompanied by declarations of willingness to resist any implementation of Home Rule by force. He announced on 27 July 1912, at a rally at Blenheim, the family home of the Churchill family, that,

> We will shortly challenge the Government to interfere with us if they dare, and we will with equanimity await the result . . . They may tell us if they like that that is treason . . . We are prepared to take the consequences, and in the struggle we will not be alone, because we will have all the best in England with us.[3]

He spoke with confidence of support from England because, at the same rally, Bonar Law, the leader of the Conservative party, had promised aid if efforts were made to introduce Home Rule.

> If the attempt be made [he said], under present conditions I can imagine no length of resistance to which Ulster will go which I shall not be ready to support, and in which they will not be supported by the overwhelming majority of the British people.[4]

Two prominent lawyers also gave voice to highly illegal sentiments. F. E. Smith, a leading Tory MP, threatened the government that an Ulster in arms to resist Home Rule 'will not stand alone' and James Campbell, colleague of Carson and Unionist MP, who was reputed to have signed the Ulster Covenant in his own blood, declared that 'though civil war might be the path of danger, it was also the path of duty'.[5] Such were the sentiments and actions that forced Pearse from a Home Rule platform. For a short time, however, it should be stressed, it was the intention of the Volunteers to mobilise in order to secure Home Rule, and there was even talk of co-operation with Carson. Indeed, in December 1913, as Pearse enrolled in the IRB and departed for a tour of America, MacNeill promised not to use the Volunteers to the detriment of Redmond and his party. He told an influential friend, John J. Horgan,

> to allow Mr. Redmond to know in the best way you can, that I pledge myself against any use of the Volunteer movement to weaken his party, which is also my party.[6]

Initially, therefore, there was no revolutionary intention in the founding of the Volunteers – one has to look to the Provisional Government in Ulster to perceive the real revolutionary movement and this was guided by Carson. Some years later MacNeill was asked how revolution was brought about in Ireland, and he replied, 'Mainly by Carson.'[7] The question was put to him by the journalist, Wickham Stead, and F. X. Martin has commented on the incident,

> The journalist thought he was being served a witty paradox, but MacNeill considered it to be the simple truth, just as he held that Carson made possible the Irish Volunteers. The facts bear out his belief.[8]

Many others have testified to the primacy of Carson and of Ulster as causes of the Easter Rising. It is fitting to conclude the discussion of the matter with the observation of Augustine Birrell, the Chief-Secretary, who described Ulster as the cause of all the trouble. 'But for the Ulster difficulty,' he wrote, 'there need have been neither gun-running at Larne, nor the rebellion in Easter Week.'[9] Reaction to Carson certainly moulded developments in the rest of Ireland, but men like Pearse who felt impelled to take up a revolutionary stance were the exception – the vast majority remained true to constitutional measures. This remained the case even after Redmond's response to Carson appeared weak and ineffective.

Redmond's apparent acquiescence in English modification of the Home Rule Bill marked the second stage of Pearse's disillusionment with the constitutional process. The incidents centred around several specific decisions of Redmond: his agreement that parts of Ireland might opt out of the Home Rule Act (21 July 1914); his promise of Ireland's unconditional support for England in the event of war (3 August 1914) – made despite the Curragh 'mutiny' and the Larne gun-running; and his call to the Irish Volunteers, in a speech at Woodenbridge, to join the British war effort (20 September 1914) – a plea made two days after the Home Rule Act had been passed but had been suspended in operation. This last call of Redmond led to a split in the Irish Volunteers. Most of them responded to Redmond's appeal and became known as the National Volunteers. It is to that organisation to which the emerging Irish-Ireland movement of the 1890s gravitated. Confidence in the constitutional promises of Redmond and the English government characterised the Irish response to Carson's revolutionary actions. In that regard the recent observation of Michael Laffan is most telling. He writes of the National Volunteers that,

> They totalled approximately 200,000 men, well over a hundred times the number of the rebels who fought against Britain in Easter Week; the volunteers who died in the Flanders trenches represented Irish national opinion more accurately than did the Volunteers who died in the general post office or Kilmainham jail.[10]

It was in the atmosphere of this split in the Volunteers that Hyde made his speech in Cork in December 1914 calling the Gaelic Leaguers moderate men. One could then judge the mood of the country accurately because men were actually making a deliberate choice — either to enroll in the Irish or the National Volunteers. Fully aware of the hordes of men rushing to enlist in British military colours, Hyde predicted a future for the Gaelic League in which members 'will be of a moderate and possibly even a conservative type, rather than of an extremist or revolutionary one.'[11] The small minority left in the Irish Volunteers, and the even smaller IRB revolutionary grouping, were clearly out of sympathy with the main body of opinion in the country. As the mass of Irishmen departed for the trenches one was faced by the strange paradox that for them the cry of Faith and Fatherland was compatible with that of King and Country. Despite Carson and despite Redmond the revolutionary group with which Pearse threw in his lot remained distinctly small. They were, however, growing more dedicated.

Further actions of the English government confirmed them in their commitment, but, once again, the evidence is that most Irishmen remained true to the constitutional process despite clear signs of English ambivalence. On 15 September 1914 Asquith made the first of a long line of pronouncements by English politicians about the coercion of Ulster. He declared that,

> the employment of force, any kind of force, for what was called the coercion of Ulster was an absolutely unthinkable thing.[12]

The disquiet of advanced nationalists was voiced by J. J. O'Kelly in the October issue of the *Catholic Bulletin*. He commented,

> We must apparently take Mr. Asquith's characteristic advice to 'wait and

see' what all this means, as Government or Acts of Parliament without the use of force is rather a novel experiment in Ireland.[13]

O'Kelly was also critical of Redmond for abandoning the ideals of Tone, Davis, Emmet and Mitchel, and for placing Ireland firmly in the British Empire. His main complaint, however, was that England, faced by illegal acts in Ulster, was unwilling to use force to uphold the democratic process of law. Pearse was motivated by the same consideration: a just solution to the Irish problem could not be secured by recourse to law. Both Pearse and O'Kelly, and many other like-minded spirits, were confirmed in their opinions by the composition of the new Coalition Government in England in May 1915. Four of the leading men in the Ulster campaign to use illegal means in opposition to Home Rule were given positions of importance – three of them in the area of justice and law. Carson became Attorney-General; F. E. Smith became Solicitor-General; J. H. Campbell became Attorney-General of Ireland (1916) and Lord Chancellor (1918); and Bonar Law became Secretary for the Colonies. In the face of this series of events some began to have doubts: doubts about the promises of England and the reassurances of Redmond concerning Home Rule; doubts, too, about England's claim to be waging the war for the rights of small nations. Some expressed these doubts publicly – the voices of Bishop O'Dwyer of Limerick and Bishop Fogarty of Killaloe were especially prominent; some distanced themselves from Redmond and his policy; but the number who embraced the IRB position still remained very small. Faith in English promises and loyalty to England's war efforts kept almost all of Ireland soundly on the constitutional path. Pearse continued to draw different conclusions from the series of events which had been initiated by the call to arms of Carson. Considerations of frustrated sexuality and of failed finances fade into insignificance as one examines the clear causal relationship between the actions of the two men. The implications for an interpretation of Pearse and the Easter Rising are considerable and will be treated shortly. For the moment, in order to appreciate more fully the character of Pearse and the Rising, it is necessary that the moves which Pearse and the IRB took in the year before the event should be considered.

PEARSE AND THE IRB PREPARE FOR THE RISING

There were two major events in 1915 in which the IRB were involved and which made a public impact: the Gaelic League Ard-

Fheis which was held in Dundalk and the funeral of O'Donovan Rossa in Dublin. Both events illustrated not only the dedicated commitment and the organisational ability of the IRB, but also the paucity and fragility of their popular support. For some years the IRB had been endeavouring to obtain more representation on the League Executive and to secure a change in the League's constitution which would include a statement of support for their nationalist aims. At the Dundalk Ard-Fheis they successfully achieved their objectives. Using unscrupulous tactics, particularly the distribution of proxies by Seán Ó Muirthile, they secured the appointment of Seán T. O'Kelly as secretary, and a statement of nationalist aspirations which led Hyde to step down as president.[14] Ernest Blythe freely admitted that,

> If the Sinn Féin or Republican forces, had been stronger than they were, they might have been content to allow the Gaelic League to stand neutral; but their numerical weakness and the hostile attitude of the popular majority towards them made it natural for them to seek to entrench themselves wherever they could do so.[15]

Right to the last, therefore, the 'popular majority' within the Gaelic League was for reform and for constitutional politics. Among the IRB themselves, there was some difference about the tactics adopted. Seán MacDermott felt strongly that the post of secretary should have been made purely on the grounds of ability. There were also indications that the role of J. J. O'Kelly was of crucial importance at the Ard-Fheis. O'Kelly had been an influential member of the Executive of the League since 1914 and at Dundalk he argued strongly for a statement of national ideals – a statement which reflected the long term principles of the Keating branch. His argument decisively influenced Hyde in his decision to stand down as president. Hyde recorded that he would have stayed in office, if he saw any chance of improving the state of the Irish language:

> I saw none [he wrote], at this very Ard-Fheis, Seán Ó Ceallaigh [Sgeilg] ... brought up a long litany of grievance against me for rulings I had given during the past year ... the remedy of this genius against being oppressed by me was to solemnly propose to the Ard-Fheis that the President should not be allowed 'to rule out of order anything that was of national importance' meaning thereby his own political resolutions!! He was soon afterwards elected a vice-President!![16]

Hyde's statement makes it clear that IRB tactics were not the only influence at work at the Dundalk Ard-Fheis; they were ably assisted by Keating branch policy. In a strange way, as Eoin MacNeill remarked, the principles enunciated in 1899 by Fr Yorke came to fruition at Dundalk in 1915. Personal considerations, going back to the days of the *Freeman's Journal* dispute, probably coloured Hyde's judgement of O'Kelly, but there could be no doubting the clear difference between Hyde's wish for no political involvement and the desire of O'Kelly and advanced nationalists that the aspiration of a free Gaelic Ireland should be written into the League's constitution.

Popular expression was given to this aspiration at the funeral of O'Donovan Rossa. Indeed, the two events had a connecting thread: the wife of O'Donovan Rossa and his daughter attended the Dundalk Ard-Fheis, and left it to attend the funeral on 1 August 1915.[17] The two events interacted as if orchestrating a ground swell of revolutionary nationalism. Pearse did not attend the Ard-Fheis. He retired in seclusion to Rosmuc in the far West of Ireland and used the time to prepare his oration to be delivered at the graveside of Rossa. His words at the funeral, delivered slowly and intently, recalled past Fenian traditions and this memory was used to inspire action in the present.

> I hold it a Christian thing [he declared], as O'Donovan Rossa held it, to hate evil, to hate untruth, to hate oppression, and, hating them, to strive to overthrow them . . . the seeds sown by the young men of '65 and '67 are coming to their miraculous ripening to-day . . . they [the British] have left us our Fenian dead, and while Ireland holds these graves, Ireland unfree shall never be at peace.[18]

These well known words, and the huge crowds that attended the funeral, have often been taken as inaugurating a mass rallying of men in arms to the Republican banner. Caution is needed. Pearse's biographer has qualified their efficacy in 1915. Ruth Dudley Edwards writes,

> He [Pearse] could stir their emotion, shape and direct them for as long as his words lasted, but there were still few among them whom he could impel to action.[19]

Her qualification is consonant with the findings of this study. Again and again it is brought home to one that only a very small fragment of nationalists — whether one labels them advanced nationalists, Fenians, separatists, Volunteers or even IRB — were prepared to commit themselves to armed revolution. The final moves of Pearse and the IRB reflected their numerical weakness.

Pearse realised that their forces were so small that they could not succeed. His writings, therefore, in the months before the Rising, attempted to justify the sacrifice of blood to which he and his comrades were committed. As early as May 1915 Patrick O'Hegarty was told by Seán MacDermott that the IRB leaders had agreed on 'a blood sacrifice for a principle.'[20] Pearse voiced this aspiration in his plays, poems and pamphlets. He also wrote to illustrate the historical antecedents of their ideas and to justify the actions that they were about to take. The shades of Emmet and of Tone had haunted Pearse since he had immersed himself in school life at Rathfarnham and he evoked them, together with Lalor and Mitchel, as the ghosts of Ireland's past who should inspire true nationalists in 1916. From the start of Carson's activities in the North, Pearse had explicitly turned his back on the affairs of the Gaelic League which had occupied his mind in earlier days. His conversion was complete. Writing in September 1913, he expressed a longing for a prophet-like figure who,

> would go through the Irish West and speak trumpet-toned of nationality to the people in the villages. I would not have him speak of Gaelic Leagues, or of Fees for Irish, or of Bilingual Programmes, or of Essential Irish in Universities: I would have him speak of Tone and Mitchel and the Hawk of the Hill and of men dead or in exile for love of the Gael; all in Irish.[21]

The thoughts that had occupied his mind and divided him from the Keating branch were laid aside. Thoughts of nationality absorbed Pearse in 1916. His last pamphlet, *The Sovereign People*, appeared the week before the Easter Rising and concluded his appeal to the Irish people. His appeal was passionate rather than practical – a call to Irishmen to emulate the sacrifice of Christ and die for their country. Most contemporaries paid little regard to his utterances. A reviewer of *Ghosts* wrote on 15 April 1916 that,

> A lack of clear insight and of practical grasp of facts has been the bane of Irish national thought at all times. It is not saying too much when we say that Mr. Pearse is not free from the same failing. . . . You must cut your coat according to your cloth, and it is hardly opportune to talk of Irish Republics.[22]

Pearse, however, was prepared not only to talk, but also to die for an Irish Republic, and he thus stood removed from the normal standards of critical reviewers. Believing, in biblical terms, that God could choose the weak to confound the strong, he was prepared to live out a dream with the conviction that he and the ghosts of Ireland's past could shape a new reality. In his poem, 'The Fool', written in 1916 just before he embarked on his mission, Pearse gave expression to his thoughts:

> O wise men, riddle me this: what if the
>   dream come true?
> What if the dream come true? and if
>   millions unborn shall dwell
> In the house that I shaped in my heart, the
>   noble house of my thought?
> Lord, I have staked my soul, I have staked
>   the lives of my kin
> On the truth of Thy dreadful word. Do
>   not remember my failures,
> But remember this my faith.[23]

Pearse, and the few others who shared this dream, realised that even in the IRB ranks they could not rely on wide support. As the organisation, therefore, made the practical plans for a military strike, the control of operations became concentrated in a smaller circle of men who were prepared to sacrifice themselves.

The IRB men who were committed to revolution and the ideal of a blood sacrifice assumed control of the military operations of the organisation in 1915. Their power was based on a Military Council and not on the officially recognised apex of authority, the Supreme Council. In September 1915 Denis McCullough from Belfast was elected president of the eleven man Supreme Council.[24] Neither McCullough, nor the Supreme Council, however, directed the plans for the Rising. These were drawn up by the Military Council which was composed of Clarke, MacDermott, Pearse, Plunkett and Kent.[25] It was these men, together with James Connolly who joined them in January 1916, who led their small band of followers numbering at the most 1,000 men – into action on Easter Monday.[26] The measured assessment of F. X. Martin concerning the origins of the Rising cannot be improved on: it was, he stated, 'the revolt of a minority, of a minority of a minority.'[27] The Irish Volunteers were a small minority of the National Volunteers, the IRB formed a small fragment of the Irish Volunteers, and the Military Council of the IRB formed only a small unit of the organisation. This analysis of the Rising has been widely acknowledged for some time. Its implications, in relation to an assessment of the cultural forces leading up to the Rising, do not appear to have been adverted to. Taken together with the re-appraisal of the character of both Pearse and the Gaelic League – a re-assessment which lays stress on their reformist rather than their revolutionary nature – one is led to evaluate the causes of the Easter Rising from a new perspective. Some aspects of this new perspective will be considered.

1916: IMPERIAL CONSIDERATIONS

The depiction of Ireland — 'southern Ireland' — as moving towards 1916 on the crest of a revolutionary wave has had important results not only in the matter of interpretation of the Rising, but also in regard to present political policies. It is argued that the revolutionary character of the Irish, fashioned by the new aspirations of the Gaelic League, divided the nation more rigidly into two separate entities. This separateness was, moreover, compounded by religious differences which influenced the character of the Gaelic League and all areas of national life. In short, it is maintained that the inherent Gaelic, Catholic, revolutionary nature of the Irish Gael explains the Rising, and at the same time justifies partition. It could not be expected, it is claimed, that accord could be found between Protestant Ulster Unionists and the revolutionary separatists of the south. Such theories, however, count for nothing once proper recognition is given to the proven constitutional character of Irish nationalists. Once that is accepted a new vista of interpretation unfolds. Instead of focussing on internal differences one is led to look to external influences as the decisive factors in bringing the Rising about — to look, in other words to England and the imperial dimension. Lyons is reluctant to place such considerations in the scales of assessment. He concludes his cultural study by stressing the primacy of internal factors as the source of division.

> During the period from the fall of Parnell [he writes] to the death of Yeats, it was not primarily an anarchy of violence in the streets, of contempt for law and order such as to make the island, or any part of it, permanently ungovernable. It was rather an anarchy in the mind and in the heart, an anarchy which forbade not just unity of territories, but also 'unity of being.'[28]

To gloss over the actions of Carson and the Tory Unionists in such a fashion is a travesty of the truth. It was precisely the 'anarchy of violence in the streets,' and the 'contempt for law and order' which made implementation of the law impossible and the country ungovernable. This fact was recognised by John J. Horgan in his celebrated contemporary book, *The Grammar of Anarchy*. Dedicated to those Unionists whose example had been a source of inspiration for the revolutionary movements in Ireland, Egypt and India, he gave a day by day account of Unionist incitements to civil disobedience. The co-operation of Tory Unionists, moreover, with the campaign of Carson gave an external dimension to this resistance to the rule of law. By methods not strictly legal, and forces not purely

Irish, Carson played a vital part in threatening the Irish 'unity of being.' At the very least it may be safely contended that in any evaluation of the factors leading to the Easter Rising, the internal influences emphasised in *Culture and Anarchy* should be qualified by an acknowledgement of the external forces stressed in *The Grammar of Anarchy*.

The profession of Lyons that there was no 'contempt for law and order' makes strange reading as one reflects on the repeated assertion of Tory party leaders that democratic majorities counted for nothing in Ireland. Lord Salisbury in 1883 declared that it would be wrong to grant 'any licence to the majority in that country to govern the rest of Irishmen as they please'; Arthur Balfour in 1893 maintained that revolt was justified against a 'tyrannical majority'; and Bonar Law in 1912 proclaimed that 'there are things stronger than parliamentary majorities.'[29] In this litany of praise for illegality, if the vital interests of the Tory party or of Empire were threatened, one can trace the direct lineage of Carsonism. The Tory intrusion into Irish affairs had another deleterious effect on the Irish body politic: it not only exploited inherent differences between Ulster and the rest of Ireland; but also it encouraged, even incited the affirmation of difference and distinction. 'Une invitation à la guerre civile' was how the French consul reported Randolph Churchill's speech of 1886 which urged Ulster to fight again against Home Rule.[30] It became part of Tory policy to foster the idea of Ulster as a separate nation and, from this prompting, the 'two nation' theory was born. The thrust of modern interpretation has been to neglect the imperial dimension as a cause of the Easter Rising and to accept the reality of the 'two nation' theory. The 'two nation' theory did not go unchallenged in the years before 1916. It was, in fact, rejected by many. As judgements about Pearse and present governmental policy decisions have been made on the premise that the theory was valid, a brief perusal of it is necessary.

THE 'TWO NATION' THEORY

The 'two nation' theory has had a lasting impact on Anglo-Irish relations. It surfaced again recently when it served as the basis of John Biggs-Davison's submission to the New Ireland Forum on 6 October 1983. He argued that 'the distinct Ulster personality' merited political expression in a separate state which, ideally, would be integrated with England. A letter from Fr Michael O'Flanagan to the *Freeman's Journal* of 20 June 1916 was used to substantiate his claim.

> Geography has worked hard [Fr O'Flanagan wrote] to make one nation
> out of Ireland; history has worked against it. The island of Ireland and
> the national unit of Ireland simply do not coincide. In the last analysis
> the test of nationality is the wish of the people.[31]

Fr O'Flanagan concluded by stating that, as Antrim and Down
looked to London as 'the centre of their patriotic enthusiasm,' it
would be wrong to compel them to love the rest of Ireland by force.
From Fr O'Flanagan's admission that 'the island of Ireland and the
national unit of Ireland' do not coincide, Biggs-Davison argued that
provision should be made for a separate entity of Ulster. Fr O'Flanagan did not. While admitting that in the immediate aftermath of
the Rising it was proper to consider the temporary exclusion of
parts of Unionist Ulster from the provision of the Home Rule Bill,
Fr O'Flanagan argued that the historic differences which made such
a suggestion reasonable should ultimately be overcome by mutual
respect and toleration — not by force — and that one nation should
be formed.

With the mention of Fr O'Flanagan, one is introduced to a leading figure in the Republican movement who lost out in the struggle
to attain the full republican ideal. His subsequent importance merits
some biographical detail of his life. Following his ordination he
threw himself with great energy and efficiency into all the movements contributing to national renewal: the Gaelic League, the Co-
operative movement and Sinn Féin. In 1904 he successfully toured
America on behalf of popular industrial interests in the west of
Ireland, and in 1910 he made a similar tour on behalf of the Gaelic
League. Highly intelligent, a great speaker and preacher — even
recognised in Rome as such by a special award — he was also a man
of action. When, at the start of the World War, local people were
faced with anxieties over fuel and food, he led his parishioners at
Cliffoney, Co Sligo, to cut turf in defiance of government regulations, and encouraged them to keep their oats in case of food short-
ages. 'Stick to the Oats' became a national slogan. In the same
year, 1915, in an incident which shows his standing in nationalist
circles, he preached in the City Hall, Dublin, as the body of O'Donovan Rossa lay in state.[32] None of these actions, nor a speech in
Cork in January 1916 against the British war aims, met with the
approval of either the British administration or of his episcopal
superior, Bishop Coyne of Elphin. He was transferred to the parish
of Crossna in North Roscommon and instructed to preach only
within the confines of his own parish.[33] His letter to the *Freeman's
Journal* in June 1916 did cause concern in nationalist circles as it

appeared that he was too willing to concede the existence of two Irelands, but his future actions showed that such a solution was far from his thoughts – he deeply desired a united Ireland based on a reconciliation of the two major traditions in the country. He made this clear in a lecture in Omagh in September 1917, entitled 'Orange and Green.' He suggested that Unionists and Nationalists should reconcile their differences in accordance with the spirit of the tricolour: Orange and Green were linked with the White – the symbol of peace. This part of his speech has not been referred to by the historian Paul Bew, in his excellent study of the period, and, in consequence he tends towards the interpretation of Biggs-Davison. Fr O'Flanagan said:

> The men who devised the Sinn Féin flag at once thought of putting the Orange colour into the flag because they believed the Orange colour stood for something which made it worthy of being put into the flag . . . it was a recognition that hidden beneath the ugly husk of Orangeism there is a kernel, a precious kernel, that Ireland needs in her future development and when we salute the Irish flag, we honour the Orange and Green both equally . . . Let us try and find out what there is in the Orange colour that makes for a democratic National movement.[34]

In part of this talk he promised 'to go to Belfast and sign the Covenant', if the Pope and the Catholic bishops interfered in politics; but despite his singular recognition of the Unionist tradition he wished to harness the north into one 'democratic National movement.' The use of Fr O'Flanagan's letter by Biggs-Davison is clearly not warranted. His argument, and those of others who advocate a partitioned Ireland, has a more grievous flaw. Constantly the point is made that if it were reasonable for southern Ireland to voice an opinion for separation from England, so too it must be reasonable for Ulster to express its wish for separation from the south of Ireland. Biggs-Davison, and others who use this argument, fail to record that in 1916 the democratic decision of Ulster, as expressed by its members of Parliament, was for Home Rule – there were 17 Home Rule members and 16 Unionists.[35] At the Derry by-election of 1913, which swung the parliamentary balance 17 to 16 in favour of Home Rule MPs, the winning candidate was a Protestant Home Ruler.[36] One is given a salutary reminder that religious differences were not all that they have been portrayed to be. Judged on the normal standards of democracy as usually applied in England, which accepts a majority based on the number of parliamentary seats obtained, it is apparent that the province of Ulster favoured Home Rule. In this decision they were at one with the vast majority of the rest of Ireland. The impression is often given, possibly to justify the action of Carson and the Tory Unionists, that Ulster was asked to abandon itself completely to the control of an Irish Parliament sitting in Dublin. Such was not the case. Ulster was being asked to take its place in a united Ireland that was firmly committed to an imperial destiny with the King of England as head of state. In order to justify their withdrawal from this imperial design, Carson and Tory Unionists propagated the 'two nation' theory — a theory which is used in the present time by Biggs-Davison and others to justify Unionist Ulster's integration in the United Kingdom. Contemporary evidence indicates not only that it is misleading to use Fr O'Flanagan in support of such a theory, but also that prior to 1916 there was little talk of two Irelands.

When the 'two nation' theory was aired in 1912 as the debate on the Home Rule Bill began, Alice Stopford Green, the historian, immediately protested at its usage. While admitting that it was reasonable to talk of two races, two religions, two factions, she bitterly resented the term 'two nations'. 'This new term', she wrote, 'seems to find favour as a convenient means of adding discredit to the notion of nationality, and thus by indirect means weakening the claim of any and every nation.'[37] John Redmond also denied the existence of two Irelands, declaring that, 'the two nation theory is to us an abomination and a blasphemy.'[38] In 1920, as plans were being made to make a reality of the 'two nation' theory by the passing of the Northern Ireland Act, George Russell (AE) maintained that the British government had deliberately promoted this divisive concept.

> It was not [he wrote] the policy of the British Government that one section of the Irish people should trust the other section; and Mr. Lloyd-George invented the 'two nations' theory to keep Ireland divided.[39]

This testimony from a Northern Ireland Protestant who was favourable to the link with England is particularly instructive. Taken together with the view of Mrs Green, another Protestant with English connections, sufficient evidence is provided to question the easy assumption of the 'two nation' theory. Biggs-Davison does not advert to the views of Green or AE; nor does Lyons. They both argue that difference justifies partition, and Biggs-Davison is happy to quote Lyons to that effect:

> The recognition of difference, especially among Irishmen, is a prerequisite for peaceful co-existence.[40]

They both ignore facts that militate against the force of their argument: they both omit to mention the manner in which the imperial factor deliberately accentuated differences among Irish people; they ignore the signs of Catholic and Protestant accord, even in Ulster; and they refer to the north in such a way that the democratic voice of Ulster, expressed in favour of Home Rule, is not introduced into the debate on partition. The tendentious nature of Biggs-Davison's submission to the Forum may be forgiven – he was after all writing to defend a cause – but the tone of Lyons' study is more difficult to excuse. His cultural analysis has shaped many modern interpretations and has had political consequences of great moment.

Lyons would appear to be a child – one might say a victim – of a particular historical perspective. He quotes with approval Sir Horace Plunkett and follows the historical pedigree of Lecky and Froude. His historical perspective is, therefore, fashioned by the same forces that accepted the English occupation of Ireland. Most significantly neither Lyons nor any of the recent cultural critics, such as Brown, MacDonagh, Garvin and Kearney, makes mention of Mgr O'Riordain's celebrated book, *Catholicity and Progress*, which refuted in minute detail the picture painted of native, Catholic Ireland by Sir Horace Plunkett in his *Ireland in the New Century*. [41] The critics have blindly followed Plunkett, neglecting the alternative historical perspective presented by O'Riordain – a perspective which fully accords with recent historical criticism on the nature of English rule in Ireland. O'Riordain also presented a positive view of Catholic learning, character and economic life.[42] The O'Riordain view, incidentally, complemented the historical perspective offered by Geoffrey Keating which was so critical of Gerald of Wales and naturally heightened the historical awareness of Keating branch members. O'Riordain's views were known to them and acted upon by them. Indeed, as Rector of the Irish College in Rome, he was to play a significant part in fostering the cause of the 1916 Rising. His opinions have been totally disregarded by Lyons and other commentators, although his rejoinder to Plunkett was so well known at the time that the two books were virtually talked about in the same breath. The result of this neglect has been incalculable. Instead of recognising the signs of burgeoning Catholic intellectual life and the Church's initiatives in economic enterprise at the turn of the century, the critics have accepted Plunkett's strictures about the weaknesses of Catholic character. As a result they lament the low level of Catholic intellectual life and condemn the Church's opposition to social reform. In short, they have accepted the classic colonial/imperial position: the native, Catholic, Irish were inferior, therefore settlement and ascendancy rule were justified.[43] From this false premise they have argued in historical terms that differences in the north of Ireland not only explain partition, but also justify it. For them the 'two nation' theory is a reality. The evidence indicates that it is a false reality based on a false historical perspective. Their view, however, has gained a wide uncritical acceptance and considerable popular support. Moreover, this approval has had important political results leading to a widespread disparagement of Pearse and the men of 1916. A critical evaluation of the recent obloquy heaped upon Pearse is long overdue.

PEARSE: RIGHT OR WRONG?

The celebration of the anniversaries of the Easter Rising affords an opportunity to measure the official and popular response to the event. In 1966 there was a truly national recognition of, and rejoicing in, the memory of the men of 1916 which continued for most of the year; in 1976 the veneration was more qualified and more limited; in 1986 the anniversary passed off almost unnoticed. An editorial in the *Sunday Tribune* of 30 March 1986 illustrated the extent of the swing away from the tradition associated with Pearse and his followers. The writer maintained that 'in 1916 there was the prospect of real political progress in the form of Home Rule once the Great War was over,' and concluded that,

> the 1916 rebellion was wrong and unjustified, that the taking of human life that it involved was indefensible, that the injustice being fought against was not of a sufficient scale to countenance rebellion and the taking of human life and that it was an elitist and arrogant action by people whose democratic credentials were suspect and, in part, for the most suffocatingly chauvinist of motives.[44]

The editorial exemplified the current trend of historical interpretation as typified by Lyons and, most recently, by Garvin. In part, too, it represented the critical appraisal of Pearse and the Rising first initiated by Fr Francis Shaw in an article entitled, 'The Canon of Irish History', which was published in 1972. He argued that Pearse was at variance with the main line of Irish constitutional opinion and that the Rising was unjustified because, as the *Tribune* editorial stressed, the promise of Home Rule was on the statute book.

It cannot be denied that the action of Pearse ran counter to the main body of public opinion: the very planning of the Rising was based on the fact that the IRB was small, select and secretive. How, in these circumstances, can the Rising be justified? By considering, I would suggest, the evidence that neither the *Sunday Tribune* nor recent cultural historians appear willing to place before their readers. Instead of focussing on the suspect 'democratic credentials' of Pearse, it is reasonable to concentrate on the deliberate denial of democratic principles by Carson and the Tory Unionists.

It was Carson and the Tory Unionists, not Pearse, who first abandoned constitutional procedures. The interpretations which have blackened the reputation of Pearse are based on significant omissions. In regard to Ulster there is no mention either of the illegality of Carson or of the imperial designs of the English government. By failing to delineate accurately these forces shaping the character of Unionism the impression is created that internal differences justified partition. In large part this delusion is created by skilful use of terminology: the terms 'Ulster', 'Unionists', and 'Northern Ireland' are used interchangeably to create the impression that they refer to the same unit. The democratic decision of Ulster in 1916 which was favourable to Home Rule is, by this mode of description, concealed. In like manner, while the promise of Home Rule after the War is offered as a reason to condemn the action of Pearse, no mention is made of the subsequent secret commitments made by Lloyd George, firstly, to Carson in 1916, and, secondly, to Craig in 1920, that in any Home Rule settlement the Unionists of Ulster would be guaranteed permanent exclusion. In 1916 Lloyd George gave the assurance to Carson that,

> We must make it clear that at the end of the provisional period Ulster does not, whether she wills it or not, merge in the rest of Ireland;

and in 1920 a similar assurance on the status of Northern Ireland was made to the Ulster leaders through Walter Long, who later recorded that, 'It was on this distinct pledge that we were able to pass the bill with the aid of the Ulstermen.'[45]

One other omission is also significant. No mention is made of the secret treaty between England and Italy, signed on 26 April 1915, which brought Italy into the War on the allied side on the expressed understanding that the Pope would not be allowed to participate in the peace treaty.[46] The signing of this treaty illustrates both the duplicity underlying England's War policy, and the simplicity of Redmond. While the English Foreign Office was negotiating with the Italian government against the Pope's interests, a newly appointed British minister to the Holy See, Sir Henry Howard, was seeking favourable consideration from the Pope for England's war aims. Redmond, English sources later admitted, 'privately aided the sending of the British mission' which was strongly opposed by Mgr O'Riordain and his assistant, Fr Hagan, at the Irish College in

Rome.[47] The treaty may have primarily served Italian interests but it served those of England as well. It meant that the Pope, who at the Versailles Peace Conference might have supported the claims of such small nations as Ireland, was barred from attending. It was evident at the Conference that, while England claimed to be fighting for the rights of small nations, these nations were confined to those outside the British Empire, and certainly did not include Ireland. Promises of Home Rule and rights to small nations 'rightly struggling to be free' inspired many Irishmen to fight for England during the War, but the promises were hollow. To be critical of Pearse for not believing in them is absurd. Broken English promises were, indeed, in the eyes of one shrewd English observer at the heart of the Irish problem.

G. K. Chesterton visited Ireland in 1918. He was saddened that Thomas Kettle and so many southern Irishmen had died at the Somme in 1916 in vain. Whenever he spoke well of them or of other Irish leaders of the past, he was told that he must have Irish blood in his veins. To which he replied that 'he did not need Irish blood in his veins to know that he did not want Irish blood on his hands.' Concerning English promises in regard to the Home Rule Act, Chesterton was equally forthright.

> Now in the political bargain with the English [he wrote] the Irish simply think they have been cheated. They think Home Rule was stolen from them after the contract was sealed, and it will be hard for anyone to contradict them. If 'le Roi le veult' [the King wills it] is not a sacred seal on a contract what is? The sentiment is stronger because the contract was a compromise. The Irish have now returned in a reaction of anger to their most extreme demands; not because we denied what they demanded, but because we denied what we accepted.[48]

In this analysis of the English denial of Home Rule, one finds the source of justification for the action of Pearse. Ireland had not received, and could not expect to receive, fair treatment from England. True justice and genuine peace could not be built on false promises. Pearse, therefore, shed his blood fighting against England because he placed no faith in her promises; Kettle shed his blood fighting for England because he believed in her promises. There is much evidence to suggest that Pearse was proven right and that Kettle, sadly, was proven wrong. Nevertheless, the tide of current opinion is flowing strongly against such an interpretation. In part, this view inimical to the heritage of Pearse, derived some stimulus from the seminal article by Fr Francis Shaw. Fr Shaw argued that the 1916 Rising was neither needed nor wanted. He wrote that,

The widespread idea that in 1916 the people of Ireland were sunken in an unpatriotic slumber could scarcely be further from the truth. The idea that for the first time in their history the Irish people had lost (or were about to lose) the consciousness of their national identity is equally false.[49]

Ireland, alert and awake to its national destiny, was about to enter the promised land: Pearse was wrong to interfere with the expected inheritance. Such is the picture commonly portrayed by press and historians alike. What, however, if the promises were not to be trusted, and the land itself was to be divided? That, indeed, was the reality of the situation in 1916. The Rising may not have been wanted, but it most certainly was needed if the promised land of Ireland's historic aspirations was to be secured. This interpretation is endorsed by an examination of the positive qualities connected with the transition of Pearse from a constitutional Home Ruler to a separatist revolutionary.

Silence concerning the conversion of Pearse has served to depict him as an irresponsible revolutionary — irresponsible and, therefore, indefensible. The silence has had a long and rather sinister pedigree. Immediately after the Rising J. J. O'Kelly as editor of the *Catholic Bulletin* attempted to assess the causes of the rebellion: he referred to the actions of Carson, and then to the character of Pearse.

> It is to be remembered [he stated] that Mr. John MacNeill and the late Mr. P. H. Pearse were among the prominent speakers who, four years ago, assisted at Mr. Redmond's monster Home Rule demonstration ... previously Mr. Pearse, as editor of the Gaelic League's official organ, was one of the few men in Ireland to urge the acceptance of the doomed Council's Bill, as a step in the direction of Irish liberty. We recall these circumstances to show how men of proved constitutional instincts may be driven from the constitutional path.[50]

The main responsibility for the Rising was bluntly laid at the door of the English government which had connived with Carson and neglected the constitutional aspirations of Pearse. O'Kelly's assessment was not published in 1916. The censor, in co-operation with the martial law authorities, decided that the editorial did not serve England's interests. These same interests are served, and Pearse is denigrated, by a similar silence today. Pearse appears as more responsible and more defensible once one considers the reasons for his conversion to a revolutionary position. Historically he rejected the 'two nation' theory; politically he resented the machinations of the Tory party in unison with the illegal forces of Carson. In such circumstances a protest in arms became not only reasonable, but also necessary to defend the threatened dismemberment of Ireland.

Fr Shaw argued correctly that the dominant expression of Irish nationalism in the nineteenth century was directed into constitutional channels; but he failed to take into consideration the fact that neither O'Connell nor Parnell had to face the possibility of a partitioned Ireland in their dealings with the British. Such a threat may well have driven them from the hustings and the conference table to the field of battle. It was that threat certainly that led Pearse on the first step which finally brought him to take up arms in 1916. He perceived that democracy was being denied and that the country was in imminent danger of division.

His early years in the Gaelic League had given him a heightened awareness of the special qualities of Irish identity. At first he had believed, and acted, as if it were possible to achieve de-Anglicisation in cultural terms while retaining the political connection with England. By the end of 1913 it was evident to him that the political settlement acceptable to England was incompatible with the cultural ideals of Irish identity. The Easter Rising was, therefore, for him a profession of belief in Ireland's historic and cultural unity, and a protest against the imperial motives and the undemocratic actions of the English government. His commitment to revolutionary action and to the sacrifice of his own life was based on principle. To write off his motives as 'suffocatingly chauvinist' is to betray a complete lack of understanding of the political and cultural forces at work in 1916. At best the *Sunday Tribune* editorial may be excused as simple naïvety, but naïve nonsense, particularly when couched in terms of abuse, serves no useful purpose in a quest for the truth. Instead of condemning Pearse for his arrogant and narrow nationalism, he merits commendation for discerning a matter of principle beneath the political chicanery of his time. He detected that, beneath the plausible promises, a principle was at stake and he was prepared to die for it. One may object to his methods and disapprove of his principles, but there are no grounds to question the sincerity of his motives. However, the cumulative effect of many recent histories has been to impugn not only his motives, but also his methods and principles — to challenge, in other words, the entire heritage of Pearse. Inevitably these histories — often set in their perspectives — have helped to shape political policies of the present. Both the histories and the political policies manifest little sympathy and respect for the ideals of Pearse, while they exhibit, at the same time, only minor criticism of the principles governing English policy in Ireland. The New Ireland Forum provides a prime example of this pattern of procedure and its treatment of Pearse will now be examined.

PEARSE AND THE NEW IRELAND FORUM

The name of Patrick Pearse does not appear in the Forum Report which was published on 3 May 1984. There is no mention either of the Easter Rising. The chapter entitled 'Origins of the Problem' begins to trace Anglo-Irish relationships from 1920, although there is, admittedly, some reference to the events concerning the Home Rule Bill of 1912. It was noted that 'faced by the unionist threat to resist this bill by, unlawful force' the English Parliament postponed its implementation.

> The message [the Report concluded] — which was not lost on unionists — was that a threat to use violence would succeed. To the nationalists, the conclusion was that the democratic constitutional process was not to be allowed to be effective.[51]

This brief notice suffices as a statement of the origins of the problems prior to 1916 and also serves as the only criticism of the Unionist and English position. Even making every allowance for the needs for brevity, the failure to find a place for the Easter Rising — the origin of the present Irish Republic — in the historical outline is, to say the least, surprising. Surprising too is the failure to mention specifically the responsibility of the Tory party in fomenting civil disobedience and armed illegality in the years before 1916. This omission is strange because even Carson admitted at the end of his days that Tory intrigues had led him on a course that was harmful to the well being of Ireland.

> What a fool I was! [he exclaimed], I was only a puppet, and so was Ulster, and so was Ireland, in the political game that was to get the Conservative Party into power.[52]

In this admission of Carson one is offered a statement which indicates precisely the root cause of the Irish problem. The Forum Report, however, did not act upon it, or upon the vast amount of historical evidence which supported the opinion of Carson. Instead it simply acquiesced in the territorial and constitutional gains made by England in Ireland through the Tory party using Carson as a puppet. The dictum of Asquith that force was not to be used to coerce Ulster, first enunciated in September 1914 and vehemently opposed by Pearse, was accepted. On 15 November 1985 the Irish Government was pleased to affirm with the English Government in the Anglo-Irish Agreement that,

> any change in the status of Northern Ireland would only come about with the consent of a majority of the people of Northern Ireland.[53]

Acceptance of majority rule in Northern Ireland was a denial of the ideals and principles for which Pearse died, namely that no such unit as 'northern Ireland' was justified either historically or politically — it was a false political entity based on a fabricated majority. One may argue that the New Ireland Forum and the Anglo-Irish Agreement are concerned with present realities, and that events in the distant past are best left forgotten, but these present realities have been shaped by their historical mould. A proper historical perspective is required to enlighten problems of the present. The evidence indicates that no such light made its presence felt either in the deliberations of the New Ireland Forum or in the negotiations of the Anglo-Irish Agreement.

Failure to identify Tory and Unionist responsibility for the problems of Ireland constitutes one major failing of the Forum Report; failure to consider, or even to contemplate, the responsibility of the Irish themselves constitutes a second major weakness in the Report. Here one touches more directly upon the heritage of Pearse. The Report does not mention the Civil War in Ireland which followed the Treaty; nor is there mention of the methods used by Fine Gael and Fianna Fáil to emerge as the leading parties in the state. No process of critical self-appraisal is entered upon. Competition between the two parties as to which is the true successor to the heritage of Pearse was avoided. It was presumed that the Irish state embodied the ideals of Pearse. The claims of Sinn Féin and the IRA that they were the true heirs of Pearse were not to be entertained. Indeed, Sinn Féin was explicitly refused permission to present its views at the Forum and is generally banned from propagating its policy by government legislation. Ironically, and, according to Sinn Féin, hypocritically, the Forum justified its intrusion into affairs in the North of Ireland,

> because of the denial of the right of nationalists in the North to political expression of their Irish identity and to effective participation in the institutions of Government.[54]

'The rights of which nationalists?', asked Sinn Féin and the IRA. Clearly the last thing envisaged by the Irish government was that rights should be conferred on their organisations. No, the only nationalists to benefit from the extension of new rights were to be the constitutional nationalists in the SDLP under the leadership of John Hume. The aims and methods of the IRA were rejected by the Forum Report.

> The conditions were thus created [the Report said of events after 1969] for revival of a hitherto dormant IRA which sought to pose as the defen-

ders of the nationalist people. . . . The negative effect of IRA violence on British and Unionist attitudes cannot be emphasised enough. Their terrorist acts create anger and indignation and a resolve not to give in to violence under any circumstances.[55]

Acting on these premises the Anglo-Irish Agreement introduced a programme of co-operation between the Gardaí and the RUC to deal with cross-border security. The IRA was to be attacked by both the English and Irish governments in a co-ordinated manner. The claim by the IRA and Sinn Féin that they are the true nationalists — the true followers of Pearse — was not up for discussion. It is, I suggest, in this contest for Republican authenticity that the reason for the strange silence about Pearse in the New Ireland Forum is to be found. Such a silence may make sense politically; but it makes for poor history. We all need, as Conor Cruise O'Brien puts it, to break free from the constraints of 'the ambiguous historical process' — to avoid engagement is to remain as prisoners of history. O'Brien further suggested that, in studying leading personalities of the period 1891-1916,

> It follows that our best rule in choosing subjects is not to be guided solely by the canon of success — acknowledged posthumous influence — but to look at those who had in fact an influence on their contemporaries.[56]

In that spirit the papers of J. J. O'Kelly are of special interest: they serve as an introduction to those who have not enjoyed the 'canon of success.' In conjunction with the research which his papers stimulated, new light is shed on the growth of the Republican movement after 1916; fresh and disconcerting information is disclosed about the activities of Collins and de Valera; and a hitherto unknown connection is revealed between Sinn Féin and the IRA with the heritage of Pearse.

3

The Emergence of a
Republican Movement
after 1916

IRELAND AFTER THE RISING OF 1916

The contention that Sinn Féin and the IRA have a special connection
with the heritage of Pearse requires examination and elucidation. In
simple terms the claim is based on the fact that the first people to
take a stand successfully for Pearse and the Rising in political terms
in 1917 were the same people who transferred their Republican
mandate to the IRA in 1938. Moreover, in the intervening years,
they showed themselves to be a clearly identifiable group with a
distinct Republican programme. Their personal idealism and their
Republican principles led them to oppose the policies of both Collins
and de Valera. In 1917, at the North Roscommon by-election Count
Plunkett became the first candidate to be elected in sympathy with
the ideals of the Rising – he was selected by Fr Michael O'Flanagan
and J. J. O'Kelly and they also masterminded his election campaign;
in 1938 J. J. O'Kelly and Count Plunkett were two of the signatories
who, as elected members of the Republican Dáil, transferred their
power to the Army Council of the IRA – Fr O'Flanagan, while not
signing the declaration, also opposed the departures of Collins and
de Valera. Rarely is any prominence given to the role of Fr O'Flanagan, Count Plunkett and O'Kelly in the North Roscommon election.
Indeed, biographers of Collins usually stress his importance at the
expense of all others. And, yet, the election, and the events that
led up to it, reveals much about the changing state of affairs in
Ireland, and the factors that led to the formation of a Republican
Sinn Féin party. These events will now be briefly considered.

The poetic verdict of Yeats on the Easter Rising has coloured the imagination of all and the historical interpretation of many. As he expressed it:

> I wrote it out in a verse —
> MacDonagh and MacBride
> Connolly and Pearse
> Now and in time to be,
> Wherever green is worn,
> Are changed, changed utterly;
> A terrible beauty is born.

While the lives of the executed leaders of the Rising were changed utterly — passing immediately into the realm of legendary renown — life in Ireland was not so utterly and immediately changed. The conflicting forces working for continuity and for change engaged in a fascinating contest over a number of years. In political terms the initiative still rested with the British Government and the first reaction of Asquith was to push forward the Home Rule Act. Paradoxically, therefore, the first result of the Rising was not to promote the Republic but Home Rule. The proposal presented by Asquith in June 1916 was in full accord with previous English policy decisions: Ulster was not to be coerced and provision had to be made for some northern counties to opt out of Home Rule. At the same time the English administration in Ireland was refashioned as a consequence of the Rising. Continuity of policy was to be enforced by martial law. The resignation of Birrell and Nathan, Chief Secretary and Under-Secretary respectively, was followed by the appointment of Sir Robert Chalmers as Under-Secretary. He had no love for Ireland or things Irish, and referred to Dublin's members of Parliament and of the Corporation as 'scrofolous swine' and 'snorters.'[1]

Chalmers may have given vent to the mood of the English administration, but effective power lay with General John Maxwell after martial law had been declared on 29 April 1916.[2] The censorship of the press which had been enforced by the Defence of the Realm Act (DORA) since the start of the War was replaced by an even more severe form of press control. A special office was established in Dublin Castle on 1 June 1916, under the direction of Lord Decies, and until August 1919 he and a staff of seventeen carefully examined all press publications and reported monthly on the feeling in Ireland.[3] Military rule and strict censorship was used to promote the government view and to suppress all dissident voices. Even before the Rising some public letters of Bishop O'Dwyer were designated as 'seditious literature' and their distribution forbidden; while on one occasion after the Rising the editor of the *Limerick Echo* was reprimanded for leaving blank spaces in his report of Bishop O'Dwyer's speech accepting the freedom of the City of Limerick.[4] Readers were not to be aware that censorship had taken place. Censorship played a vital part in the struggle for popular support. The *Catholic Bulletin*, for instance, tried to evade the directive that no mention was to be made of the Rising by printing obituaries of the dead and tributes to those who had participated. In September 1916 Lord Decies complained that special problems were raised by the *Bulletin*'s obituary of Sir Roger Casement.

> It cannot fail [he wrote] to stir the sympathy of a large section of the readers of the *Catholic Bulletin* who would probably be unaffected by matter of an openly insidious nature. Although this article is an insidious attempt to keep alive resentment at Casement's fate, it preserves moderation of tone, and since it purports to be written with a religious motive, is most difficult to censor.[5]

It was finally decided to allow publication after consultation with General Maxwell. Month after month the battle for the minds of the people was waged as the government propaganda machine attempted to portray the rebels as extremists in the pay of Germany while the *Bulletin* described them as devout Catholics and Irish of the Irish. In November 1917 the *Bulletin* submitted to the Censor's office a photograph of a painting, 'The Rebels in the Post Office', which they wished to reproduce. Sir William Byrne, who had succeeded Chalmers as Under-Secretary in October 1916, in recommending rejection of the request, observed that,

> It is an artistic production, very well grouped and designed and would probably become popular and help to spread sedition over Ireland. After some years, it might be allowed to become part of 'history', when circumstances have changed.[6]

The *Bulletin* in April 1917 made it clear that it was explicitly attempting to provide a counter to the official government history — 'to place in its true perspective the lives and the methods and the motives of the men of Easter Week.'[7] Contemporary accounts indicate that the *Bulletin* was successful in its objectives and was, indeed, a major influence in making the Rising acceptable. Many modern historians have failed to recognise the context in which O'Kelly and the *Catholic Bulletin* operated. While most writers acknowledge the importance of the *Bulletin* in shaping opinion favourable to the Rising, their acknowledgement is tinged with more than a trace of disparagement. O'Farrell criticises the 'kind of canonisation' conferred upon the rebels by the *Bulletin*; Lyons, too, relying heavily on O'Farrell, is critical of the 'semi-religious cults' nurtured by writings such as the *Bulletin*; and Garvin has echoed the same sentiments — 'the *Bulletin*,' he notes, 'was quick to generate a cult of the martyrs.'[8] None of these writers, and few others, mention the climate of censorship which dictated the pattern of publication adopted by the *Bulletin*. While O'Kelly clearly wished to portray the rebels in an acceptable light, he was not allowed to argue their case in political terms; he was forced to focus on their social and religious qualities; and he was twice imprisoned without trial for his activities. Disregard for the conditions surrounding the publication of the *Bulletin* has led Garvin, in particular, to general conclusions far removed from the reality of the situation.

> Messianism and the sense of external menacing evil, [he declared] which seem to be elements in the psychology of fascism, emerged clearly in the *Catholic Bulletin* after 1916.[9]

There was no Messianic intent, or primeval fascist purpose, in O'Kelly's praise of the rebels of 1916. To engage in such speculation is to indulge in a flight from reality which is harmful not only to the reputation of J. J. O'Kelly, but also to the heritage of Pearse. The reality is more precise and prosaic: O'Kelly emphasised the religious aspects of the rebels' lives because the censor left him no other alternative. O'Kelly and the *Bulletin* deserve recognition as presenting an historical account of the Rising in the most difficult of circumstances.

In the immediate aftermath of the Rising, however, the majority of the people were still content to follow the well established constitutional path. The Irish Party remained the only organised political grouping in the country and, under the direction of Redmond, it was still prepared to co-operate with the English proposals for Home Rule made in June 1916. Many Catholics, Sir William Byrne being one, were quite prepared to assist the English administration in Dublin Castle. And the Catholic Church, despite the strong declarations of Bishop O'Dwyer, remained the ally of the Irish Party. Unlike Bishop O'Dwyer most Catholic clerics believed, and preached with great effect on their parishioners, that the Rising was incompatible with the Church's prerequisites for a just rebellion. It was noted that the *Irish Catholic*, much to the annoyance of advanced nationalists, 'continues to publish sermon after sermon quoting St. Paul and St. Thomas Aquinas against the Rising.'[10] The policy of the *Irish Catholic* was carried out with the approval of Cardinal Logue. His own views were strongly against Sinn Féin. On 22 June

1916, while speaking at Maynooth, he mentioned that it was being said that the younger clergy were supporters of Sinn Féin. 'I think this a calumny on the younger clergy', he declared, 'These things are said and they should not be allowed to go unchallenged.'[11] His words were greeted with applause. Other Bishops publicly condemned the Rising as 'unlawful', 'mad' and 'foolish'.[12] The prevailing clerical opinion was for the status quo: the Catholic Church wanted to repair the damage done by the Rising and to return to the well trodden ways of parliamentary negotiation. The promise of Home Rule, attendant on co-operation in the World War, still appeared to be the only path for the Irish to pursue. Such were the forces operating in favour of continuity and conservatism. They represented the majority of the people; they were organised; and, in the case of the British Government, they were backed up by military force and by effective control of public opinion. In comparison, the forces operating in favour of change were tiny; they lacked any form of organisation; and were devoid of any military capacity. And yet in ten short months these forces which sought change – which wished to implement the ideals of 1916 – won the by-election at North Roscommon. In seeking the reason for this transformation one becomes aware of the factors that determined the shape of Sinn Féin and of the distinct Republican lineage associated with Fr O'Flanagan and J. J. O'Kelly.

In general it may be said that the tiny number who sought an alternative to the Irish Party were slowly augmented by an ever increasing awareness that Pearse was right and the Irish Party was wrong. More and more people gradually became convinced that the partitioned Home Rule settlement did not meet Ireland's aspirations; that England's promises in the War were meaningless; and that no self-respecting Irishman could ally himself with a policy that was sustained by the brutal execution of sixteen fellow Irishmen. Efforts were made to expose the nature of English rule and the futility of Redmond's policies – slowly and imperceptibly progress was made on that front; but to co-ordinate the ensuing opposition into some organised form of protest was another, and more difficult, matter. An examination of the nationalist groups that survived the Rising and the emerging new groups after the Rising both illustrates the problem and helps to identify the people who brought about the new Sinn Féin.

The Sinn Féin party of Arthur Griffith offered no base on which to build an advanced nationalist opposition. It was moribund before the Rising and, after the Rising, Griffith was imprisoned in Reading gaol. It was only English ignorance of the role of the IRB that led to the common description of the Rising as the Sinn Féin Rebellion. The small group in the IRB, which had masterminded the Rising, was eliminated in the ensuing executions. The Irish Volunteers also suffered from the executions of some of their leading members. Many rank and file members of the IRB and the Irish Volunteers were among those imprisoned after the Rising. Inevitably the death and dispersal of these men also affected the nationalist character of the Gaelic League. The group which had planned the Rising was small and had established its links in the IRB, the Irish Volunteers and the Keating branch of the Gaelic League. With the small body of leaders either executed or imprisoned, the remnant of like-minded nationalists was exceedingly minute. Their task of rebuilding the decimated nationalist organisations was made more difficult by the omnipresence of the army, police and intelligence officers, all working in the interests of English rule.

In August 1916 several steps of significance were taken to restore the advanced nationalist position. Seán Ó Muirthile, who had enjoyed a prominent position in the Keating branch, recalled that in August meetings of the branch were resumed.

> The Gaelic League [he wrote] again proved useful, and under the guise of Gaelic League work we were able to hold frequent meetings throughout the Autumn.[13]

The pattern of communication was the same; so also was the geographical area in which contact was made — the region of Parnell Square. Progress was rapid. The Gaelic League Oireachtas was held in August at the Minerva Hotel, Parnell Square. A commitment was made to the men who died in the Rising. Hyde confided in his memoir that,

> Sceilg [J. J. O'Kelly] proposed a resolution to the effect that there was nothing in the chequered history of Ireland that they were so proud of as the heroes who died in the Rising.[14]

This general profession of approval was given a practical dimension when, during the week, a Provisional Supreme Council of the IRB was established. Ó Muirthile became secretary of the Council. In the same month contact was renewed with John Devoy in America. The contact was made through John Archdeacon Murphy. Ostensibly he visited Ireland to help in the co-ordination of American aid to the Irish relief organisations for prisoners and their families. Secretly he was on a private mission from John Devoy.

> He had been commissioned [Ó Muirthile noted] by the Clan na Gael to

look round and ascertain what was being done to recreate the Republican movement on a Physical Force basis.[15]

Both his public and private missions were successful. A meeting was arranged with the widow of Tom Clarke and she conveyed to the Supreme Council of the IRB the names of those men most trusted by her husband. While these developments were taking place within the IRB a move was also made to revive the Irish Volunteers. In September 1916 Cathal Brugha was released from hospital. Although still suffering from the wounds he had received in action at the South Dublin Union, he was prepared to continue the fight. Ó Muirthile and Diarmuid O'Hegarty visited him in his house at Rathmines and were instructed to convene a meeting of the Irish Volunteers. As a result, in the words of Richard Mulcahy,

> a group of Volunteers representing the country — about 50 of them — came together in Fleming's Hotel some time in November or December and Cathal came there on crutches and presided over the meeting and gave them some heart. The initiative and coming together went on through the country.[16]

Fleming's Hotel was situated some 100 yards from Parnell Square, just opposite Belvedere College, and its proprietor Seán O'Mahony — a friend of J. J. O'Kelly and Brugha — had been active in 1916. By December 1916, therefore, a start had been made to revitalise the two organisations most involved in the Rising — the IRB and the Irish Volunteers, and a connection had been re-established with the Clan in America. The unity of purpose was not, however, complete. Brugha, in the words of Ó Muirthile, 'seemed to have lost some of his old faith in the Brotherhood.'[17] He was not alone in his doubts. Denis McCullough, the President of the IRB, and de Valera felt that the organisation should be disbanded after the Rising.[18] All three felt that the secret policy of the Military Committee had not produced the best military effect. Brugha may also have felt, and with some justification, that as president of the Keating branch and a senior and loyal member of the IRB he had some claim to the inner corridors of power — his proven record was, for example, far superior to that of Pearse. This difference of opinion in regard to the IRB had momentous consequences at the signing of the treaty. Already by December 1916 some indication was given of the trouble that lay ahead. Collins, still 'but little known' according to Ó Muirthile, returned from imprisonment and dedicated himself to the restoration of the IRB. In origin, therefore, the renewal of the IRB and the Irish Volunteers contained within itself the seeds of discord, and the grounds for the personal animosity that developed between Brugha and Collins.

The organisation in which Collins established his reputation and built up his contacts immediately after the Rising was the Irish National Aid and Volunteer Dependents' Fund. Soon after the Rising two organisations were active in Dublin in providing relief to those who had suffered as a result of participating in it. On 11 August 1916, representatives of these two groups met at the Gresham Hotel in Dublin. It was this meeting that was chaired by John Archdeacon Murphy as representative of the Irish Relief Committee of America. The two groups – the Irish National Aid Association and the Irish Volunteer Dependents' Fund – amalgamated as the Irish National Aid and Volunteer Dependents' Fund.[19] Formal approval was given to the title of the organisation – a title chosen by Archdeacon Murphy – at an executive meeting on 15 August, and at the same time it was agreed that five representatives of the Dublin Trades Council should have places on the executive.[20] Archbishop Walsh accepted the position of Honorary President and Fr Richard Bowden, the administrator of the Catholic pro-cathedral, was appointed president. New people from all social backgrounds, many of them women, were drawn into the nationalist movement. John Archdeacon Murphy stressed this point in his confidential report to Devoy. He stated that 6,000 dollars a week was being administered to 1,300 families and said of the organisation: 'It has no connection with the parliamentary party and is holding the unanimous nationalist support and confidence of all Ireland.'[21] Murphy correctly identified the wide national support for the organisation. Very rapidly its influence spread throughout the whole country. Special committees were set up to deal with the particular problems of education, employment, civil servants, as well as for the prisoners themselves, and in the space of three years over £130,000 was raised and distributed to the victims of Easter Week. J. J. O'Kelly was a treasurer of the society and Patrick Keohane, secretary at Gill's, was a vice president. It was no mere coincidence that the pages of the Catholic Bulletin promoted the cause of the society and that the photographs, used to telling effect in December 1916 to portray the sad condition of women and children left to mourn their dead husbands and fathers, should be reproduced in the souvenir fund raising programmes of the society. By the time that Collins became secretary of the Irish National Aid and Volunteer Dependents' Fund, in February 1917, it was a flourishing concern, and the ready made contact with released prisoners made it an ideal base on which to rebuild the IRB.[22] Murphy made no mention of the IRB in his report to Devoy. He did, however, refer to a meeting with Bishop O'Dwyer — he called him 'the Bishop of Ireland' — and this allusion serves as an introduction to the first political organisation to challenge the policy of the Irish Party — the Irish Nation League.

On 4 August 1916 the Irish Nation League (INL) had been formed to resist the acceptance of any Home Rule Act which included a temporary provision for the partition of Ireland. In large part it was a direct response to the decision of the Irish Party at the Belfast convention of 17 June which, on the advice of Redmond, Dillon and Devlin, had agreed to accept the English offer of partition. The INL was centred in Omagh and its leading figures were George Murnaghan and F. J. O'Connor. Both men had been members of the Irish Party and many critics felt that its aims did not embrace sufficiently the ideals of the Easter Rising.[23] One eminent member of the Irish Party, Lawrence Ginnell, known as the 'member for Ireland' because of his immediate acceptance of the cause of the rebels, was of that opinion. He had many conversations with John Archdeacon Murphy and had drawn up a draft project with a more advanced programme for the INL. On 16 August 1916 Ginnell wrote to Stephen O'Mara, junior, of Limerick telling him that 'immediate action' was required and asking his help in the foundation of a 'new national organisation.' 'Limerick would,' he declared, 'for many reasons, be the best place to launch such a project.'[24] Quite logically the Bishop of Limerick figured prominently in his plans — this may explain Murphy's visit to the bishop — and he asked Bishop O'Dwyer for 'public episcopal approval.' O'Dwyer replied that although he had no objection to the project, he was not willing to 'father' it.[25] Despite Ginnell's doubts about the INL it made a considerable impact on Irish affairs. On 10 September 1916 it arranged in the Phoenix Park the first public demonstration to be held in Dublin since the Rising.[26] Many attended the demonstration and many who were dissatisfied with the Irish Party were happy with its draft constitution which was published on 24 October. The declared aims, while not embracing the Republican ideals of 1916, were sufficiently advanced to win over many supporters. The stated policy was,

> to secure complete National Self-Government for Ireland without any partition of the Nation; to secure the release of all Irishmen and Irish women imprisoned in connection with the Easter Rising or the Volunteer movement; to resist the imposition of compulsory military service on Ireland; ... to preserve and cherish the National ideals of Ireland by fostering her language and traditions, sports and pastimes, and promoting the study of her history.[27]

Stephen O'Mara was sufficiently attracted to the programme to join the Provisional Supreme Council of the society as was Michael O'Callaghan, also of Limerick. Gavan Duffy, and eventually Ginnell himself, also joined the Council. J. J. O'Kelly was also a member. The appeal of the INL was wide, but the leadership and organisation was to prove too weak. However, in chanelling able and influential men of affairs into organised opposition to the Irish Party, it made a significant contribution to the growth of the Sinn Féin party. Other organisations, notably the 'Repeal League' of Michael Judge and the 'Sinn Féin' party of Herbert Pim bear witness rather to the weaknesses of the nationalist cause after 1916 than to its strengths.

Michael Judge who boasted of a Volunteer pedigree stretching back to 1798, was the first in the field. His weekly journal, *The Irish Nation*, appeared on 24 June 1916 and a policy based on the repeal of the Act of Union was quickly formulated.[28] Efforts were made to establish branches of the League throughout the country but with very limited success. For a short time he considered amalgamating with the INL, but, after attending the INL demonstration in the Phoenix Park, he conducted a policy of open opposition towards it.[29] He also opposed publicly the Sinn Féin policy advocated by Herbert Pim. Pim, a convert from Unionism, had joined the nationalist ranks and been imprisoned. On his release, he declared, on 16 September 1916, that *The Irishman*, the journal which he directed, would be 'a genuine Nationalist organ.'[30] His main claim to recognition derived from his assertion that he was preaching the Sinn Féin policy of Griffith and was acting in accordance with the wishes of his fellow prisoners in Reading gaol. On 4 November 1916 he declared,

In Reading Jail the prisoners of war held several conferences on the subject of what action they would take when released. The procedure of *The Irishman* has been based upon these conferences, and, as will appear later, upon the last urgent admonition which the Editor received from Arthur Griffith.[31]

Fortified by this mandate Pim attacked the Irish Party, Judge's Repeal League and the INL with great confidence and few signs of tolerance. The policy of Home Rule was derided as being 'the outcome of helotry and ignorance,' while Judge was ridiculed as the 'self-appointed Pope' of a movement of which he, himself, made up 100 of the 200 branches.[32] This assessment of Judge and the Repeal League was probably correct, but the gadfly prompting of Pim served only to create divisions in the nationalist ranks. By November 1916, when a by-election became necessary in West Cork, the parties claiming to represent nationalist interests — the INL, Sinn Féin and the Repeal League — were well and truly at variance with each other. Pim attempted to intervene in the election in the interests of his Sinn Féin party and, on 4 November 1916, received a reply from William O'Brien, leader of the All-For-Ireland League, who was running a candidate in the election. O'Brien, a former colleague of Redmond and Dillon, was an experienced politician who perceptively analysed the diverse elements which were adopting a nationalist position.

> The term 'Sinn Féiner' [he wrote] has three different meanings. Firstly, it is used to describe Irish Republicans, whose appeal is to armed force alone: secondly, 'Constitutional Sinn Féiners' who have revived the programme of withdrawal from Westminster originally formulated by Mr. Griffith's organisation which has, I believe, for several years ceased to exist; and, thirdly, the far larger number of Nationalists, neither physical force men nor abstentionists . . . who received with a thrill of gratitude the proof given by the Rising that there are thousands of young Irishmen as ready as ever to die for pure love of Ireland's nationality.[33]

O'Brien's analysis cannot be improved on: the motives that led Irish people to abandon the Irish Party and to adopt a more nationalist policy are accurately delineated. But in November 1916 the disparate motives had not been fused together into one organisation. The West Cork election was won by a supporter of Redmond; there was no nationalist candidate.[34] The fundamental weakness of the nationalist cause could not be more dramatically underlined.

Following this by-election some attempts were made to heal the manifest divisions, but without success. On 18 November, Louis J. Walsh of the INL urged Pim to implement Griffith's Sinn Féin policy as a member of the INL organisation. Pim's arrogant and public reply left no room for compromise.

> True Nationality, like True Religion [he wrote], cannot compromise . . . As Sinn Féin cannot compromise, it remains for the members of the Nation League to add a little to their national principles, and Sinn Féin will gladly welcome them, and reinstate them in the estimation of the Irish people.[35]

At the same time Judge published a letter which indicated that Pim had been in touch with the English administration, and he commented laconically on 2 December that Pim 'may be more fool than knave, but whether he be knave or fool he is equally impossible as a leader of our people.'[36] The files of the Press Censorship Office reveal that Pim was, indeed, in secret contact with Lord Decies, the Censor. They also reveal much about the real aims and the true mentality of Pim. He wanted to avoid a repetition of Easter week; he wished to restore the 'old Sinn Féin'; and he envisaged himself as leading the country in a new constitutional movement.

> I sincerely wish [he wrote on 12 October 1916] that they would liberate Professor MacNeill, with his assistance I could pacify the country.[37]

Lord Decies did not trust Pim.[38] Nor, with good reason, did many other nationalist leaders. Nevertheless his erratic and unstable behaviour, which eventually led him back into the fold of Unionism, was a factor to be reckoned with in the evolution of Sinn Féin until the end of 1917.

When, on 22 December 1916, James J. O'Kelly, the MP for North Roscommon, died, there was no nationalist party in existence sufficiently organised to contest the vacant seat. While the rebirth of the IRB and the Irish Volunteers offered hope for the future, and the burgeoning growth of the prisoners relief society was also a sign of brighter prospects to come, the basic political organisation was lacking. More seriously, the political groupings that had appeared — the INL, the Repeal League and Sinn Féin — were in open conflict with each other. In this political power vacuum there was scope for an individual of enterprise and initiative to make his presence felt. Fr Michael O'Flanagan was such a man and, as a curate of Crossna in the vacant constituency of North Roscommon, he was in the right place at the right time. It was in this context, and in these circumstances, that the first political grouping to declare successfully for Pearse and the Rising was born.

COUNT PLUNKETT AND THE NORTH ROSCOMMON BY-ELECTION

Soon after the death of James J. O'Kelly, Fr O'Flanagan paid a visit to Gill's at 50 Upper O'Connell Street, close to Parnell Square. There he talked with J. J. O'Kelly and Patrick Keohane. They discussed the North Roscommon election. O'Kelly recalled later that,

> After half an hour's conversation Father O'Flanagan concluded that Count Plunkett was the man. His son had been martyred . . . and he was himself a man with a fine national record and high accomplishment intellectually . . . He was very active in 1916 and he was the passport to the situation at the time. I wrote to Count Plunkett that evening . . . and I had a letter back from him to the effect: Yes, he was prepared to go forward as Ireland's representative at the Peace Conference . . . It was really as Ireland's representative for the Peace Conference that Count Plunkett was nominated for Roscommon.[39]

Behind this factual account lies a network of inter-connecting personal relationships which made it possible, and credible, for a small group of men to select a parliamentary candidate. The initiative lay with Fr O'Flanagan. He was, as has already been indicated, a national, if controversial, figure. His speech in June 1916, which accepted two contrasting traditions in Ireland, was seen by some to show a lack of national understanding. However, his speeches against conscription, for which he had been effectively silenced by his Bishop, Coyne of Elphin, had conferred upon him wide popularity. Locally he was regarded as the champion of the people and his word could command instant support. Although ordered by Bishop Coyne to preach only within the confines of his own parish, Fr O'Flanagan decided that the national good required his intervention. In a private memorandum to the bishop he later justified his actions on the ground that 'salus populi, suprema lex' — the well being of the people is the supreme law.[40] Fr O'Flanagan was concerned about the condition of the nationalist cause in Roscommon. It was known that the Irish Party was well organised in that area and could mount an efficient campaign. The effectiveness of the nationalist campaign was immediately threatened by the decision of Michael Judge to run his own candidate, Jaspar Tully, in the interests of the Repeal League. Moreover, Dr Michael Davitt, who had originally been nominated by a small group of nationalists in the area, expressed an unwillingness to contest the election. Deciding that a national figure was required to enhance the nationalist cause, Fr O'Flanagan made contact with J. J. O'Kelly and Patrick Keohane at Gill's. There were good reasons for contacting these men, especially O'Kelly.

Through a family contact at Maynooth, Fr O'Flanagan had been on friendly terms with O'Kelly since the turn of the century. As an active Gaelic Leaguer, Fr O'Flanagan would also have been aware of O'Kelly's influential role in that society. Personal associations would have made the visit understandable but the purpose of the visit was based on eminently practical considerations. Both O'Kelly and Keohane, through the medium of the *Catholic Bulletin*, offered unrivalled opportunities for promoting the claims of a candidate; and, as leading figures in the prisoners relief society, they were in close contact with all those connected with the Rising. O'Kelly, in particular, was on friendly and intimate terms with Count Plunkett. Both men were in the Society for the Preservation of the Irish Language (SPIL) and in the years before the Rising they had worked closely together — Plunkett, as president since 1906, and O'Kelly as secretary since 1914.[41] The private letters of O'Kelly reveal that after the Rising this contact was retained. The Count, following his deportation, wrote to O'Kelly in his capacity as treasurer of the Irish National Aid and Volunteer Dependents' Fund, and O'Kelly visited him in England. A letter of 7 January 1917 makes clear that Plunkett fully recognised and supported O'Kelly's editorial policy in the *Catholic Bulletin*: 'I hope', he wrote, 'the Bulletin keeps up its abnormal success.'[42] O'Kelly, therefore, provided an ideal channel of communication with Count Plunkett. In this way a distinctive voice was added to the Republican lineage which had its roots in the Roscommon election. The traditional picture presented of Plunkett is generally far from flattering: at best he is described as merely a symbolic figure; at worst he is written off as an old buffer who became caught up in something which he did not really understand. The reality is far different and contains many surprises.

Plunkett was, indeed, an old man. He was born in Dublin in 1851 and had received the title of Papal Count from Pope Leo XIII in 1884. Politically he was sympathetic to the views of Isaac Butt and Parnell, and had contested a parliamentary seat in the interest of the Irish Party. He enjoyed a European reputation as a man of learning and it was fitting, as a member of the Royal Irish Academy and of the Royal Dublin Society, that he should be appointed Director of the National Museum in 1907.[43] In many ways he was an establishment figure. He had good reason however, after the Rising of 1916 to turn his back on the establishment. One son, Joseph Mary, was executed, having been married on the eve of his execution; two other sons, George and John, were sentenced to death before this was commuted to ten years penal servitude; and he, himself, was dismissed from his post at the National Museum, expelled from the RDS, and deported to England with his wife. These traumatic events were sufficient to bring about a genuine conversion to the ideals of Easter Week. And yet there are surprising indications that the conversion came some time before the Rising. O'Kelly, when writing of the Count as being 'very active in 1916,' hints at some prior involvement in the activities of his sons. This suggestion is confirmed by the revelation of his daughter, Geraldine, that he 'was sworn into the Irish Republican Brotherhood early in April 1916.'[44] Acting on behalf of the IRB, Count Plunkett went to Berne where he met the German ambassador and through him sent a letter to Roger Casement on 5 April 1916. The letter announced that the Rising was fixed for Easter Sunday; that arms and German officers would be needed; and that 'a German submarine will be required in Dublin Harbour. The time is very short, but is necessarily so, for we must act of our own choice and delays are dangerous.'[45] The letter was signed 'a friend of James

Malcolm' — the code name of Plunkett's son, Joseph Mary, on his missions to Germany. Count Plunkett then visited Pope Benedict XV in Rome. Asquith had had an audience with the Pope on 31 March in which he had tried to justify England's policy in regard to Ireland, on the grounds that Home Rule would be granted after the War. Plunkett attempted to expose the falsity of Asquith's promises. He informed the Pope that the partition of Ireland was to be part of the Home Rule settlement and added that such a partition would permanently endorse the initial wrong caused by the Protestant plantation of Ulster. The Pope appears to have been impressed for according to the Count, he returned to Ireland with the papal blessing for the Volunteers.[46] Having regard to these important activities of Count Plunkett in the weeks before the Rising, one cannot but conclude that the man who accepted the candidacy for North Roscommon was a far more committed nationalist than he has been given credit for — worthy indeed to be 'the passport to the situation at the time.' Plunkett's family connections also reveal another invaluable contribution to the Roscommon campaign. Dr Thomas Dillon who was sworn into the IRB by Joseph Mary Plunkett, and who later married Geraldine Plunkett, maintained that the Irish Volunteers were committed by Brugha to endorse Plunkett's candidacy and to engage actively in his election campaign. Granted O'Kelly's close links with Brugha, it was understandable that they should see eye to eye on the choice of Plunkett. They may even have discussed the matter between themselves. What is certain is that by January 1917 Count Plunkett was appointed the nationalist candidate and that Fr O'Flanagan, J. J. O'Kelly and Cathal Brugha were especially identified with his candidature. It is this group of people who form the basis of a distinct Republican lineage. While it is true that both Collins and Griffith assisted in the campaign, they had no say in the selection of Count Plunkett. Both men had just been released from prison when the election issue arose and neither had had time to find their feet in Ireland: Collins, as has been noted, only became secretary of the prisoners aid society in February 1917; and Griffith, who also called into O'Kelly's office at Gill's, admitted that he had no party funds, no party organisation, and no newspaper to put at the disposal of Count Plunkett.[47] The INL did support Plunkett's candidacy and campaigned for him effectively. The election campaign, however, was masterminded by Fr O'Flanagan and J. J. O'Kelly.

Fr O'Flanagan was the driving force in Roscommon. He funded the election; he mobilised clerical support for Plunkett; he organised assistance in Plunkett's interests at all the polling stations throughout the county; and he braved the severe cold weather to speak on many platforms on Plunkett's behalf.[48] O'Kelly made himself responsible for the paperwork and the promotion of Plunkett. His letter of invitation to Plunkett served as his election address and was reproduced for propaganda purposes. He also wrote some light hearted ballads which were critical of Plunkett's opponents; but, perhaps most important of all, he produced in the February issue of the *Catholic Bulletin* — available to a wide audience some few days before the vote — a well written lengthy tribute to the Count with a fine photograph of him wearing his papal decorations.[49] Those with inside knowledge of the campaign recognised the value of O'Kelly's contribution. Soon after the election Gavan Duffy wrote that 'Sceilg did more than anyone for the Count at the election and in fact took charge of practically all his correspondence.'[50] The primacy of Fr O'Flanagan's efforts in the field was recognised by the secret police reports of Sinn Féin activities. He, Count Plunkett, Lawrence Ginnell and Louis Walsh were listed as being responsible for making very disloyal and seditious speeches.[51] Their endeavours were rewarded with success. On 3 February Count Plunkett was elected with 3,022 votes; Tom Devine, Irish Party candidate, secured 1,700 votes; and Jaspar Tully 587 votes. Newspapers, significantly, in announcing Plunkett's victory described him as an Independent candidate, not as a member of Sinn Féin. The result had a dramatic effect on the political life of Ireland. For the first time the supremacy of the Irish Party had been successfully challenged and the ideals of Pearse and 1916 convincingly asserted. A clear sign was given that the old order could be changed — changed utterly. Rarely is fitting prominence given to the men who made that change possible — hence the need for an outline narrative to establish their credentials. Their contribution to the events that culminated in the creation of a republican Sinn Féin organisation will now be considered.

COUNT PLUNKETT AND HIS CONVENTION OF APRIL 1917

Signs of differences in the nationalist ranks appeared on the very evening of the declaration of Plunkett's victory. A meeting, chaired by Count Plunkett, was held in Boyle. When he announced that he was not going to take his seat at Westminster representatives of the INL expressed their displeasure. Controversy about the policy of abstention loomed large in future discussions of all nationalist groups. At the same time the memoir of Dr Thomas Dillon sheds light on the progress of the nationalist cause on another front.

Having participated in the election campaign, he wrote,

> I had been recalled to Dublin before the declaration of the poll, by Cathal Brugha to meet some people from the country to advise them on the matter of explosives.[52]

Brugha was clearly prepared to take action to make the Volunteers effective across the country. Dr Dillon and Rory O'Connor were leading advisers on the making of explosives: Dillon was a member of the chemistry department of UCD and O'Connor, a graduate of the Royal University, was a qualified engineer with scientific knowledge. Both men, interestingly enough, followed the pattern of conversion experienced by Pearse and others. Dillon had been president of the Young Ireland branch of the Irish Party at UCD and O'Connor, in the midst of the Home Rule controversy, had declared, 'Concentrate on Home Rule. Never mind unessentials!'[53] Both became disillusioned with the Irish Party; both joined the IRB; both were active in 1916; and both played important roles in the plans of Brugha and Plunkett. They were close friends; O'Connor was best man at Dillon's marriage to Geraldine Plunkett.

The first step to fashion unity among the nationalist forces was taken by Count Plunkett. On 15 February 1917 a meeting was held at his house at 26 Upper Fitzwilliam Street. Among those present, apart from the Count himself, were Fr O'Flanagan, J. J. O'Kelly, Rory O'Connor, Lawrence Ginnell, Alderman Tom Kelly, Arthur Griffith, F. J. O'Connor, Thomas Farren, William O'Brien, Darrell Figgis, Séamus O'Doherty and Michael Collins.[54] Plunkett was appointed chairman and Rory O'Connor was made temporary secretary. Most cross sections of nationalist opinion were thus represented. Sinn Féin by Griffith and Figgis; the INL by F. J. O'Connor and Ginnell; the labour movement by Farren and O'Brien; the IRB by Collins and Séamus O'Doherty; and the Volunteers by Rory O'Connor. Many at the meeting had more than one title to be present. O'Kelly, for example, was vice-president of the Gaelic League, a council member of the INL as well as being treasurer of the INAVDF – of which organisation Collins, Farren and O'Brien were also officials. Despite their highly vocal claims for recognition, neither Judge nor Pim was at the meeting. There was no immediate agreement beyond the setting up of a small committee of five which was to examine the possibility of unity. The members of the committee were Plunkett, Griffith, William O'Brien, Séamus O'Doherty and J. J. O'Kelly.[55] On 22 February the nationalists involved in these discussions were given a sharp reminder that ultimate power lay with the British Government. On that day J. J. O'Kelly, while walking home from a meeting with Griffith, was seized, arrested and deported without trial.[56] He was not alone: 27 other nationalists were deported with him under the terms of martial law which were still in operation. Among those arrested with him were Seán T. O'Kelly, Darrell Figgis, Seán Ó Muirthile, Dr Patrick McCartan, Séamus O'Doherty, Thomas MacCurtain, Terence MacSwiney, M. P. Colivet and Michael Brennan. The names of those deported, in what became known as the first 'German plot', testify to the efficiency of British intelligence, for all those seized were playing a prominent part in the nationalist revival throughout Ireland. Having struck at the resurgent nationalist forces, the British attempted to implement their own policy.

The English policy was aimed at winning acceptance from the Irish Party and the Irish people for a partitioned settlement. Despite Lloyd George's secret pledge to Carson that partition would be permanent, the Home Rule proposals made in June 1916 had proved a failure. The success of Count Plunkett made a new initiative necessary. Pressure from America, whose help was urgently required in the War, ensured that some new English action would be taken. The answer of Lloyd George to this new situation was to call a convention of all the Irish people. Publicly it was proclaimed that the Irish people held their fate in their own hands; privately it was stressed that no resolution from the Convention would be allowed to subvert the secret pledge made to Carson and the Unionists. Duke, the Chief Secretary, began consultations with the Irish Party to ensure the Convention's success, and Sir Horace Plunkett was chosen as chairman. Ironically two Plunkett Conventions were held in 1917: Count Plunkett called his for 19 April; Sir Horace summoned his for 25 July. The contrast between the two conventions could not be more complete or revealing: Count Plunkett stood for a united Ireland and attempted to attain his ideal despite the restrictions of martial law and censorship of the press; Sir Horace accepted, somewhat reluctantly, the idea of partition and was happy that censorship of the press should assist the work of his convention.[57] The battle for the minds and hearts of the people was thus enjoined on these markedly unequal terms.

On St Patrick's Day, 17 March 1917, Count Plunkett summoned a convention of nationalists to meet in the Mansion House, Dublin, on 19 April. He called the meeting as if the mantle of leadership had fallen on his shoulders. 'The duty has been cast upon me,' he wrote, 'of inaugurating a policy for Ireland.'[58] The manner of his announcement was not designed to reconcile the INL and Sinn Féin to his side. Archbishop Walsh, whom Plunkett had approached for support, tactfully pointed this out while declining the chance of closer involvement with the movement. The further stipulation that membership at the convention was 'reserved for bodies that commit themselves to the principle of "abstention from Westminster" ' raised particular barriers to the attendance of the INL.[59] Between the summoning of the convention and the actual meeting itself a flurry of activity took place. Griffith representing Sinn Féin and F. J. O'Connor representing the INL made common cause against the authoritarian methods of Plunkett. Since Griffith had begun to republish *Nationality* on 17 February 1917 he had been content to carry advertisements for the INL.[60] It was understandable, therefore, that while differences existed between the two groups, co-operation on specific issues should be quite possible. The record of their conflict with Plunkett is encapsulated in the correspondence of Gavan Duffy. Not only was Duffy on friendly terms with Griffith and a council member of the INL, but also he was a lawyer with special access to the Irish prisoners and deportees in England. His letters to Fairford, especially to Figgis, McCartan, Seán T. O'Kelly and J. J. O'Kelly, informed them of developments in Ireland; sought their advice; and, in regard to J. J. O'Kelly, requested his assistance in getting Count Plunkett to change his mind. On 30 March O'Kelly, writing as a member of the INL and admitting that the organisation had grounds to be upset with Plunkett, said of the situation,

> It looks hopeless . . . but by no means past redemption. The Count being the best man we were able to put up, we cannot think of turning him down now without the certainty of the new movement being practically still born.[61]

O'Kelly attached much attention to Bishop Fogarty's public endorsement of Plunkett's election policy of sending an Irish representative to the Peace Conference. 'This will,' O'Kelly noted, 'help to smooth the way for priests all over the country.'[62] The feeling from Fairford was that no policy difference, or manifestation of personal rancour, should be allowed to impair the general growth of the movement across the country. Good will and common sense should prevail. To a limited extent they did. The convention was not sabotaged but the unity expressed was fragile and based on tactical expediency. On the one hand Plunkett was adamant that no concession should be made over the question of abstention, thus making an official INL representation impossible; on the other hand, Duffy, on 10 April, approved of a suggestion by Darrell Figgis that the INL attend as individuals as 'I think that it is quite possible we might carry the meeting against Plunkett.'[63] Practical difficulties were added to these differences of principle. Plunkett's invitation had been delivered to local councils and other public bodies in a general capacity, but many of these organisations were controlled by the Irish Party. It was only due to the initiative of Rory O'Connor, who contacted many individuals and assumed responsibility for attendance; and to Dr Thomas Dillon, who drew up the agenda and the list of speakers, that a representative gathering of any size was assembled.[64] Privately there was great discord in nationalist ranks – Griffith, for example, told Dillon bluntly that, 'I am not going to that meeting' before finally consenting to attend, but not to speak.[65] Publicly every effort was made to present a harmonious unity.

Griffith, despite his personal feelings, hailed the success of the convention. It was, he proclaimed in *Nationality*, 'the most important held in Ireland since November, 1905, when Sinn Féin were established.'[66] Over 150 clergy, 70 public bodies and 1,000 delegates attended the assembly in the Mansion House. Of the clergy a typed list of 49 names is to be found in Count Plunkett's papers with a hand written note at the top of the page inscribed, 'Turbulent priests. Supplied by Fr O'F.'[67] Among these priests were several associated with J. J. O'Kelly in the language movement or with the *Catholic Bulletin*. Notable among them were Frs Brennan and Ferris from Kerry; Fr Fullerton from Down and Connor; Fr Wall from Limerick; and Fr Kelleher from Waterford. In popular estimation there was unity of purpose. Count Plunkett and Fr O'Flanagan were greeted as they appeared on the platform with cries of, 'Up Sinn Féin! Up Roscommon.'[68] There was little public awareness that 'Sinn Féin' and 'Roscommon' represented two different policies. The issue was raised, however, in the ensuing debate. Count Plunkett argued that there should be a new national organisation, named the Liberty League, which embraced the ideals of Easter Week. So little value did he attach to Sinn Féin that Dillon observed that 'on me he left the impression that he did not know of the existence of Sinn Féin.'[69] Naturally representatives of Sinn Féin argued for the retention of their own organisation and policies inside a wider national framework. Gavan Duffy, speaking as an individual, made the case for the INL. Faced by these signs of discord and acrimony one of the priests present, Fr Fullerton, proposed that in order to safeguard unity, Fr O'Flanagan should consult with Griffith and produce an agreed statement.[70] This suggestion was acted upon. The result was a compromise: the affirmation of such aims as 'we proclaim Ireland to be a separate nation,' and 'we demand representation at the Peace Conference,' represented a success for the views of Plunkett: but the setting up of a committee, the Mansion House Committee, to decide on the formulation of future policy ensured that the case of Sinn Féin and the INL could still be made.[71] The composition of the committee reflected the compromise on policy. On the one hand there were Count Plunkett and his wife, Fr O'Flanagan, Cathal Brugha and Dr Dillon who, significantly described this grouping as the Volunteers — a title that may well indicate Brugha's growing influence in the movement; and on the other hand there were Griffith, Seán Milroy, Alderman Tom Kelly, William O'Brien and Stephen O'Mara — a grouping which reflected Sinn Féin, INL and Labour interests.[72] This hard-won unity, however, did not serve as the foundation for future co-operation: rather it served as the focal point from which issues of confrontation between Plunkett's Liberty League and Griffith's Sinn Féin might be resolved.

COUNT PLUNKETT AND HIS DIFFERENCES WITH ARTHUR GRIFFITH

Fortunately, from a nationalist point of view, few people realised the differences that existed between the Liberty League and Sinn Féin. Ironically, however, while the mood in the country was moving towards the aspirations of Count Plunkett, it was expressed by joining not the Liberty League but Sinn Féin. There were good reasons for this: Griffith's Sinn Féin had a central organisation based at 6 Harcourt Street, and a weekly journal in *Nationality*; it also benefitted by the British labelling of the Rising as the 'Sinn Féin Rebellion.' It was some time before the Mansion House Committee saw it as necessary to tackle the problem posed by a party with a non-republican programme attracting republican-minded voters. Their first efforts were made in unison to support Joseph McGuiness in the Longford by-election of May 1917.[73] The choice of McGuiness was made by Collins and not without some opposition. McGuiness lived in Longford; he was a prisoner at Lewes; and he was a member of the IRB. The IRB in Lewes gaol were divided over the choice: Thomas Ashe advised him to contest the election; de Valera, Seán McGarry and others were opposed to his standing.[74] Any weaknesses in the nationalist position caused by these differences were more than compensated for by the public declaration on 12 May, the eve of the vote, by Archbishop Walsh 'against the partitioning of Ireland.'[75] He explained why, a few days previously, sixteen Catholic and three Protestant bishops had opposed partition in any form, and lamented the fact that it still held 'a leading place in the practical politics of to-day.' He concluded: 'I am fairly satisfied that the mischief has already been done, and that the country is practically sold.'[76] It was a clear attack on the policy of the Irish

Party and was used by the supporters of McGuiness. At the polling stations copies of Walsh's letter were distributed with the appendage:

This is a clear call from the great and venerated Archbishop of Dublin to vote against the Irish Party traitors, and to vote for Joe McGuiness.[77]

Undoubtedly the appeal of Archbishop Walsh helped to undermine the support of the local bishop and his senior clergy for the Irish Party and to secure victory for McGuiness by 37 votes. The momentum initiated by Plunkett's election victory at Roscommon was maintained. Formal unity within the nationalist groups was also preserved.

Archbishop Walsh was correct in his fears about proposals of partition to solve the Irish question. On 21 May 1917 Lloyd George announced the terms of Sir Horace Plunkett's convention. Count Plunkett immediately convened a meeting of the Mansion House Committee. They rejected Lloyd George's convention.

A Convention to have the right of formulating a system of government for Ireland [they declared] must be freely chosen for that special purpose by the people of Ireland, upon a basis of adult suffrage, free from English influence, and free, if it so decides, to declare for the complete independence of Ireland.[78]

The signatories were William O'Brien, Griffith, Brugha, Count and Countess Plunkett, Milroy, Stephen M. O'Mara, Fr O'Flanagan, and Dr Dillon. Differences between Sinn Féin and the Liberty League did not interfere with this condemnation of English policy. The police reports indicate that they were not aware of any differences or difficulties in the nationalist ranks. Owen Brien, the superintendent of the DMP, submitted his report to the Under-Secretary under the subject heading of 'Sinn Féin and National Convention,' and referred to the signatories as 'the Sinn Féin Republican Committee'.[79] A republican Sinn Féin was far removed from the designs of Griffith and below the surface differences did exist – and they were growing more serious. The day after the joint declaration the Sinn Féin executive in Tralee reported that, 'We nearly broke up our organisation here as a result of trying to decide between Liberty Club or Sinn Féin.'[80] On that very day, 22 May, the executive of the Volunteers had met and had acted decisively. Members of the Volunteers were informed that while they were free 'to join any other movement that aims at making Ireland a separate and independent nation,' they were warned against abandoning physical force as a policy.[81] They were urged to give their first allegiance to their own organisation. Such advice was necessary as in Cork too there was trouble. On 2 June Liam de Róiste sent a circular from the Cork Sinn Féin executive to all members of the Mansion House Committee.

> If our forces are split up into possible rival organisations [he complained] it will have a disastrous effect upon the whole movement and will give an opportunity to the pro-English faction to return to power.[82]

The Cork Sinn Féin executive was in favour of Plunkett's policy and, in fact, wanted the Mansion House Committee to organise a provisional parliament. On 30 May another voice from Cork expressed itself to be in sympathy with Plunkett; it was that of Mary McSwiney. Significantly she referred to his movement as the Volunteers and to him as the 'trump card.'[83] In the short term she counselled him to build up his organisation in Cork on the Volunteers and Cumann na mBan — advice that reflected the Volunteer directive of 22 May; in the long-term she was to prove the most influential adherent to the republican cause expounded by Plunkett and Brugha.

It was not until the third meeting of the Mansion House Committee that Brugha raised the differences between the policy of himself and Plunkett with that of Griffith. He felt strongly that Griffith's Sinn Féin was undermining the republican position. So angry was Brugha that he 'threatened that if Griffith stumped the country for Sinn Féin, he would get the Volunteers to stop him.'[84] A fourth meeting of the committee was, therefore, called in which an attempt was to be made to resolve all difficulties. By that time the composition of the committee had been significantly changed: William O'Brien had announced his departure from it on 28 May to concentrate on building up the Labour Party; and, early in June, F. J. O'Connor had died — 'his loss to the Nation League', O'Kelly commented, 'is irreplaceable.'[85] The meeting took place at Brugha's house in 5 Fitzwilliam Terrace, Upper Rathmines Road. According to Dr Dillon who attended as secretary of the Mansion House Committee,

> the difference between the sections of the movement stood out very clearly. The argument might be described as hot and strong, without being too acrimonious.[86]

Dillon recalled that as well as members of the Mansion House Committee, Rory O'Connor and Michael Collins were also present. A compromise was reached. It was agreed that the name of Sinn Féin should be retained and that for a provisional period Griffith should remain as its president and that its constitution should remain unchanged. These arrangements were designed to meet the requirements of Griffith. To meet the requirements of Count Plunkett and Brugha it was further agreed that a provisional committee should be formed to draft a new constitution which, together with proposals for a new leader, would be voted on at a National Convention later in the year.[87] The provisional committee was composed of six members from the old Mansion House Committee, six members of the Sinn Féin executive and six members from the Liberty Clubs, again referred to by Dillon as the Volunteers.[88] The full committee was Arthur Griffith (President), Count and Countess Plunkett, Milroy, Brugha, O'Mara, Fr O'Flanagan, W. L. Cole, M. Collins, Liam Ó Cléirigh, Eamonn Price, Seán Brown, Charles Murphy, Joseph McGrath, Rory O'Connor, James Whelan, M. J. Lennon and Seán Ó Tuama. Dr Thomas Dillon and Seán Campbell were Honorary secretaries.[89] At the same time an invitation was sent to the INL to send six representatives but the invitation was not acted upon until 11 September.[90] The INL Council then agreed to amalgamate with the new Sinn Féin and nominated Lawrence Ginnell, Michael Lynch, George Murnaghan junior, Joseph Murray, Michael O'Callaghan and J. J. O'Kelly to places on the 'temporary provisional executive'.[91] Six released prisoners were also co-opted on to the committee. It was that provisional committee composed of representatives of the Mansion House Committee, Sinn Féin, the Liberty League (also called the Volunteers), the INL and the released prisoners which finally hammered out the terms of the new Sinn Féin constitution. Meeting at 6 Harcourt Street twice a week for six weeks they engaged in doctrinaire debate of crucial importance to the nationalist cause. However, their discussions were vitally affected by other events that had taken place after the formation of the committee in June.

4

The Ideals of Republican Sinn Féin

DE VALERA ENTERS THE ARENA

The amalgamation in June 1917 of all the leading nationalist groups under the banner of Sinn Féin, despite all the obstacles to unity, offered hope of future progress. The release of the remaining prisoners from English gaols on 16 June 1917 added a new dimension to the nationalist cause and served as a major impetus to the nationalist campaign. By chance the release of the prisoners coincided with a by-election in East Clare. The opportunity, therefore, existed for a renewed public statement of nationalist aims. De Valera was chosen as the nationalist candidate. As a surviving commandant of the 1916 Rising it was fitting that he should stand for the ideals of Easter Week. His campaign was marked by a striking assertion of the nationalist demand: 'he stood there for a principle' (he told the voters of Ennis on 23 June) 'for the Irish Republic'; 'he owed allegiance only to the Irish Republic.'[1] Wearing the Volunteer uniform throughout the campaign, de Valera was escorted to and from meetings by Volunteer companies who sang The Soldier's Song at the conclusion of his meetings. By word and image the revolutionary message of the Republic was conveyed and conveyed successfully. The result was 5,010 for de Valera and 2,035 for Patrick Lynch, the Irish Party candidate. 'It was a victory,' de Valera declared, 'for the independence of Ireland, and for an Irish Republic.' The *Irish Times* interpreted the election result in the same manner: 'The Sinn Féin policy as explained by Mr. de Valera, with the utmost frankness demands an independent Irish Republic.'[2] In the eyes of the *Irish Times* de Valera had defeated not only the Irish Party but also 'the authority of the Catholic Church.'[3] The victory was complete, and yet some signs indicate that the unanimity in nationalist ranks was far from absolute. Doubts had arisen concerning even the choice of de Valera as candidate. Oliver Snoddy writes as if the decision to select de Valera took place on 14 June in the Old Ground, Ennis, and that he was informed by telegram while leaving Pentonville prison. Such a sequence of events may well have taken place but other sources suggest that the definitive choice was made on 18 June 1917, on the day that the released prisoner arrived in Dublin. It was made in Fleming's Hotel. According to Ó Muirthile, Fr O'Kennedy of St Flannan's College headed a deputation from Clare which met de Valera in the hotel and sought his acceptance. A problem seems to have arisen because, of the twenty-five prisoners who attended the meeting in Fleming's, a majority wanted Ashe to be the candidate. Ashe, who had claims to recognition as President of the IRB and the Commander of the successful ambush at Ashbourne in Easter 1916, explained that he was reluctant to go forward, 'Because a small but solid group is supporting de Valera with great persistance. If I accept I believe it may cause disunity in our ranks.'[4] This observation by Ashe indicates that, from a very early stage, de Valera had determined political ambitions, not withstanding Ó Muirthile's feeling that he was lacking in such aspirations. More significantly, perhaps, one can detect differences between the IRB, who supported Ashe, their president, and the Volunteers who supported de Valera. Indications of division between the military wings of the nationalist cause were matched by similar signs of difference on the theoretical side. While de Valera was proclaiming the Republic and Count Plunkett and Brugha were leading the argument in its defence, Griffith refused to acknowledge the republican dimension of the Clare election victory. Writing in *Nationality* on 14 July he attempted to associate de Valera's campaign with that of Charles Dolan who had stood unsuccessfully for Sinn Féin in 1908. Griffith even reprinted his own 'Letters to the men of Leitrim' in order to show the continuity of policy – a policy which accepted the 'King, Lords and Commons' of Ireland.[5]

These inchoate signs of difference and of future difficulty were subordinated for the time being to a united opposition to the Irish Party and to a genuine attempt to forge a truly homogeneous nationalist party. Following de Valera's election success in Clare the nationalist movement was marked by a new aggressive momentum – military parades of the Volunteers became common. The impetus in the nationalist movement was maintained by the election of W. Cosgrave for Kilkenny on 10 August – an election in which Gaelic Leaguers, having finished their Oireachtas at Waterford, joined the Volunteers. The British authorities moved to curtail the progress of the nationalists. Their main concern was to promote the National Convention, which had opened on 25 July, as the most reasonable answer to Ireland's problems. Both the Irish Party and the Catholic hierarchy, with some qualification, co-operated in the British plans which were further reinforced by the strict use of censorship. The acceptance by the Catholic Church of a place at the conference table separated it from Sinn Féin and posed a potential threat to popular support. The death of Bishop O'Dwyer on 19 August further weakened the cause of Sinn Féin in Church circles. Every effort was made to redress the loss of Bishop O'Dwyer's support. Michael Staines, a member of Sinn Féin and a Volunteer, visited Bishop Fogarty of Killaloe on the eve of O'Dwyer's funeral and successfully sought from him the promise that he would assume the mantle of Bishop O'Dwyer as the protector of Sinn Féin.[5] Bishop Fogarty was as good as his word. In his panegyric at the funeral mass, he said,

> From first to last his [Bishop O'Dwyer's] own political principle, if I may venture to mention it here, was the sterling one of 'depending on ourselves.'[7]

Encouragement of the Sinn Féin ideal could not be more clearly given. However, in August 1917, the forces working for change and those working for the old order were finely balanced. Bishop Fogarty and Archbishop Walsh may have expressed themselves as sympathetic to Sinn Féin, but the majority of bishops, while opposed to partition, were still prepared to engage in debate on the assumption that British promises could be believed. The Irish Party, too, having committed itself to British promises had little option but to lead its followers along the same path. Wait until the end of the war, they argued, and all will be granted. To accept the republican policy of de Valera, they argued, was unrealistic and could only be achieved by armed revolution. Were people prepared to face that consequence? Sinn Féin argued that there was another way. The Peace Conference, Sinn Féin maintained publicly, was the answer to Ireland's problems; secretly the military wing of the nationalist movement prepared to fight.

Early in August a meeting had taken place of the Volunteers at 46 Parnell Square, the headquarters of the Keating branch, to plan their own reorganisation under the cover of the Sinn Féin Convention. Present at the meeting were de Valera — he had assumed primacy in the organisation after his release from prison — Brugha, Ashe, Diarmuid O'Hegarty, Diarmuid Lynch, Collins, Staines, Mulcahy and Seán McGarry.[8] The gathering included leading representatives of the Volunteers and the IRB. Ashe was president of the IRB and Collins, Mulcahy, McGarry, O'Hegarty and Lynch were also members. It was estimated that some fifty to sixty thousand young men had enrolled locally as Volunteers and it was proposed, in the words of O'Donoghue,

> to lay down guidelines for their internal problems of organisation, training and arms, and for their relation to the political wing of the movement in which many of them were deeply involved.[9]

It was agreed that the Volunteer Convention should take place on 27 October 1917 – the day after the Sinn Féin Convention. While these discussions between the various nationalist bodies were taking place Ashe and other leaders were imprisoned. Many of them began a hunger strike. On 25 September it was announced by the authorities at Mountjoy that Ashe had died after being forcibly fed. His death dramatically affected the mood in Ireland. A broad feeling of sympathy for his nationalist ideals was generated and an attendant feeling of revulsion for British rule in Ireland was created. Archbishop Walsh insisted on taking part as a 'public protest' in the huge funeral procession to the republican plot in Glasnevin.[10] His participation in the funeral was striking. Membership of the IRB was forbidden by Church law – a restriction which had prevented many young men from joining its ranks – and, yet, here was the Archbishop identifying himself prominently with the dead president of the organisation. Bishop Fogarty also spoke out publicly against the death of Ashe and English treatment of other hunger strikers.

> The world [he wrote on 26 September] sees already in these hideous atrocities what the triumph of English culture means for small nations.[11]

The mood in the country first engendered by the executions after the Rising was renewed with a fresh intensity. Ashe, like those who died in the Rising, symbolised a Gaelic Ireland, a united Ireland, and the ideals of Faith and Fatherland. English rule and English promises were shown to be ruthlessly opposed to these ideals. In prison it was reported that Ashe had encouraged his fellow hunger strikers to 'Pray to Bishop O'Dwyer and the Dead who died for Ireland;'[12] and the linking of his sacrifices with those of Christ and of other dead Irish patriots, as with Pearse, struck a chord in many Irish hearts. The song which Ashe composed in Lewes gaol, 'Let me carry Your Cross for Ireland, Lord,' embodied these sentiments and enjoyed wide popularity. The first verse reads:

> Let me carry your Cross for Ireland, Lord!
> The hour of her trial draws near,
> And the pangs and the pain of the sacrifice
> May be born by comrades dear.
> But, Lord, take me from the offering throng,
> There are many far less prepared,
> Though anxious and all as they are to die
> That Ireland may be spared.[13]

For four days his body lay in state in the Mater Hospital and in the City Hall before the Volunteers in uniform escorted his body to the grave. At the graveside Michael Collins, representing the IRB, declared, after the firing of a volley over the grave, 'That volley which we have just heard is the only speech which it is proper to make above the grave of a dead Fenian.'[14] Irish observers felt that the death of Ashe had transformed the national scene. Shrewd British commentators frankly admitted that such was the case. Lord Decies, in his secret report for the month of October, observed that, 'The death of Ashe has given an immense stimulus to the whole movement, which had begun to show signs of decline.'[15] And yet the question remained; what was Sinn Féin? The impetus derived from the death of Ashe did not automatically confer on his republican ideal an undisputed claim to recognition in the debate on the Sinn Féin constitution.

THE SINN FÉIN AND VOLUNTEER CONVENTIONS OF OCTOBER 1917

The evidence is clear that in the debate on the future constitution of Sinn Féin, Arthur Griffith defended his partiality for the 'King, Lords and Commons' of Ireland until the last. Dr Thomas Dillon, who was secretary to the provisional standing committee of Sinn Féin, expressed the view that,

> Griffith was a strong theoretical monarchist and would have preferred at the time to have the King of England as King of Ireland, with a completely independent parliament, to an Irish Republic.[16]

J. J. O'Kelly was left with the same impression after attending the meeting of the composite committee. Griffith, he felt, 'did not desire the Republic but Cathal Brugha would have nothing but the Republic;' he (Brugha) felt that 'provision should be made for the declaration of independence in 1916'; and O'Kelly was convinced that Brugha 'got a majority of support.'[17] The new Sinn Féin constitution adopted by the Convention on 25 and 26 October 1917 signalled the end of Griffith's Sinn Féin. Although Griffith managed to preserve the name of the organisation he had founded, it was given a new republican reality owing to the insistence of Brugha and the grouping associated with Count Plunkett that it should reflect the values of those who had acted in 1916. At first glance the victory of Brugha over Griffith was complete. The constitution read:

> Whereas the Proclamation of an Irish Republic, Easter 1916, and the supreme courage and glorious sacrifices of the men who gave their lives to maintain it, have united the people of Ireland under the flag of the Irish Republic, be it resolved that we, the delegated representatives of the Irish people, in Convention assembled, hereby declare the following to be the Constitution of Sinn Féin:—
>
> 1. The name of the organisation shall be Sinn Féin.
> 2. Sinn Féin aims at securing the International recognition of Ireland as an independent Irish Republic.
>
> Having achieved that status the Irish people may by referendum freely choose their own form of Government.[18]

The aims and ideals of Sinn Féin were identified with the republican aspirations of the Rising; but, on second glance, the qualifying sentence to clause two, allowing the Irish people to choose their own form of government after they had secured their independence, ensured that the debate about a republic could be continued. Dr Dillon explained that this 'extraordinary statement' was devised by de Valera to reconcile Griffith and Brugha.[19]

> We then discovered [another participant at the conventions wrote] that de Valera had found a formula to satisfy Brugha [who wanted a clear-cut declaration for the Republic] and Griffith [who had been insisting on the old Sinn Féin programme].[20]

The fight for the Republic was seen as a contest between Brugha and Griffith and the carefully constructed constitution, despite its inherent contradiction, served as the basis of unity and of joint action in the immediate years ahead. Unity was also fostered by the unopposed election of de Valera as president of the Sinn Féin organisation. Other candidates representing diverse manifestations of the nationalist movement, were elected to the executive body. Their names and the votes they received tell an interesting story. Vice-Presidents were Arthur Griffith (1,197) and Fr O'Flanagan (780); Honorary Treasurers were W. Cosgrave (537) and L. Ginnell (491); Honorary Secretaries were Austin Stack (857) and Darrell Figgis (510); other executive members were MacNeill (888), Brugha (685), Dr Hayes (674), Milroy (667), Countess Markievicz (617), Count

Plunkett (598), Béaslaí (557), McGuiness (501), F. Lynch (475), H. Boland (448), Dr Kathleen Lynn (425), J. J. Walsh (424), J. McDonagh (421), Fr Matt Ryan (416), Fr Wall (408), Mrs Tom Clarke (402), D. Lynch (390), D. Kent (385), Seán T. O'Kelly (367), Dr T. Dillon (364), Mrs J. Plunkett (345), Seán McEntee (342), E. Blythe (340) and Collins (340).[21] Membership of the Sinn Féin executive reflected the entire spectrum of nationalist bodies which had shaped developments in Ireland after 1916: some had been active in 1916; some involved in the prisoners associations; some members of the Liberty League, or of Sinn Féin, or of the INL; some were members of the Volunteers, or of the IRB – or both organisations; some were members of the Gaelic League; and a significant number of women and priests merited election on account of their association with these nationalist bodies. The votes cast, however, may not reflect accurately the standing of any one individual in nationalist circles because a process of canvassing was conducted. Figgis led a campaign for Griffith and Sinn Féin members, while Collins not only canvassed for de Valera, but also issued to all members of the IRB a typed list of candidates whom they were meant to select for the executive.[22] Of the canvassing de Valera commented critically, 'Beginning a new Ireland it will not be necessary to resort to such methods anymore.'[23]

The signs are, however, that Collins and the IRB exercised a dominant influence at the Volunteer Convention held on Saturday, 27 October 1917, at Jones' Road, now Croke Park. The aim of the Convention was, in the words of Mulcahy, to establish

a representative National Executive which would provide and control machinery for stimulating, co-ordinating and directing a Volunteer military organisation in the spirit of its 1913 foundation.[24]

The aim of the IRB was to secure as much representation on the Volunteer Executive as possible. They were not successful in the two senior appointments: de Valera was appointed President of the National Executive and Brugha was elected Chairman of the Resident Executive; but the IRB secured election to other leading positions. Collins was appointed Director of Organisation; Diarmuid Lynch, Director of Communication; Mulcahy, Director of Training; McGarry became General Secretary. Other members of the executive were Rory O'Connor, Director of Engineering, and Michael Staines, Director of Supply. Co-options to the Resident Executive of such men as Diarmuid O'Hegarty, Gearóid O'Sullivan and Dick McKee, all members of the IRB, strengthened its influence in the Volunteers.[25] It would be misleading, however, to stress the importance of Collins at this stage. In March 1918 Brugha, acting in his capacity as Chairman of the Resident Executive, called members of the executive to a meeting in the rooms of the Keating branch. Mulcahy, not Collins, was elected as Chief of Staff of the Volunteers. The name of Collins was raised but Mulcahy observed, significantly, that 'as he was not very well known, it was easy to decide that I would be C. of Staff so that was done.'[26] Mulcahy appointed Austin Stack as his Deputy Chief of Staff. On the many occasions in later years when Mulcahy related the progress of Sinn Féin in the years immediately after 1916 he was at pains, despite his close and friendly relationship with Collins, to minimise the importance of his friend at that time. Of the address made by Collins at Ashe's graveside, Mulcahy wrote that it was 'a kind of a small overture to the guns that were fired over Ashe's grave',[27] and he noted that it caused some surprise as Collins was not a leading member of the IRB.[28] Of the election to the Sinn Féin Executive, Mulcahy observed that, 'Collins was the last person of the people elected on the Sinn Féin Executive, so that he wasn't very well known at the time.'[29] Privately Collins, as a member of the IRB and as secretary of the prisoners relief association, certainly exercised some hidden influence, but Mulcahy's caveat as to the degree of his importance in both the upper echelons of the Sinn Féin and Volunteer organisations cannot be ignored.

If doubt is cast on the power of Collins in 1917, confusion also exists as to the fighting strength of the Volunteers and the IRB. Ó Muirthile who, as secretary of the IRB, was at the centre of affairs, gave the Volunteer strength at the end of 1917 as 200,000 – a figure which bears some relationship to O'Donoghue's estimation of Volunteer numbers in the Munster area of 31,000 in 1921; but no correlation with Townshend's figure of 5,000 as the total IRA strength in 1921.[30] Likewise there are discrepancies about the membership of the IRB: Ó Muirthile records that by the end of 1917 there were some 4,000 members centred in 350 circles – 'each circle formed a nucleus for a Volunteer company' – and these circles were directed by a Supreme Council of fifteen members. These figures correspond in some measure to O'Donoghue's estimation of IRB strength in Cork, Kerry and Waterford as 1,170 in 1921; but there is no correlation of these figures with O'Broin's total of 1,617 for the entire IRB membership in 1921.[31] Possibly the discrepancies may be resolved by distinguishing between simple membership and actual operational strength. Fortunately there is more unanimity about the strength of Sinn Féin. By the end of 1917 there were 1,300 registered clubs with membership of 250,000.[32]

One other association merits recognition: the Gaelic League. The number of branches affiliated to the League increased dramatically after 1916: in 1915 there were only 262 branches – a sharp decline from the heady days of 1905 when almost 1,000 branches were registered; in the year 1916-17 there were 312 branches; in 1917-18 there were 551 branches; and by 1920 there were 700 branches enrolled.[33] J. J. O'Kelly was Vice-President of the League in 1917 and he deliberately declined nomination to the Sinn Féin Executive in order to build up the language movement on a national scale.[34] In August 1919, when O'Kelly succeeded MacNeill as President of the League, he became head of a vigorous national movement. Numbers dropped in 1921 owing to legislation which classified the League as an illegal association, but in 1917 the Gaelic League was a virile and vibrant organisation fully prepared to play its part in harmony with Sinn Féin, the Volunteers and the IRB in proclaiming the cause of Irish nationalism.

If one compares the situation at the end of 1917 to that immediately after the Rising, the changes are striking. As late as November 1916 William O'Brien had rightly claimed, as preparations were being made for the West Cork by-election, that Sinn Féin did not exist. It meant different things to different people: there were physical force Sinn Féiners, constitutional Sinn Féiners and ordinary Irishmen who resented the English actions over Easter Week. By the end of 1917 these disparate elements had formed a well-organised alliance which enjoyed the backing of a revitalised military organisation. The steps, from Count Plunkett's by-election at Roscommon via his April Convention to the Mansion House Committee, and from then on to the election of de Valera, the death of Ashe, and the Sinn Féin and Volunteer Conventions, had been arduous and tortuous. Ultimately the interplay of ideological and emotional forces had combined to fashion a national movement which, in the short term, at least, was equipped to challenge both the Irish Party and English rule in Ireland. Beneath this hard-won unity, however, one can detect signs of acute difference concerning the republican ideal; and, on closer examination, it is apparent that the group which argued most firmly and consistently for the ideals of Easter Week and the Republic was that associated with Count Plunkett, Cathal Brugha, Fr O'Flanagan and J. J. O'Kelly – not the groupings which rallied around de Valera, Collins or Griffith.

GRIFFITH, COLLINS, DE VALERA AND REPUBLICAN SINN FÉIN

There can be no doubting Griffith's undeviating attachment to a political settlement with a monarchical character. He stood for the 'King, Lords, and Commons' of Ireland. From his release from prison in December 1916 he had defended the original aims of his Sinn Féin party with passionate intensity — an intensity which has been but little recognised, and yet was manifested in his youth when he horse-whipped a journalist for writing critically of Maud Gonne. To the end of his days, notably in his vicious attack on Erskine Childers, he defended his ideals with the same burning, and some-times bitter, resolution.

Of Collins much has been written in adulatory terms. He has been described as playing a leading part in the North Roscommon election — a role not substantiated by the facts; he has been praised for his part in the Sinn Féin Convention of October 1917 — a role of dubious character and of slight effect; and, following the obser-vations of Mulcahy, it would appear that he has been accorded a degree of prominence by the end of 1917, which was in advance of his actual status. In large part, the elevation of the status of Collins has been caused by the singular treatment accorded to him by Piaras Béaslaí, his colleague and biographer.

A contemporary reviewer of Béaslaí's book gave the salutary warning as long ago as 1927 that, 'He goes out of his way to mini-mise the importance, . . . and to question the motives of certain persons from whom he and his associates parted later.'[35] Robert Brennan, one of those who parted company with Collins, presented a less flattering portrait of him.

> Collins [he wrote] had really little political 'savoir faire', and this was clearly shown when, after 1916, he almost wrecked his own cause by trying to capture a young and fast growing national movement by secret devices. He had great faith in the secret conclaves of the few, as if he despised the intelligence of the many.[36]

The IRB was the real power base for the influence that Collins exercised. He was Secretary of the Supreme Council of the IRB briefly on the death of Ashe in 1917 but, according to Leon Ó Broin, he did not become President until some time in 1919 — following three successors of Ashe, Seán McGarry, Harry Boland and Patrick Moylett.[37] Despite the objections of de Valera and Brugha, Collins was resolved to pursue his ambitions for Ireland within the IRB — within 'the secret conclaves of the few.' Strangely, granted his commitment to the IRB and its republican ideals, Collins showed little awareness in 1917 that the Republic was an issue. Speaking to his biographer, Hayden Talbot, of the North Roscommon by-election, Collins declared that 'as for the Irish Republic, so far as that campaign was concerned, it had ceased to exist.' He showed a similar reluctance to accept the republican implications of the Sinn Féin constitution.

> But again let me emphasise [he said] the fact that the cause was not the Irish Republic . . . the declaration of a Republic by the leaders of the rising was far in advance of national thought . . . our real want was . . . liberation from English occupation.[38]

Collins expressed the same sentiments in the Treaty debates. For him the main concern was freedom from English rule rather than a commitment to any political theory, be it republican or otherwise.

De Valera, even in the earliest stages of the growth of the nationalist movement, emerges as an equally complex character. As a surviving commandant of the Rising, an aura of distinction and eminence had been thrust upon him. His actions immediately revealed a shrewd awareness of the qualities required to preserve his position of distinction. For example, his call to the prisoners in Dartmoor to salute MacNeill as their president when he was placed in the gaol may have been simply a generous gesture to a man whose services for Ireland de Valera admired; but, in the light of subsequent events, it is probable that it was also an attempt to assert the Volunteer influence against the IRB. Not only did de Valera resolutely sustain a minority grouping of prisoners to challenge the candidacy of Ashe and the IRB for the East Clare by-election, but also he distanced himself from the Ashe funeral procession. Representing the Irish Volunteers he had directed the removal of Ashe's body to the Pro-Cathedral on 27 September, but he spoke in Ennis on the day of the funeral itself. Possibly this speaking engagement may provide sufficient reason for his absence, but de Valera's actions and his declared policy statements make it clear that he wished to advance Ireland's cause without any IRB assistance. The support of MacNeill was an invaluable asset in this contest for influence. Not only did he command the respect of countless Volunteers who had not been active in 1916, but also he was held in high regard by most of the Catholic Church authorities. This latter consideration was of major importance to de Valera. The secret report of the Sinn Féin Convention obtained by the British 'at some cost' contained de Valera's statement that 'There is only one thing that might be in our way and that is the Catholic religion if we are trying to get our freedom.'[39] With that in mind de Valera renewed his links with MacNeill after the prisoners had been released from prison. 'Don't forget', he told his colleague Robert Brennan, 'that the clergy are with MacNeill and they are a powerful force.'[40] During the East Clare election de

Valera and MacNeill stood shoulder to shoulder on the election platform. A solidarity that, despite the opposition of many senior clergy,
was seen in the popular mind to be blessed by the Catholic Church.
A blessing that was effectively symbolised by MacNeill calling from
the election platform in Ennis to a priest to say the Angelus in Irish.
This striking event was evocatively commemorated by a popular
poem describing the incident:

> De Valera had spoken in manly appeal
> To the gallant Dalcassians, and up stood McNeill;
> And his pleading for Erin with eloquence fell,
> Hark, sweet came the tones of the Angelus Bell.
>
> A reverent pause as the sound reached his ear,
> Then he called out aloud to a priest standing near;
> 'The Angelus, Father' and bowed was each head
> As the message to God in the old tongue was said.
>
> O Mary, O Mother, the stainless, the blest,
> Look down from thy throne on this land of the West;
> Be with us, O Mary, and help us to free
> Our country so loyal to God and to thee.[41]

The Catholic Church and the language movement, two hallowed
repositories of Ireland's true values, were claimed to be with Sinn
Féin. Towards the end of November, Cardinal Logue publicly dis-
puted this claim of unity based on politics, language and religion.
The Sinn Féin policy, he declared, was 'a dream which no man in
his sober senses can hope to see realised.'[42] The British administration was pleased with the results of Logue's letter to the press. Lord
Decies, in his secret report of developments, noted that 'the effect
of this letter on the moderate Sinn Féiner has been undoubtedly
good.'[43] That was in December 1917; in July 1917 the Sinn Féin
movement was still gathering momentum. The progress of the movement seemed assured. For de Valera, as for Collins, it is reasonable
to ask if it were progress towards a Republic. MacNeill, reflecting
on de Valera's aspirations during the Clare campaign, observed that,

> I gathered from him that he, no more than I was myself, was not a doc-
> trinaire republican, and all that happened since shows that I was right in
> that view.[44]

Despite the republican rhetoric in Clare and at other meetings, de
Valera was fully prepared to accept Griffith's qualification to the
republican dimension of the Sinn Féin constitution. Indeed, prior
to the Sinn Féin Convention de Valera had hinted at a compromise
in a speech at Rathfarnham where he stated that, 'Once freedom

was attained, the Irish people could choose a monarchy or a republic.'[45] 'Not a doctrinaire republican,' such was the verdict of Mac-
Neill. The description was soon to be happily used by de Valera
of himself. On 16 August 1921 he gave the Dáil his opinion of the
people's vote in the 1918 election:

> I do not say that that answer was for a form of government so much,
> because we are not Republican doctrinaires, but it was for Irish freedom
> and Irish independence.[46]

The emphasis on freedom and independence was strongly redolent
of the language of Griffith and Collins; but de Valera, as if to keep all
options open, added that 'Irish independence could not be realised
at the present time in any other way so suitably as through a Republic.'[47] Beneath the opaque utterances so characteristic of de Valera,
the message was clear: other times might bring a more suitable
solution; the Republic was not sacrosanct. Careful calculation of
the forces shaping the evolution of the nationalist movement —
forces political, military and clerical — marked de Valera's ascending
path to the Presidency. In this progress to a position of power he
exhibited from as early as 1917 a willingness to compromise with
the republican ideal — an inclination which brought him close to
the equally ambivalent attitudes of Griffith and Collins. This tendency also served to separate him from those nationalists associated
with the names of Brugha, Plunkett, Fr O'Flanagan and O'Kelly.
These men, all closely associated with the Roscommon election,
argued most strenuously for the republican character of Sinn Féin
in 1917, and subsequently they claimed to be the most firm up-
holders of the Republic. That claim will now be considered.

COUNT PLUNKETT, FR O'FLANAGAN, BRUGHA, J. J. O'KELLY AND REPUBLICAN SINN FÉIN

Without a doubt the chronicling of events after 1916 reveals that
instead of conferring on Collins and de Valera unqualified acclaim
for the resurgence of a republican movement, it is fitting to acknowledge the contribution of Count Plunkett, Fr O'Flanagan, J.J. O'Kelly
and Cathal Brugha. If they had not intervened at Roscommon in
February 1917 a vital lead would not have been given to the country;
if they had not defended the Republic in the debates before the
Sinn Féin October convention the constitution may well have reflected, to an even greater degree, the monarchical views of Griffith.
In regard to both primacy of action and purity of purpose they
have a fair claim to recognition as champions of the ideals of Easter

Week. Undoubtedly they have had a bad press. Even before the Rising, Brugha and J. J. O'Kelly had suffered from the critics' ill-founded condemnation of the Keating branch – a condemnation which failed completely to recognise the positive qualities of the branch and its central role in the Easter Week Rising. After the Rising the continuing influence of the Keatng branch headquarters and of Keating branch members has, apart from the work of Leon O'Broin, largely been ignored. It was in this branch that Brugha, as president until his death in 1922, and O'Kelly met regularly and established themselves in the national movement. O'Broin's otherwise valuable study of the period is coloured, however, by an uncritical admiration of Collins which manifests itself in an antipathy to Brugha and his part in the national movement. In large part this is a reflection of the treatment accorded Brugha in the Béaslaí biography of Collins. Having been sworn into the IRB by Brugha and having co-operated with him enthusiastically in the cause of the Irish language, often in opposition to Pearse, Béaslaí committed himself to Collins after the Rising. He questioned the judgement of Brugha; characterised it as 'sheer wrong-headedness;' and was critical of his 'taurine obstinacy.'[48] Personal prejudice against Collins, Béaslaí felt, had distorted Brugha's clarity of thought. Countless biographers of Collins have reproduced this damning picture of Brugha – and without justification. Brugha was critical of Collins because he refused to submit the secret organisation of the IRB to the democratic process after 1916. Brugha wanted the IRB to be disbanded: Collins resolutely supported the reconstitution of the IRB as a separate entity from the Irish Volunteers. Brugha wanted the Volunteers to take the oath to the Republic and Dáil Eireann. Collins did not. While it is reasonable to engage in debate as to the effectiveness and propriety of the means adopted – arguments for the democratic as opposed to the secret development of the nationalist movement – it would appear altogether unreasonable to attribute Brugha's dislike of Collins to merely personal considerations. Moreover, the indications are clear that Brugha was committed to the ideals of 1916 with far more integrity than Collins. Regrettably the case for Brugha has not been put to a wide audience. It was made by J. J. O'Kelly in his life of Brugha which was written in Irish. Of this book General Richard Mulcahy wrote, 'Sgeilg's book which is written in very fine Irish, epitomises a particular type of mentality which it is important to notice.'[49] Mulcahy knew what he was talking about. He had participated at close quarters with Brugha and O'Kelly since 1907 and his opinion may be treated as objective as he opposed them over the Treaty. With commendable historical detachment he stressed the importance of giving them, and their point of view, fitting recognition. Their special and singular part in the events from the Rising to the Sinn Féin Convention in 1917 cannot be gainsayed. Following the Convention, Brugha, as chairman of the resident executive of the Volunteers and Minister of Defence, and O'Kelly as editor of the *Catholic Bulletin*, President of the Gaelic League, Speaker of Dáil Eireann and Minister of the National Language, continued to make their specific and influential contributions to the attainment of the Republic. One other person of note associated himself with their vision of the Republic – Austin Stack. It was a connection based on personal ties as well as on those of political principle. Stack had been a friend of O'Kelly from the earliest days because of their Kerry backgrounds. This friendship led to contacts with Brugha, and mutual love of Gaelic games – Stack was a celebrated player on the Kerry team – resulted in friendship between Brugha and Stack. Eventually, in 1908, Brugha enrolled Stack in the IRB. After the Rising, O'Kelly kept in touch with Stack and saw him in prison in 1916, and at the Ashe inquest in 1917.[50] Owing to his standing in the Kerry Volunteers and his prominence in prison disturbances, Stack had been elected to the Sinn Féin executive as Honorary Secretary. More significantly, in March 1918 he had been appointed by Mulcahy to be Deputy-Chief of Staff of the Volunteers. Unlike Brugha, and possibly because of his continued time in prison, Stack remained in the IRB. The particular mentality of Brugha, Stack and O'Kelly was, of course, shared by Count Plunkett and Fr O'Flanagan.

Count Plunkett, like Brugha and O'Kelly, has also been a victim of partisan criticism. The opinions of his adversaries have been freely quoted to illustrate his limitations. Griffith declared of him that he was 'not a safe guide in Irish national political matters;' and F. J. O'Connor of the INL lamented the fact that 'there is no National party, no leader, or leaders, no settled programme' – only Plunkett.[51] Both statements were made on 4 April 1917 on the eve of Plunkett's Convention, and were made by men opposed to the republican character of Plunkett's proposals. Ironically, in relation to the ideals of 1916, it was Griffith, rather than Plunkett, who was not a safe guide in Irish political affairs. Those who accepted the republican dimension of the Rising respected the aspirations of Plunkett, although they may have disagreed with his methods. Some time in 1917, the exact date is uncertain, Seán Ó Muirthile and Patrick McCartan of the IRB consulted Plunkett about sending greetings to the revolutionaries in Russia. Ó Muirthile observed that,

We discussed the idea with Count Plunkett, who was then the recognised leader of Sinn Féin, Arthur Griffith not having yet grown into sufficient favour after the Rising, and the Count approved.[52]

There can be no doubt that both immediately before and after the Rising, Count Plunkett had an advanced idea of Irish nationality. Recognition of his IRB mission to the Pope and his message to Casement on the eve of the Rising require that he be regarded in a new perspective. He not only symbolised the ideals of 1916 at the Roscommon election, but in a very real and effective manner defended these ideals at his own Convention; at the Mansion House Committee meetings; and, finally, contributed to their insertion in the Sinn Féin constitution. His personal contacts with his sons, George and John, both released prisoners from Lewes gaol, ensured his continued contact with the military side of the struggle against England. A contact which was to have considerable consequences in 1938. His commitment to the nationalist cause was no mere sentimental association based on the memory of his executed son; it was a commitment forged and fashioned in the furnace of spiritual dedication. Count Plunkett was a man of deep religious feeling. His poems, largely unknown, bear comparison with those of his son, Joseph Mary. Following his election at Roscommon one of his poems was published in *Studies*. It reads:

> World-wounded, standing at the Cross's foot,
> I looked into the face of the meek Christ.
> Railing I said, while He hung still and mute,
> 'To heal man's ill one drop of Thy blood sufficed:
> Is it so? Then heal the sinner at Thy feet.'
> One gout fell on my brow and made me whole.
> Ah, God, punish me not with a smile so sweet!
> Nay, with Thy spear of love slay not my soul![53]

The sincerity and the fine sentiments are evident. Such qualities inspired Plunkett and, indeed, his closest colleague throughout their lives. Fr O'Flanagan certainly possessed them in abundance. He was a decisive figure, possibly the most influential in nationalist affairs, immediately after 1916. Mention has been made of his influence in the years prior to the Rising and an explanation given of his statements in relation to the 'two nation' theory. Certainly, in June 1916, he realistically admitted that historical and geographical reasons did not combine to produce a harmonious unity in Ireland; but his wish was to resolve conflicting loyalties by toleration and understanding. His intervention in the Roscommon election was the single most important factor leading to the election of Count Plunkett, and his subsequent actions were designed to promote unity in the nationalist ranks. Without him it is doubtful if unity could have been preserved at Plunkett's Convention and fostered, despite all the difficulties, at the meetings of the Mansion House and provisional Sinn Féin committees. By September 1917 he was arguing for a united Ireland and a nationalist party which accepted the ideals of 1916. He wanted an Ireland in which the traditions of Orange and Green could happily live together, and he denied England's right to occupy Ireland. 'England's only claim to retain Ireland', he wrote in September 1917 when opposing the offer of colonial Home Rule, 'is geographical.'[54] As the most prominent Catholic priest to support the Sinn Féin movement publicly his opinions had an incalculable effect on popular support for the emerging party. Fitting recognition was given to his influential role in the development of the national movement when he was elected Vice-President of the new Sinn Féin party in October 1917. The position was no mere honorary one. The arrests of de Valera and Griffith, and de Valera's absence in America, ensured that there was plenty of scope, as well as great necessity, for Fr O'Flanagan to act. He continued to make his contribution to the growth of the Republic in his own inimitable manner, until finally his style and his concept of the Republic brought him into conflict with Collins and de Valera. While it would be wrong to stress unduly the signs of division in the Sinn Féin party – a genuine unity of purpose did exist in the struggle for independence from English rule – one can detect differences about the ultimate goal of the organisation as early as 1917. Even in the October Convention itself, the secret police report claimed that Fr O'Flanagan discerned division in the recommended voting lists for the executive which were masterminded by Collins and Figgis.

> One list [Fr O'Flanagan said] appears to represent the desires of what I might call the Extreme Right of the movement, and the other the Extreme Left.[55]

Many years later, in 1934, when Fr O'Flanagan was President of Sinn Féin, he elaborated on the origins of division in the movement and on the reasons for the split at the time of the Treaty. 'The split was there from the start,' he maintained.[56] He traced its beginnings as far back as the committee formed after Plunkett's April Convention. The attempt to reconcile the republican aims of Count Plunkett with the non-republican proposals of Griffith were, he felt, the source of all future controversy and of personal conflict. The impact on the Sinn Féin Convention in October was immediate and disastrous, Fr O'Flanagan's analysis, although long, makes instructive reading:

> The duality that was put into the provisional committee at the originating conference in April, 1917, was inevitably repeated and emphasised at the first National Convention in October of the same year. The two vice-presidents elected [Arthur Griffith and Fr O'Flanagan] were the two men of opposite views who formed the nucleus of the provisional committee. The two secretaries elected were Austin Stack and Darrell Figgis. The two treasurers were Laurence Ginnell and William Cosgrave. The highest votes for membership of the standing Committee were given to John MacNeill and Cathal Brugha. When the so-called Treaty came, one of the original vice-presidents of the organisation [Arthur Griffith] became its foremost champion. The other [Fr O'Flanagan, himself] remained on the side of the Republic. One of the secretaries [Figgis] became an eloquent spokesman of the Free State cause, the other [Stack] fought against it to his last breath. One of the treasurers [Cosgrave] became for many years the leader of the Free State majority party. The other [Ginnell] died in harness in the ranks of the Republic. Of the two who came first in the list for the Standing committee, the name of one [Brugha] will go down into Irish history as that of the outstanding hero martyr of the Republican cause; that of the other [MacNeill] as the leading intellectual champion of the policy of compromise. We had only one president. The president found it impossible to divide himself into two.[57]

In attempting to account for the split in 1922, Fr O'Flanagan focussed on the two different groupings which had appeared at that time. In fact, consideration of the events leading up to October 1917 enable one to discern four distinct alignments: Griffith with his willingness to accept a monarchical solution; Collins with his emphasis on fighting for an independent Ireland; Brugha dedicated purely and simply to the Republic; and de Valera prepared to qualify the complete republican demand, if circumstances required it. In the light of these aspirations it was not so surprising that the least revolutionary group (that of Griffith) should combine with the most military-minded group (that of Collins) and accept the Treaty — their main concern was independence for Ireland, not the Republic; and subsequently it was not surprising that the group prepared to compromise its republican demands (that of de Valera) should find it possible to enter the Free State, while those who stood for the strict republican ideal (the followers of Brugha) should refuse any compromise to the last. The most dedicated republican group has become the most neglected body of men in modern Irish history. A similar silence has characterised the treatment of their contribution to the election of 1918 and to the first meeting of Dáil

Eireann in 1919. Their impact on these events will now be briefly considered.

THE REPUBLICAN ELEMENT IN THE FIRST DÁIL EIREANN OF 1919

Admirers of Collins generally attribute to him, in association with Harry Boland, the unique credit for the direction of the 1918 election which preceded the first meeting of Dáil Eireann. 'Boland and Collins and the "secret organisation" made the selection of candidates' declared Patrick O'Keeffe in his memoir of events, and his views have gained a wide acceptability.[58] In fact there are good reasons to be sceptical of O'Keeffe's testimony: not only was he motivated by a blind adulation of Collins, but also he was in prison during the election campaign — one of about 80 leading Sinn Féiners arrested at the time of the German plot in May 1918. Most importantly, however, his reminiscences of events do not accord with the detailed accounts of the Sinn Féin standing committee for that period, now available in the Mulcahy collection. The minutes of the meetings reveal that the organisation as a whole planned and carried out the election programme of 1918: Robert Brennan was made temporary director of elections on 21 May 1918; James O'Mara replaced him on his arrest in November; Fr O'Flanagan was appointed to special responsibility for propaganda and publicity as well as being acting-president; and the names of almost all election candidates were discussed individually by the committee.[59] Significantly Collins did not attend any meetings of the committee from 21 May, the day Brennan was appointed in charge of elections, until 7 November. His absence during this period may have been caused by illness, Béaslaí notes that he had pleurisy at this time, but, whatever the reason, it is evident that he could not have influenced the election campaign in the manner envisaged by O'Keeffe.[60] The primacy of Brennan in the direction of election is further illustrated by the fact that, from his prison cell in England, he accurately predicted that Sinn Féin would win 73 seats.[61] Moreover, he attributed the election success not to Collins and Boland, but to James O'Mara.

> The credit was not mine [he wrote]. It was in large measure due to the splendid election scheme which was the work of James O'Mara and Dan McCarthy, and which was based on a directorate system.[62]

The life of James O'Mara by his daughter, Patricia Lavelle, provides detailed corroboration of Brennan's opinion.[63] Where the influence of Collins may be clearly traced to any one candidate, it does not always redound to his credit. For example in the controversial decision to accept Cardinal Logue's proposals for a division of the nationalist seats in the north – a decision that led to some losses for Sinn Féin – Collins was in favour of the proposal, while James O'Mara argued against acceptance.[64] While Collins may have influenced the choice of some candidates, it is clear that, in the main, the selection of candidates and the election campaign were directed by the official Sinn Féin organisation. Of Fr O'Flanagan's part in the campaign the British were in no doubt: it was the most vital factor affecting public opinion. The secret report from the press censor's office admitted that most of Fr O'Flanagan's pronouncements had been heavily censored, and further expressed the view that,

> He is undoubtedly the one platform speaker of power in the party . . . and he remains the first apostle of the anti-British faith, and no one has laboured more strenuously or effectively against recruiting.[65]

Every effort was made to silence Fr O'Flanagan. Cardinal Logue was requested to see the Lord Lieutenant; he was suspended from his priestly duties; he was banned from his church in Crossna. It was as a suspended priest, motivated by the injunction 'salus populi, suprema lex,' that Fr O'Flanagan made his contribution to the election success of 1918. The role of Collins was minimal. It would appear eminently reasonable to confer on Fr O'Flanagan and on the backroom election workers of Sinn Féin, Brennan and O'Mara, the major credit for making the assembly of Dáil Eireann of January 1919 possible. In that assembly the role of Fr O'Flanagan and his colleagues, Cathal Brugha, Count Plunkett and J. J. O'Kelly was of paramount importance and merits recognition.

Count Plunkett, as chairman of the Republican Representatives, summoned republican members of the Irish constituencies to meet as Dáil Eireann in the Round Room of the Mansion House on 21 January 1919. On that day he led into the chamber the Sinn Féin elected members who were free to attend. Count Plunkett then proposed that Cathal Brugha should be appointed Ceann Comhairle (Speaker) for the session. Brugha, in turn, called on Fr O'Flanagan to lead the assembly in prayer. Brugha then read out the provisional constitution of the Dáil and a Declaration of Independence. The Declaration was unreservedly republican. It looked back to the Proclamation of the Republic in 1916 and declared that

> the Irish electorate has in the General Election of December, 1918, seized the first occasion to declare by an overwhelming majority its firm allegiance to the Irish Republic: Now, therefore, we, the elected Representatives of the ancient Irish people in National Parliament assembled, do,

in the name of the Irish nation, ratify the establishment of the Irish Republic and pledge ourselves and our people to make this declaration effective by every means at our command.[66]

J. J. O'Kelly then read, in Irish, an Address to the Free Nations of the world which also expressed unqualified republican sentiments. Ireland, it declared, 'calls upon every free nation to uphold her national claim to complete independence as an Irish Republic against the arrogant pretentions of England;'[67] and three delegates – de Valera, Griffith, and Count Plunkett – were appointed to state that claim at the Peace Conference in Paris. The final measure to be introduced was the Democratic Programme. Again it referred back to the Republican declaration of Pearse and it was designed to implement the reforms called for in regard to land, labour, living conditions and education. Amongst other things it stated that, 'We, in the name of the Republic, declare the right of every citizen to an adequate share of the produce of the Nation's Labour.'[68] Granted Griffith's hostility to Larkin and his objectives in 1913, and granted the commitment of Collins to the financial order of the establishment, it is not unreasonable to connect the social content of the Democratic Programme with Brugha and his colleagues who dictated the tone of the assembly. Fr O'Flanagan was renowned for his activities to secure basic rights and land for his people, and J. J. O'Kelly, while no socialist, favoured land reform and, gave prominence in the *Catholic Bulletin* to a large number of articles calling for social reform and fresh economic initiatives in Ireland. One writer of such articles, Fr Peter Coffey, a professor at Maynooth, merits brief attention, as his views shed light on the attitude of the Catholic Church to the question of social reform. Ordained in Maynooth in 1900 he was greatly influenced by Cardinal Mercier while he studied for his doctorate at Louvain.[69] When he returned to Ireland he brought with him an awareness of European developments in social thinking, and he endeavoured to devise a social programme which would reconcile Catholic teaching with socialism. Almost certainly his views were presented to the labour leaders who visited Maynooth and saw Fr William Moran, another priest with concern for social problems, whose advice is said to have influenced the formulation of the Democratic Programme, which was ultimately drafted by Seán T. O'Kelly.[70] Catholic Church authorities, however, were not happy with the writings of Fr Coffey. A series of articles entitled 'James Connolly's Campaign against Capitalism', which attempted to reconcile the writings of Connolly with Catholic teaching, did appear in the *Catholic Bulletin* in April 1920; but other books, such as *A Sinn Féin Money Policy, The Financing of Industry*, and a *Catechism of the Labour Question* were banned from publication.[71] The silencing of Fr Coffey effectively began at the signing of the Treaty in 1922. His views lost out to a Catholic Church which had adopted Pius X's condemnations of social modernism. Both those who accepted the Treaty in political terms and the Church authorities had no wish to see the implementation of the Democratic Programme. The silenced voice of Fr Coffey merits recognition as it bears witness to a new social order in Ireland which might have seen the light of day, if those who conducted the first assembly of Dáil Eireann had ever exercised power. Not only a republican dimension was lost in the failure of Brugha and his colleagues to secure a hearing, but also the vision of a new social order in Ireland compatible with Catholic social principles. Frequently it is alleged that the Democratic Programme was mere lip service paid by the new Sinn Féiners to the memory of Connolly, or part of a deal done with the Labour Party. The lesson drawn from this study of Fr Coffey is that the lips which gave utterance to the Democratic Programme did mean what they said. It was, however, other nationalist lips which dictated the social policy after the Treaty. Undoubtedly the content of the proceedings of the first Dáil and the manner of its conduct – almost without exception all the business was carried out in Irish – reflects well on the group of men who came together in the North Roscommon election of 1917. Even British agents were impressed. They reported back that 'the solemn air of the meeting seems to have produced an almost sacramental effect on sympathisers who were present.'[72] No greater tribute could be paid to Brugha and his colleagues than to describe their deliberations in religious terms, for they viewed their task as a sacred and holy trust. The first meeting of Dáil Eireann marked the apogee of this distinctive group of republicans. They received no opportunity to implement their particular brand of republicanism from a position of authority for they opposed both the moves of Collins and de Valera which took them and their supporters into power inside the framework of the Free State. They became the losers in modern Irish history, and, as losers, they have had a bad press. The winners write the history. Rarely is mention made of their unique contribution to the North Roscommon by-election; of their special role in creating Republican Sinn Féin; of their endeavours in the 1918 election campaign; or of their decisive part in placing the Republican proclamation of Pearse into the programme of Dáil Eireann. Griffith, Collins and de Valera certainly did play important parts in the transformation of Ireland after

1916; but all too often they have been credited with too much influence, while Brugha and his colleagues – their adversaries at the end of the day – have been criticised for countless failings. As the Keating branch before 1916 has been described as the 'wrecker party' by historians happy to accept the verdict of the branch's enemies, so too Brugha, Fr O'Flanagan, Count Plunkett, J. J. O'Kelly and Austin Stack have been harshly judged by historians equally happy to accept the hostile views of their opponents. On the one hand the republican tradition associated with these men has been either neglected or disparaged, while, on the other hand, a cult of hero worship has evolved around the personalities of Collins and de Valera. The evidence indicates not only that Brugha and his fellow republicans merit rehabilitation, but also that the untarnished images conferred on Collins and de Valera conceal, beneath their god-like glitter, a more base metal. The republicans aligned with Brugha made specific charges against Collins and de Valera which are rarely raised, let alone discussed, and yet they are central to any understanding of the two men and the political situation in Ireland today. They alleged, in regard to Collins, that he was in touch with a leading British official in the Castle for a full year before the Treaty; and, in regard to de Valera, they claimed that he was secretly planning his entry into the Free State while pretending to build up an alternative republican government. The charges against Collins will be considered first.

5

Collins and the Republic

COLLINS AND COPE

As early as 22 December 1921 J. J. O'Kelly in his speech against the Treaty suggested that Collins was unduly influenced by an official at the Castle.

> I opposed strenuously [he said] the proposal to send a Delegation to London. I opposed it until it became only too obvious that the insidious counsel of Cope of the Castle had permeated our whole body politic.[1]

The Cope referred to was Alfred Cope, generally known as 'Andy', the assistant Under-Secretary at the Castle. Stories about Cope's influence on Collins were rife both before and after the Treaty. Collins, naturally enough, was extremely sensitive about them. In April 1922 he wrote to Seán T. O'Kelly asking him to comment on the charge that 'Collins is a drunkard and spent the time during the truce boozing with Cope', reportedly made by O'Kelly in Rome.[2] O'Kelly replied immediately. He denied the allegation categorically, but added

> I have told or more probably joined with others in telling some of the stories of the tentative negotiations of last year and adverted to the fact — as told to me over and over again last Autumn — that you and others saw Cope frequently even before the Truce and that there was a good story in circulation in Dublin of your having on one occasion carried him to bed. The converse I have never told and may I say could not tell.[3]

Collins replied on 2 May: 'I don't know who has told you that I met Cope before the Truce', he declared, 'and I should like to meet the man who says it or repeats it.'[4] There the matter ended. Seán T. O'Kelly agreed to accept the explanation of Collins concerning the dating of his meetings with Cope, but clearly there was a marked distrust and bitterness between them. Certain questions remain, however. Even if we accept the statement of Collins that he did not meet Cope until after the truce on 11 July 1921, it is necessary to ask whether he was in contact with him before that date. The story begins with the appointment of a new British administration to Dublin in May 1920.

The tone of the Dublin Castle administration after the Rising reflected the changing aims of English policy: Duke, as Chief Secretary, attempted to conciliate moderate Catholic and nationalist opinion while the English Government pursued a path towards a solution of the Irish problem through the Plunkett Convention — he was recalled on 4 May 1918; Edward Shortt, his successor, and the new Lord Lieutenant, Lord French, engaged in a more aggressive policy as they tried to impose conscription and to prevent the electoral success of Sinn Féin — Shortt was recalled on 13 January 1919; Ian MacPherson, his successor, still acting with Lord French, implemented an even more severe policy as they attempted to come to grips with the military attacks that had accompanied the meeting of Dáil Eireann — he resigned in April 1920. By this time a new policy to solve the Irish question had been agreed upon by the British Cabinet. The deliberations of the Irish Committee, under the chairmanship and direction of Sir Walter Long, had proposed two separate parliaments for Ireland: one for the six unionist counties of Ulster, the other for the twenty-six counties. This proposal had been endorsed by the Cabinet; had passed its second reading in the House of Commons on 29 March 1920; and Lloyd George had given a secret pledge to the northern unionists that the boundaries of their six counties would not be tampered with.[5] The task of the new Chief Secretary, Sir Hamar Greenwood, in consultation with Lord French and with General Macready, the newly appointed commander of the army, was to prepare the ground for this settlement by partition, and, at the same time, to mobilise the army to crush the Sinn Féin rebels. Both objectives required an able and efficient Castle administration. It was widely known that such an administration did not exist. Lloyd George, therefore, instigated an inspection which was conducted by Sir Warren Fisher, secretary of the Treasury and head of the Civil Service. His report, published on 12 May 1920, was damning: the Chief Secretary's office had lost its grip on the civil government of Ireland and the military were left to their own devices — basically he found that 'the Castle administration does not administer.'[6] A new régime was established. While Greenwood remained Chief

Secretary and the Castle administration remained intact, a select group of civil servants was sent out from London to assume responsibility for all governmental services. The leading figure in this group of officials was Sir John Anderson, who was appointed Under-Secretary, and by Mark Sturgis, whose status was comparable to that of assistant Under-Secretary. Anderson worked harmoniously with James MacMahon, who had been appointed Under-Secretary by Shortt, but had been isolated and suspect under the régime of MacPherson. As a Catholic and a friend of Cardinal Logue he had a specific role to play in the administration of Anderson — he was to be the main liaison with the Catholic Church. This role was to prove important; but by far the most controversial role was played by Cope.

The significance of Cope was recognised by friend and foe alike. He had been a member of Sir Warren Fisher's team of inspection and his appointment to a position in Ireland was made directly by Lloyd George. In the words of Anderson's biographer he was,

> The Prime Minister's personal and secret envoy for the purpose of establishing contact with the Sinn Féin leaders with a view to negotiating peace.[7]

Prior to his appointment, Cope had been a detective with the Customs authorities. 'A calling which', again in the words of Wheeler-Bennett, 'had taught him the intricacies of under-cover work and the technique of dealing on terms of intimacy with gunmen and law breakers.'[8] On the one hand the administration, nominally under Greenwood but effectively under Anderson, upheld law and order and attempted to crush the rebellion; on the other hand efforts were made to contact the Sinn Féin leaders and to secure a compromise peace settlement. Cope was responsible for this latter policy. With the approval of Lloyd George he could, and did, act independently of Greenwood and General Macready as he pursued all channels available to contact the Sinn Féin leaders and influential members of the Catholic hierarchy. His background equipped him admirably for his task. Not only was Cope familiar with secret service work, but also he knew how to use a gun. A strange, but true, story is told of his car being seized by anti-Treaty forces in 1922. Cope commandeered another car, gave chase, and at gun point retrieved his brief case from the open car. Not the action of an ordinary civil servant![9] Nor could the other actions that he took to establish links with Sinn Féin be called ordinary. That he did establish such links is indisputable. General Macready, in his memoirs, recorded that Cope 'was a "persona grata" with the leaders of the rebellion,' and maintained that he himself, 'was ignorant or only partially informed' of these contacts.[10] The editor of the diaries of Thomas Jones, assistant secretary to the British Cabinet and confidant of Lloyd George, observed that

> Partly due to the indefatigable work of A. W. Cope, assistant Under-Secretary at Dublin since 1920, channels of communication were kept open between the Sinn Féin leaders and Lloyd George.[11]

Others, while accepting that Cope made contact with the Sinn Féin leaders, were bitterly critical of his conduct. Lord Muskerry publicly made the grave allegation that Cope, having attended secret departmental meetings, then

> having obtained full information, he at once proceeded to convey that information to the leaders of the Sinn Féin organisation, with the result that these plans devised by His Majesty's officers came to naught and in many cases His Majesty's officers lost their lives.[12]

The fact is clear: Cope made contact with the Sinn Féin leaders. It would be easy, if facile, to argue that, as Collins was one of those leaders, he must have made contact with him. Other evidence exists, however, to link Cope and Collins in a more compelling and conclusive manner. Initial contact, it would appear, was obtained through William Wylie, the legal adviser to the Government, who formed an integral part of the team established by the administration of Anderson. Wylie was held in high regard by those involved in the English administration. Soon after his arrival in Ireland General Macready urged Lloyd George to see him as 'he strikes me as being the one who knows the country and the feelings of the people best;'[13] and Lord French, not without some disquiet, informed the Prime Minister that Anderson and Cope 'have been advised and "coached" in Irish affairs during the last two months entirely by Mr. Wylie whose opinion always commands great respect over here.'[14]

COLLINS AND PEACE INITIATIVES

The biographer of Anderson simply states that the first meeting of Sinn Féin representatives with Castle officials took place on Sunday, 26 September 1920, in a solicitor's office in St Andrew's Street. Wylie, he observed, played a leading part in setting up the meeting.[15] Beneath that bald statement lies a nexus of personal relationships which made contact possible between the two warring parties. Wylie had been Chief Prosecutor at the trial of the 1916 rebels. His memoir, of whose contents I was made aware through the generous and invaluable advice of Dr Leon O'Broin, is a veritable treasure chest of information. He talks of the dignity of Clarke, Pearse, MacBride, McDonagh and Kent as they faced the court martial tribunal, and he reveals that, contrary to common legend, Countess Markievicz pleaded for leniency because she was a woman.[16] Apart from comments on people of note, Wylie also mentioned other prisoners. One of these was a solicitor named Corrigan. Acutely conscious that there was no counsel for the defence, Wylie, as in other cases, placed before the court martial points in Corrigan's favour, as a result of which he was acquitted. On being told by the court martial that he seemed to be impressed by Corrigan, Wylie replied that he had acted for Corrigan before the Rising, and that he still had a cheque to cash! Laughter ensued.[17] The humour was to have momentous consequences. In 1919, at the height of the troubles, Corrigan met Wylie on O'Connell Bridge. He promised to contact him, and to intervene, if he was to be shot! It was in Corrigan's offices in 3 St Andrew's Street that the first meeting of the Castle administration and Sinn Féin took place. The connecting link with Sinn Féin does not end there; rather it may be said to begin. Corrigan was no ordinary solicitor. He acted on behalf of the Irish National Aid and Volunteers Dependents' Fund.[18] Collins, as we have seen, was secretary of that influential society and was in regular contact with Corrigan. Under the name of Murray – his name was actually on the door of the house – Collins occupied a room on the top floor of Corrigan's office.[19] Collins did not attend the meeting that took place on 26 September 1920, but, in the circumstances, he must have been aware of it. According to Wylie, Arthur Griffith, acting-President of Dáil Eireann in the absence of de Valera, met both himself and Sir John Anderson and exchanged views for about an hour.[20] Several other peace initiatives were also made at this time – all involving Griffith and Collins – so that British sources in early November felt 'that Michael Collins had secretly joined Griffith in his anxiety for a truce.'[21]

One of these peace overtures involved the Dublin business man Patrick Moylett. Following an exchange of letters in the press in early October by Brigadier General Cockerill, MP, and Arthur Griffith, which publicly aired possible lines of a truce, Moylett went to England on 7 October. He saw Cockerill and visited the Foreign Office. On October 15 he returned to Dublin and met Griffith, Collins and Bishop Fogarty in Alderman Cole's house.[22] Bishop Fogarty had been appointed a trustee of the Dáil Eireann loan and his regular contacts with Collins, as Minister of Finance, had led to familiarity and friendship. This friendship had an enduring influence on the

Treaty negotiations. Of Collins's support for this peace initiative there can be no doubt. Moylett commented later that Collins 'expressed his delight with all I had done.'[23] Another and more significant initiative occurred in early November. General Macready and Anderson met Dr W. M. Crofton and General Wanless-O'Gowan and received from them, in Macready's words, 'very important proposals from Sinn Féin.'[24] Anderson was encouraged to inform Bonar Law that

> A very influential section of Dáil Eireann is definitely prepared to accept the essential conditions outlined by the Prime Minister before the recess.[25]

Anderson was optimistic. It was, he said, 'the first definite indication of a "Sinn Féiner on the bridge" '. Cope was even more hopeful and wrote enthusiastically to Lloyd George.[26] Although Crofton and Wanless-O'Gowan did have an interview with Lloyd George, Bonar Law and Greenwood, the initiative came to naught. In the midst of these negotiations a letter from Crofton and Wanless-O'Gowan to Anderson on 2 November raises disconcerting questions about the relationship of Collins and the Castle authorities. Anderson was advised in a post script to warn the Lord Chancellor that 'they are at the moment raiding Dublin for Michael!'[27] The Irish Lord Chancellor at this time was Sir James Campbell, the close ally of Carson in the crisis years of Home Rule. Interestingly enough Collins was regularly referred to as 'Michael' in official British correspondence. The implication of the letter to Anderson is, presumably, that the raids on Collins should be curtailed. Although the peace moves mentioned do not substantiate a direct personal connection between Collins and Cope, it is inconceivable, granted the specific mission of Cope to supervise overtures with Sinn Féin leaders, that contact was not established in some form. That feeling is confirmed by the truce negotiations which began in December 1920 and involved Archbishop Clune of Perth, Australia.

COLLINS, COPE AND ARCHBISHOP CLUNE

Archbishop Clune's mission was fully backed by Lloyd George. He saw Clune on 1 December and described him as 'thoroughly loyal.'[28] Clune's arrival in Dublin on 3 December showed the level to which both sides were willing to put aside the horrific incidents of recent months in order to secure peace. Indeed, the manner in which both sides continued to maintain avenues of negotiation open while waging war was a feature of the truce talks from the very first. The talks went on despite the sack of Balbriggan by Black and Tans (20 September 1920), the death of Terence MacSwiney on hunger strike (25 October), the execution of Kevin Barry (1 November), the assassination of fourteen British secret service agents and the indiscriminate killing of twelve spectators at Croke Park by Black and Tans (21 November), and the killing of eighteen auxiliaries at Kilmichael (28 November). Archbishop Clune, himself, was personally affected by the atrocities that were taking place. His nephew, Conor Clune, was shot in captivity on 21 November along with two leading IRB men, Peadar Clancy and Dick McKee. If his record in Australia made him acceptable to Lloyd George, this incident gave him the sympathy and respect of the Irish leaders. He was in many ways an ideal mediator. The account of his mediation tells us much about Collins and Cope. The latter's role in the English administration remained the same, but a new initiative was launched on 27 November: Griffith, Duggan, Staines and subsequently, MacNeill were arrested and confined to Mountjoy gaol. The IRB were reluctant to admit the significance of Griffith's arrest. 'It was said,' Ó Muirthile reported, 'that he was placed there so that he could be easily got at by Peace Agents!'[29] Despite the exclamation mark, the arrest was used to facilitate peace talks. The status of Collins was changed by the arrest of Griffith. He became acting-President of Dáil Eireann; he was also president of the IRB. J. J. O'Kelly chaired the meeting of the Dáil executive at which the appointment of Collins was made, and he recalled that both Brugha and Stack were offered the position by Griffith but declined the office. O'Kelly also remembered that on the way to the first meeting of the Dáil executive after the arrest of Griffith,

> a friend informed me that already agents of Dublin Castle — including under-secretary Cope — had visited Mountjoy Jail with satisfactory proposals for a settlement.[30]

The Sturgis diary reveals that the rumours, which O'Kelly was not inclined to believe, were, in fact, true. The diary also reveals that not only was Cope the guiding influence behind the Clune talks, but also that he was mainly responsible for the final truce and Treaty settlement. Sturgis recounted that Cope took Clune twice to Mountjoy to see Griffith and MacNeill and that provision was also made for Clune to see Michael Collins.[31] According to Tim Healy, Cope 'placed a Government car at his [Clune's] disposal in order that he might inform Collins' of his talks with Griffith.[32] In these circumstances it is impossible to believe that Cope was unaware of the whereabouts of Collins. Sturgis, indeed, was provoked to wonder how it is that the Archbishop sees Collins apparently without difficulty in Dublin and our intelligence fails to find him after weeks of search.[33]

They met at Louise Gavan Duffy's school on Stephen's Green.[34] The implications for the portrait of Collins hunted from pillar to post in Dublin are considerable and will be treated later. For the moment it is sufficient to record the outcome of the Clune peace talks. Collins consulted his Cabinet colleagues, Brugha, Stack, and Diarmuid O'Hegarty, secretary of the Dáil ministry and a member of the IRB, and on 4 December the conditional terms for a truce were accepted. On the same day Collins met Archbishop Clune.

> If it is understood [the formula read] that the acts of violence . . . are called off on both sides, we are agreeable to issue the necessary instruction on our side, it being understood that the entire Dáil shall be free to meet, and that its peaceful activities be not interfered with.[35]

Unanimity among Cabinet colleagues was, despite the secret influence of Cope, preserved. Fr O'Flanagan, however, was not happy with developments and intervened decisively. Collins believed disastrously.

Fr O'Flanagan, at exactly the same time as the truce formula was drawn up, sent a telegram as vice-president of Sinn Féin — effectively head as de Valera was still in America and Griffith in prison — to Lloyd George. The telegram was made public on Monday 6 December.

> You state [Fr O'Flanagan declared] that you are willing to make peace at once, without waiting for Christmas. Ireland is also willing. What first step do you propose?[36]

Collins was furious with Fr O'Flanagan's telegram. He wrote immediately to Patrick O'Keeffe, acting-Secretary of Sinn Féin, and requested him to make it clear publicly that Fr O'Flanagan was acting entirely on his own account.

> We must not allow ourselves [Collins said] to be rushed by these foolish productions, or foolish people, who are tumbling over themselves to talk about a 'truce', when there is no truce.[37]

On 8 December, O'Keeffe wrote to the *Irish Independent* and repudiated the initiative of Fr O'Flanagan: his views were merely 'a statement of personal opinion.'[38] Collins also wrote to the press implicitly criticising the letter of Fr O'Flanagan and other similar calls for peace by the Galway County Council and by Roger Sweetman. Parts of his letter, which was not published, were disingenuous.

Mr. Arthur Griffith [Collins wrote] has been seized and thrown into prison, where he is no longer free or able to confer with his colleagues.

He denied a suggestion that,

Mr. Griffith was taken into custody in order that he might negotiate more freely and safely. Does anybody think that Mr. Griffith will be so foolish as to negotiate with anybody from behind prison bars, away from his followers, and from his movement?[39]

This letter was written on 7 December. At this time Collins was in regular contact with Griffith through Archbishop Clune. This contact was made with the connivance and assistance of Cope and the Castle authorities, and Collins must have had some inkling that the arrest of Griffith was intended to serve as a prelude to a period of negotiation. He was arguing, therefore, rather dishonestly, for his peace initiative at the expense of that of Fr O'Flanagan. When Archbishop Clune returned to London to report to Lloyd George on his mission, the telegram of Fr O'Flanagan certainly acted as an influential factor on the minds of Lloyd George and his Cabinet colleagues. Signs of a peace wish among the Irish were seen by the hard-liners in the Cabinet and by the military as justification for harsher terms in the settlement of a truce. Nevertheless Clune was induced by Lloyd George to return to Dublin and to continue his mission. On 13 December and on several days following, he saw Bishop Fogarty, Griffith, MacNeill and Duggan. Cope again enjoyed a central role in these negotiations. According to Sturgis he was again Clune's 'faithful attendant' on the visits to Mountjoy, although 'he does not join the converzatione.'[40] Clune also saw Collins again on 17 and 18 December.[41] On his return to London, Clune was informed by Lloyd George that a consensus in the Cabinet required that republican forces would surrender their arms as part of the truce. Clune replied that further talks on those terms made a truce impossible. On 3 January 1921 Cope visited Clune and told him that 'negotiations had now been opened in another direction.'[42] Fr O'Flanagan was to visit London on the next day to discuss, it was claimed with de Valera's approval, a settlement on the lines of Dominion Home Rule. The initiative on the Irish side had passed from Collins and Arthur Griffith to Fr O'Flanagan and de Valera who had returned to Dublin on Christmas Eve.[43]

Béaslaí concluded his account of the Clune negotiations with the observation on Fr O'Flanagan that 'it is unnecessary to follow the abortive efforts of this self-accredited amateur diplomat.'[44] This view of Fr O'Flanagan has received general acceptance: he is referred to as the man who wrecked the Clune mission, and is held responsible for so doing. There can be no doubt that his actions contributed to its collapse; but can they, on any count, be justified? Neither in Fr O'Flanagan's own personal statement of his political career, nor in the memoir of Austin Stack is there mention of his intervention in the Clune negotiations. Evidence does exist, however, to show that he acted deliberately and consciously to break the peace initiative directed by Collins. Despite the approval of Brugha and Stack for the truce formulas that emanated from Clune's discussions with Griffith and Collins, Fr O'Flanagan was convinced that the talks were too much under the influence of the Castle — he feared for the terms of a final settlement. In April 1922 when Béaslaí was publicising his point of view on behalf of the Treaty supporters in the United States, Fr O'Flanagan, also in the States, was asked to comment. He replied that

> he sent the telegram to Lloyd George not to secure peace but with the deliberate intention of spoiling the great negotiations that were being carried on between Collins in Ireland and George in England.[45]

J. J. O'Kelly had given public expression to this view in the *Catholic Bulletin* of January 1922. He wrote of Fr O'Flanagan's efforts to prevent a false peace and added

> Fr. O'Flanagan was roundly censured at the time because, on the one hand, he retarded if he did not jeopardise the realisation of Dublin Castle's deep designs and, on the other, he all but exploded the little game behind the scenes.[46]

O'Kelly concluded by prophesying an 'imperial reward' for Cope 'for his immortal part in creating the present Anglo-Irish situation.' Any judgement concerning the correctness of Fr O'Flanagan's action will be influenced by the value one places on the relationship between Collins and Cope. Significantly Béaslaí only mentions Cope in the Clune negotiations in regard to Fr O'Flanagan. In this context Béaslaí does record some comments of Collins in early January 1922 about Cope. Collins advised Archbishop Clune that 'he should not allow himself to be made a tool of by pleasant gentlemen like Cope;' and he added, in regard to Fr O'Flanagan's new initiative, that

> there has been no interview with Mr. Griffith in connection with this new departure of Mr. Cope's, but Mr. Griffith is in daily touch with myself.[47]

The personal judgement concerning Cope and the admission that Cope could easily and regularly contact Collins via Griffith confirms the earlier impression furnished by the Clune negotiations, namely that Collins was in close touch with Cope, at the very least, since the beginning of the truce talks. Collins was, moreover, acting with a far greater guarantee of personal security than has generally been recognised. Compelling evidence exists to show that, although wanted by the police, there was no price on his head. While this fact does not impair the integrity of his intentions during the Clune negotiations, it does raise questions about his personal image.

COLLINS: A PRICE ON HIS HEAD?

Evidence concerning a price on the head of Collins is to be found in the correspondence between General Macready and Sir John Anderson. On 5 March 1921 Macready wrote giving the views of leading army officials that a reward for Collins would be desirable. 'Brind is very anxious, and so is Boyd,' he said, 'that rewards should be offered for Michael and certain other people.'[48] It was suggested that £10,000 be offered for Collins, Brugha, and Mulcahy; and that £3,500 be offered for William Cosgrave, Austin Stack, Gerald O'Sullivan and Joseph McDonagh. Anderson replied on 8 March rejecting the request. He gave four reasons: rewards had not worked with Dan Breen; they made heroes; they showed up the military organisation as being weak; and awkward questions might be raised concerning rewards for government officials who tracked down rebels.[49] Cope was aware of the policy outlined by Anderson and approved of it. When, in March of the following year, Churchill suggested that the introduction of rewards might be helpful, Cope replied that, 'We found it useless ourselves during hostilities. There is more likelihood of information without reward.'[50] Apparently Macready either did not receive Anderson's reply, or did not take it as conclusive, because on 8 April he repeated his request.

> You have never [he wrote] replied to the query I put up to you some little time ago about offering head money for Michael and others. I do not suppose for a moment it will be done, but what about it?[51]

To this letter Anderson replied immediately. He had placed the request before Ministers but 'they were not disposed to move' for the same reasons as he had given on 8 March.[52] There the matter rested. Indeed further directives were made by the administration to promote conciliation. Apart from the recall of Lord French in May and the appointment of a Catholic, Lord Fitzalan Howard, as his successor as Lord Lieutenant – a general pointer towards compromise – there was a specific instruction by Anderson to the Chief of Police on 28 June concerning the Sinn Féin leaders. He explicitly ordered that none of them should be arrested without consultation with either himself or Cope.[53] It seems unlikely, granted that this well considered policy of co-operation was in force at the highest level, that an alternative policy of 'head money' should have been introduced in the short period before the truce of 11 July.

Where, it is reasonable to ask, did the story of a £10,000 reward arise? Cathal Brugha gave the answer in a speech against the Treaty on 7 January 1922. It was a bitter speech containing many personal attacks on Collins. His bitterness was caused by his conviction that Griffith and the Treaty supporters were using the press to promote the reputation of Collins in order to advance the case for the Treaty. Collins was the man who won the war; it was, therefore, right to let him dictate the terms of peace. Thus argued Griffith in the Dáil debates; thus was the matter presented in the press. Brugha was furious with this distortion of the truth and at the way it was being used to manipulate support for the Treaty. On what authority, he asked, did the *Freeman's Journal* inform the public that 'there was a reward of ten thousand pound offered by the British Government for the corpse of Michael Collins'?[54] No reply from the Treaty side was forthcoming. The text of the *Freeman's Journal* bears out all that Brugha implied — and more! The editorial of 5 January 1922 blamed de Valera and Erskine Childers for resistance to the Treaty: of de Valera it declared 'he has not the instinct of the Irishman in his blood;' and Childers was condemned as 'an Englishman who has achieved fame in the British Intelligence Service.' An allegation later used with devastating effect by Arthur Griffith.[55] It concluded:

> When the fight was on Mr. de Valera and Mr. Erskine Childers fell acci-
> dentally into the hands of the military. They were immediately released.
> That was at a time when there was a £10,000 reward for the corpse of
> Michael Collins. The Irish people must stand up, and begin their freedom
> by giving their fate into the hands of their countrymen.[56]

The purpose of the editorial was exactly as claimed by Brugha — to extol Collins and to encourage the passing of the Treaty. So pronounced was the support of the *Freeman's Journal* for the Treaty that Seán McEntee called it the 'chief propagandist organ for the Treaty Party', and added that there were, at times, meetings of the staff of the *Freeman* with the Treaty side at the Gresham Hotel to plan strategy.[57] This latter remark led to laughter and derisive talk of spies. Collins interjected dismissively with the comment, 'the Gresham spy.'[58] The impression was created that McEntee's charge was ridiculous. In fact the rumours were far from fanciful. The

Sturgis diary reveals that he met Collins for the first time in the Gresham Hotel on 13 November 1921 and that Collins made a good impression on him. He was 'strong, brave and quite ruthless' — 'just like the big young pleasant prosperous self-satisfied cattle dealer in a big way of business with which Ireland is full.'[59] The Castle connection with the Gresham reveals a more sinister side to the articles in the *Freeman's Journal.* Cope was particularly friendly with Martin Fitzgerald, the owner of the *Freeman*, and through him could influence the contents of the paper. Sturgis had no doubt on the matter. He noted on 15 August 1921 that the plans of the administration had received excellent press coverage and, of the line taken by the *Freeman*, commented 'this is clever — Andy at the bottom of that, I expect.'[60] Cope, himself, admitted an ability to control the paper. On 24 November 1921, when there was fear of a breakdown in the Treaty talks, he called to see Thomas Jones and suggested travelling to Dublin immediately as 'he was certain he could get the *Freeman* to oppose such a break.'[61] Of Cope's influence at the *Freeman* there can be no doubt. One is left with the disturbing impression that the image of Collins projected by the paper was not only fully approved by him, but also possibly fashioned by him as well.

As long ago as 1935, Frank Pakenham, in his excellent study of the Treaty, drew the conclusion that 'the British assessed the value of Collins dead or alive at £10,000 but set no reward for Brugha.'[62] The same story, with the same implications as to the relative value to the war effort of Collins and Brugha, is repeated by Leon Ó Broin.[63] Other biographers of Collins have repeated the story. A new picture of Collins emerges once it is recognised that there was no price on his head and that, from December 1920 onwards, he was working in co-operation with a Castle agent who had no wish to see him arrested. The often told story of Collins bravely confronting Auxiliaries in the Gresham Hotel on Christmas Eve 1920 takes on a new perspective. Photograph of Collins in hand, Béaslaí and other biographers of Collins tell us, the officer 'ran his hand through Collins's hair, and compared his face with that in the photograph.'[64] 'A perfact photograph,' Seán Ó Muirthile, the close IRB colleague of Collins informs us.[65] How, in this situation, could Collins escape detection? Even the closest friends of Collins were baffled. Ó Muirthile wrote:

> There must, I think, have been a certain amount of luck on his side also in his recklessness, because when they did get him they did not know him, and he was let off with an apology for having been even suspected of being himself.[66]

The Auxiliaries were not fools and a more likely answer for his regular escape, an answer given by some on the anti-Treaty side, was that Collins had secured a pass from the Castle. It would have been relatively easy to obtain such a pass from Neligan, his spy in the Castle; but in the light of the connection between Collins and Cope it is reasonable to raise questions about the status of Neligan in the Castle — was he so unknown to Cope? — and to ask whether Cope may not have been responsible more immediately for the security of Collins. It was Cope who interviewed Neligan for his transfer from G Division of the DMP to the Secret Service at the end of 1920, and it was Cope who secured for him a special pension after the signing of the Treaty.[67] A picture emerges of Collins, from December 1920 onwards, as a man not in danger because of a price on his head, but secure in the knowledge that, even if he did not have a pass in his pocket, he could appeal directly to a top Castle official if he was arrested. Further examples of the influence of Cope confirm the fact that his power was such that he could guarantee protection to Michael Collins.

Cope's power over the military and the police forces in matters pertaining to Sinn Féin was absolute. The army chiefs, Sturgis noted, 'regard Andy as a complete Shinn' and treat him in much the same way as they would Michael Collins.[68] This reputation was earned by Cope's decisive intervention on several occasions to protect his Sinn Féin contacts. For example, on 22 June 1921, Cope was furious when he was informed that de Valera had been arrested and, according to Sturgis, 'personally effected De Valera's release over the protests of the military.'[69] This episode so incensed one British sympathiser, possibly a soldier or an intelligence agent, that he asserted that it was 'unfair to ask myself and also my colleagues to go on.'[70] Soon afterwards, on 30 June, Cope visited Mountjoy and 'insisted on the immediate release' of Griffith, Mac-Neill, Staines and Duggan.[71] He did this completely on his own initiative, wiring Anderson from Mountjoy and getting his approval. Subsequently Anderson informed Greenwood that 'I am quite satisfied that we did the right thing,' and concluded that 'Cope has been wonderful.'[72] There was a planned purpose behind the release of these men who had figured so prominently in the Clune negotiations: it was intended that they should press de Valera to go to London to see Lloyd George. Duggan, significantly in the light of his future role as liaison officer on the Irish side during the Treaty talks, said to Cope 'our labours were nearly over.'[73] The months in prison would appear to have created a unity of purpose between Cope and his captors. To the very last, Cope's influence was vital to securing the truce. Even on 11 July the Sinn Féin leaders, especially Collins, held out for the release of Seán McKeown before the terms of the truce could be implemented. Cope again intervened. He sent a telegram to London and it was reported to Collins that Cope 'urged his release to-day at noon exactly!'[74] McKeown was not released until August, but on 14 July, Collins, using the name Mr Grey, was allowed to visit him in his condemned cell at Mountjoy.[75] Such was the power of Cope and, as he conducted his secret negotiations, it was to be presumed that his protection should extend to the Sinn Féin contacts vital to his purposes — not only Collins, but also de Valera.

His power to secure personal protection was matched by his capacity to influence Lloyd George and policy decisions. In the days before the truce, both Greenwood and Anderson were out of the country and he became *de facto* head of the civil Government in Ireland. It was he who co-ordinated the arrangements of the army and of Sinn Féin forces prior to the truce. Of the truce, itself, Sturgis observed that 'Everybody who counts knows he is the author of the whole thing and Macready himself would be amongst the first to admit it.'[76] When Lady Greenwood asked Sturgis 'who made the truce — Smuts or the viceroy?' he replied, 'Neither, but one Cope.'[77] Macready was quick to acknowledge the vital role of Cope in securing the truce. It was made possible, he declared, by 'Cope's subterranean activities.'[78] 'Probably no other man', he added, 'could have carried the matter through.'[79] Tim Healy who was involved in the various attempts of settlement throughout this period, and was, indeed, in touch with Cope and the Castle, gave it as his opinion that,

> the services of Sir Alfred Cope at this time cannot be overestimated ... to him is due, perhaps, more than to any other man on the English side the negotiations for the Treaty.[80]

Of Cope's adversaries on the Irish side, J. J. O'Kelly was not the only one to voice his critical recognition of Cope's leading part in the path to the Treaty. Austin Stack also expressed the view that 'Cope was England's chief instrument in bringing about the signing of the treaty.'[81] To Cope, therefore, in the eyes of his friends and his enemies went the credit not only for the truce, but also for the Treaty. In that period, from the truce to the Treaty, Collins admitted to Seán T. O'Kelly that he met Cope. The circumstances of the first meeting and subsequent contacts again indicate that Cope had an unusual relationship with Collins.

COLLINS MEETS COPE

They first met soon after the signing of the truce. The account given by Seán Ó Muirthile, who as a leading IRB man and friend of Collins was certainly in a position to know, reads like a passage from a spy story. Collins and Duggan, he related, were driving back to Dublin from Kildare when their car was struck by an English military vehicle containing some Auxiliaries and some women. Following the crash, Ó Muirthile recounts,

> Mr. Duggan who was then acting as Chief Liaison Officer in connection with the Truce, rang up the Castle, and Cope himself motored to the scene of the accident. Another car was supplied to replace the broken one, and Cope and Collins met for the first time.[82]

Possibly it was a genuine accident, but the easy manner in which Duggan was able to ring up the Castle and contact Cope speaks volumes about his stay in prison. On the admission of Collins, Cope and himself met frequently after this first encounter. While Cope endeavoured to keep as many contacts as necessary going, it would appear that he was particularly at ease with Collins and convinced by the Clune negotiations that a deal could be done with Collins and Griffith. De Valera was willing to communicate but difficult to pin down; Brugha, Stack and O'Kelly — despite a strategic imprisonment in O'Kelly's case — refused to communicate; Fr O'Flanagan broke ranks with his closest allies but, while engaging in consultations, lacked the authority to enforce a policy decision. Cope was acutely aware of these differences in Sinn Féin ranks. A secret service report of 16 July 1921 also made him aware of the lengths to which Collins would go to monitor the actions of de Valera and Griffith. It was recorded in July 1921 that during the Mansion House Conference Collins had a special watch placed upon them and tapped their telephones.[83] Perhaps such tactics, so familiar to Cope, may have served to endear him to Collins. Whatever the reason, the links forged between Cope, on the one hand, and Collins, Griffith and Duggan, on the other, proved to be of vital importance in the Treaty negotiations. It was reported on 24 October 1921, as the seventh session of the Treaty talks resumed, that 'Cope, at the request of Griffith and Collins, had arranged a private meeting with Lloyd George and Chamberlain before the afternoon session.'[84] In this fashion the splitting up of the Irish Treaty delegation began. A further type of individual meeting took place on 30 October. Cope and Duggan discussed such a meeting in the presence of Thomas Jones on the evening of 29 October and on the following day Griffith met Lloyd George alone in Winston Churchill's house while Collins, who had accompanied him, talked with Churchill and Lord Birkenhead.[85] In this splitting of the delegation, so criticised by Brugha, there can be no doubt that Cope played an important part. In many ways it may be said that the ties, formed at the Clune negotiations, developed in prison confinement, and strengthened in social contacts from July onwards, came to fruition in the Treaty talks.

Moreover, following the signing of the Treaty, Cope continued to play a decisive part in securing its implementation. He acted under the direction of Winston Churchill who, as Secretary of State for the Colonies, was responsible for the affairs of the Provisional Government of Ireland. In this capacity Cope, despite the strong objections of Churchill, attempted to defend the pact policy of Collins and de Valera which was ratified on 20 May 1922; and he intervened actively to obtain British guns and ammunition to strengthen the Provisional Government, especially in regard to the planned attack launched by Collins against Rory O'Connor in the Four Courts on 28 June. To all intents and purposes, he acted as a liaison officer between Collins and General Macready. Macready openly admitted that such was the nature of Cope's work. 'Through representations to London by Cope,' he declared, 'I received instructions to hand over two 18-pounder field guns to the Provisional Government with a reasonable supply of ammunition.'[86] The primacy of Cope in all dealings with the Provisional Government, especially in the matter of armaments, was officially recognised. On 27 June 1922 a memorandum stated that, 'The authority responsible for signing importation permits for arms and ammunition to be landed in Southern Ireland is Mr. Cope.'[87] This formal authorisation permitted Cope to act with an amazing amount of flexibility. Collins simply approached Cope when he was in need of more armed support, and Cope made every effort to facilitate him. This was made clear in a letter of Churchill to Collins on 4 August 1922. He stated that he had discussed the question of extra munitions with Cope, 'and I have given him further latitude in regard to the issue of arms and ammunition. We are very anxious to give you all reasonable support.'[88] Even more important than this specific assistance in military matters afforded by Cope to Collins was the overall tenor of his reports to the English Cabinet. Constantly, often in the face of strong and influential opposition, he argued the case for Collins: he could be trusted to honour the Treaty; he must be supported. There was no need for British military intervention. Faced by the forceful character of Churchill it was no small achievement to sustain such a policy throughout so many critical situations.

Whereas Churchill was willing, almost eager, to embark on armed intervention over the Pact, the occupation of the Four Courts, and the apparent reluctance of the Provisional Government to confront the anti-Treaty republicans, Cope recommended that England's interests were best served by caution and by co-operation with Collins. On 1 July 1922 Churchill, in a rare admission of error, acknowledged that his approach was wrong and that Cope was right.

> I consider the events of the last three days [he declared] and the actions of the Irish leaders constitute a striking vindication of the judgement and instinct which you have displayed in Irish affairs and justify the advice which you have consistently given for many months.[89]

Churchill was so impressed and grateful that he promised to recommend Cope for civil honours. Further and final confirmation of the importance of Cope was revealed after the death of Collins on 22 August 1922. Cope was informed by the Provisional Government that Collins had died at 3 a.m. on 23 August. From then until the funeral of Collins, Cope was in constant communication with the surviving leaders of the Provisional Government. He encouraged the English authorities to meet all their requirements. He contacted the Admiralty to ensure that a boat would be sent to Cork to recover the body of Collins; he arranged that the War Office should make available a British gun carriage and trained horses for the funeral procession in Dublin; and he made detailed recommendations for condolences to be sent by the King and the Prime Minister. In the midst of the crisis Cope gave clear and unequivocal expression to the closeness of his ties with Collins. When it was suggested that he might attend a Cabinet meeting on the day of the funeral, he replied,

> I would only point out that the top officers of the Army and also the Ministers know I was on intimate terms with M.C. and they may think my absence from the funeral somewhat strange.[90]

He attended the funeral of his friend Michael Collins on Monday, 29 August. His attendance provided conclusive and fitting testimony to a remarkable relationship; and his dealings with both Collins and Churchill provide abundant evidence of his powerful influence in the shaping of Anglo-Irish affairs. From control of the keys of the prison cells in December 1920 to master of the hands that pulled the triggers of the guns against the Four Courts, Cope was a dominant figure in the English administration in Ireland. Unknown to most other republicans he exercised his power in close co-operation with Collins. One cannot but conclude that this strange

Keating Branch Players who performed Douglas Hyde's Casadh an tSúgáin *at the Gaiety Theatre, Dublin in 1901. Back, from left: Miss N. Murphy, J. Murphy, R. A. Foley, Miss M. Murphy, H. O'Geary (?), Douglas Hyde, Seán Ó Cuiv, Tadhg O'Donoghue (Torna). Front, from left: Eamonn Ceannt, Miss F. O'Sullivan, Miss O'Kennedy, Miss O'Donovan, Miss Jessop, Senator (?) Healy, Phil Ryan, J. J. O'Kelly (Sceilg). (Courtesy of Mortimer O'Kelly collection)*

Group of nationalists at Fairford, Gloucestershire after deportation in February 1917. Standing, from left: D. Figgis, G. O'Sullivan, J. J. O'Kelly, Unknown, Unknown. Seated, from left: Unknown, M. Foley, M. P. Colivet, B. Mellows, S. T. O'Kelly. (Courtesy of Mortimer O'Kelly collection)

The O'Kelly family as it appeared in the Catholic Bulletin *of March 1917 after J. J. O'Kelly (inset) had been deported without trial. From left: Sean (1908-75), Máire (1910-37), Mrs Nora O'Kelly (née O'Sullivan) (married 1904, died 1949), Catherine (b. 1914), Mortimer (1912-89), Padraig (1906-28). The* Catholic Bulletin *published many groups such as this to show how the English policy of execution and imprisonment after 1918 was affecting ordinary families.*

Count Plunkett (centre with beard) with J. J. O'Kelly on his right, at Liverpool in August 1920, waiting in vain for the arrival of Archbishop Mannix, as representatives of Dáil Eireann. Mannix was taken from his liner, Baltic, *by a British destroyer and put to shore at Penzance. (Courtesy of Mortimer O'Kelly collection)*

Dublin Castle administration that was created after Sir Warren Fisher's report of May 1920. Standing, from left: Basil Clarke, G. N. Crutchley, L. N. Blake Odgers, M. T. Loughnane, J. P. Fairgrieve. Seated, from left: Geoffrey Whiskard, Alfred Cope, John Anderson, Mark Sturgis. (Sir J. W. Wheeler-Bennett, John Anderson, Viscount Waverley, London, 1962)

J. J. O'Kelly (left) and Austin Stack on their tour of the United States (March-May 1922) as representatives of Cumann na Poblachta. (Courtesy of Mortimer O'Kelly collection)

J. J. O'Kelly, Fr Michael O'Flanagan and John Clancy, as portrayed in a publicity photograph for their tour of Australia beginning in March 1923 and ending with their arrest and deportation in July 1923. (Courtesy of Mortimer O'Kelly collection)

Members of First Dáil Eireann, 21 January 1919. Seated, from left: J. O'Doherty, S. Hayes, J. J. O'Kelly, Count Plunkett, C. Brugha, S. T. O'Kelly, P. O'Malley, J. J. Walsh, T. O'Kelly. Standing, from left: S. MacSwiney, K. O'Higgins, R. Barton, D. Buckley, R. Mulcahy, E. Duggan, C. Collins, P. Beazley, P. Shanahan, Dr J. Ryan, Dr Crowley, P. Ward, J. A. Burke, P. J. Maloney, R. Sweetman. Although this photograph shows the men who were mainly responsible for the conduct and content of the First Dáil, the later photograph of April 1921, with Griffith, Collins and de Valera in attendance, is regularly (and incorrectly) presented as the first assembly of Dáil Eireann. (Courtesy of Mortimer O'Kelly collection)

J. J. O'Kelly (Sceilg) while in the United States in 1923 as de Valera's republican envoy. (Courtesy of Mortimer O'Kelly collection)

Mgr John Horgan, Vice-Rector of the Irish College, Rome, 1904-1920; Rector of the College, 1920-30 (left) and Mgr Michael O'Riordain, Rector of the Irish College, Rome 1905-1919. (Catholic Bulletin)

Assembly of the Republican Second Dáil Eireann taken in the grounds of Fleming's Hotel, Dublin, 1928. Back, from left: Tom Maguire, Seán MacSwiney, Seán O'Farrell, Brian Mellows, Mrs Cathal Brugha, Miss Tieberd (stenographer), Joseph Clarke (courier). Centre, from left: Count O'Byrne, Eamon Dee, Séamus Lennon, M. P. Colivet, Austin Stack, Charles Murphy, Seán O'Mahony, Dr Ada English, Thomas O'Donoghue, Judge D. Crowley. Front, from left: Phil Shanahan, Professor W. P. Stockley, Mrs K. O'Callaghan, Art O'Connor, J. J. O'Kelly, Miss Mary MacSwiney, Dáithí Ceannt, Count G. N. Plunkett, Brian O'Higgins. The photograph was taken with the explicit purpose of showing that not all republican deputies had joined Fianna Fáil. (Courtesy of Mortimer O'Kelly collection)

Seán O'Mahony, known as 'Big John', proprietor of Fleming's Hotel, Dublin, where meetings of nationalists took place after 1916, including secret meetings of Dáil Eireann. O'Mahony was elected to Dáil Eireann for South Fermanagh in 1918; he voted against the Treaty and against de Valera's policy on the oath; he remained an active member of the Republican Second Dáil until his death in 1934. (Courtesy of Mortimer O'Kelly collection)

General Thomas Maguire; born 1892; led ambush at Tourmakeady in May 1921 as General Officer Commanding the Second Western division, IRA; same year elected to Dáil Eireann; voted against the Treaty, 1922; voted against de Valera's proposals on the oath, 1926; signatory of the republican Dáil's delegation of power to the Army council of the IRA, 8 December 1938; last survivor of the pro-Treaty Republican Dáil Eireann. (Photo by Liam Lyons, Westport, September 1989)

association was not only extremely effective, but also presents the activities of Collins in a totally new perspective.

COLLINS, THE IRA AND THE CATHOLIC CHURCH

However much one attempts to justify the policy of Collins and Griffith – it was realistic on account of British military might; it was supported by the Catholic Church; and so on – one has to accept that it was made possible through secret communication with a British agent in the Castle. Moreover, the justifying reasons for their policy are open to question: the motives of realism may be challenged on many grounds, and the support of the Catholic Church was obtained, to some degree, by the unseen influence of Cope and his colleague at the Castle, James MacMahon, the Under-Secretary. My research brought me into contact with two men, both in their nineties, of contrasting backgrounds, whose stories shed significant light on the policies of Collins and Griffith. General Tom Maguire provided me with information on the fighting strength of the IRA – an issue central to the appraisal of a policy based on realism; and Fr John MacMahon, SJ, provided equally valuable information as to the role of the Catholic Church. The matter of military capacity will be considered first.

Collins, in his time, and defenders of the Treaty ever since, argued that, as the IRA could not last out for much longer against the might of the British Army, it was realistic and right to come to terms. The statements of Collins on this theme are well known: his remark to Sir Hamar Greenwood that 'you had us dead beat. We could not have lasted another three weeks', is frequently used to justify a settlement.[91] General Maguire told another story. One of the few IRA commanders to be officially appointed a general, he directed the South Mayo brigade until he was severely wounded in an ambush at Tourmakeady on 3 May 1921. While wounded he was elected to Dáil Eireann – formally to the British Parliament – on 24 May 1921. He maintained that, contrary to many common assumptions, the war effort in the west of Ireland was directed, and well directed, by a chain of command from Dublin which centred around Brugha, as Minister of Defence, and Mulcahy, as Chief of Staff of the IRA. Collins and the IRB played no part in planning military strategy. Maguire also believed that the strength of the IRA was so secure and the support of the people so solid that the war effort could have continued at the time of the truce.[92] Endorsement of his opinion has been provided on the Irish side by Florence O'Donoghue and Tom Barry who maintained that the IRA in South Munster were willing and able to continue the war. O'Donoghue explicitly denied the allegation by Béaslaí, often repeated, that Liam Lynch had visited the General Headquarters and informed them that the Southern Command could not fight on. Collins, O'Donoghue asserted, did not consult Lynch as to his military capacity.[93] On the English side too there is compelling evidence to support General Maguire's contentions. General Macready's memorandum to the Cabinet written on 23 May 1921 stated that,

> I am convinced that by October, unless a peaceful solution has been reached, it will not be safe to ask the troops to continue there another winter under the conditions which obtained during the last.[94]

Macready was so depressed that he suggested that men and officers should be removed from the Irish atmosphere for some time. Towards the end of May, soon after Macready's dire predictions, Cope made the astonishing announcement to Patrick Moylett on a further abortive mission that, 'We are willing to acknowledge that we are defeated militarily.'[95] Extermination, Cope argued, might be possible using extreme measures of repression, but public opinion, both in England and throughout the world, would not sustain such a policy. To talk of defeat in the field was not surprising in the light of the Chief Secretary's report to the Cabinet for the week ending 16 May 1921. It read:

> I regret to state that the crime statistics for the week are exceptionally bad ... the highest on record for any week since the rebellion of 1916.[96]

The week had witnessed 60 attacks on Crown forces, 55 casualties and 23 deaths. The situation had not improved by 24 June 1921. On that day the Secretary of State for War presented to the Cabinet a report from Colonel Elles, a Colonel in the Tank Corps, who had recently returned from a tour of Ireland. 'The British army in Ireland is besieged,' he declared, and added that unless more troops were made available 'we shall be beaten.'[97] In the light of these well-documented reports to the British Cabinet on the military situation in Ireland at the time of the truce, it appears reasonable to cast doubt on the authenticity of 'a secret "report on the military situation", made in September, [and] intercepted by Collins'.[98] This report stated that,

> Three months ago the Rebel organisation throughout the country was in a precarious condition, and the future, from the Sinn Féin point of view, may be said to have been well nigh desperate.[99]

This alleged report was given prominence by Béaslaí, one of Collins's most loyal supporters, as early as 1926 to justify the truce, the Treaty, and the policy of Collins as a whole. It has been used regularly ever since, notably by Leon Ó Broin, to serve the same purpose.[100] It is sufficient to note here that it has been used to prove a point and that its contents are not supported by other well-authenticated documents. Space prevents a more comprehensive account of the military situation, but enough evidence has been cited to indicate that the realism detected by Collins and Griffith in Dublin, where admittedly conditions were extremely difficult, may well have to give second best to the reality experienced by General Maguire on the mountain sides of Mayo. Such indeed is the considered conclusion of the finest study of the British campaign in Ireland in the years before the truce. Townshend writes,

> It was commonly said after the truce, and is often accepted now, that the IRA was reaching the end of its tether. Such a conclusion . . . seems exaggerated. There is no reason to doubt that, given time, strength, and public support, the British forces could have reduced rebel operations to negligible proportions. But these quintessential conditions were missing.[101]

This conclusion fully accords with the fresh substance and colour which were added to the military scene by the recollections of General Maguire. Fr John MacMahon's recollections serve as a similar catalyst in the area of clerical diplomacy.

Fr John MacMahon was ninety-three when I met him in March 1987. He was called to the Irish Bar in 1916 before he entered the Jesuit order. He was, therefore, well able to provide reliable and mature recollections of his father, the Right Honorable James MacMahon, in his role as Under-Secretary at the Castle from 1918 to 1922. MacMahon had been retained as Under-Secretary in the re-structuring of the Castle administration in May 1920 with the express purpose of retaining Catholic sympathies and, if necessary, of serving as a contact with the Roman Catholic hierarchy. The strange nature of this contact with the hierarchy was revealed in an admission made later by MacMahon to Seán T. O'Kelly. He confessed that during the preparations for the 1918 election he had telephoned the Sinn Féin headquarters and, pretending to be Cardinal Logue's secretary — with the Cardinal's permission, he successfully altered the allocation of Sinn Féin seats in Ulster. This was the sharing of seats between Sinn Féin and the Irish Party to which Collins gave his consent. In May 1920 the Fisher report had been critical of MacMahon's lack of initiative — a deficiency possibly caused by his isolation under the Macpherson administration — but

Wheeler-Bennett has written not only of his 'charm and urbanity,' but also of his experience and adaptability in blending in with the new team under the direction of Sir John Anderson.[102] Mark Sturgis also came to admire his good sense and professional competence. MacMahon did not initiate the shaping of policy; he acted as directed by Anderson and by Cope, especially by the latter in clerical matters. Sir James O'Connor, who was closely involved in the peace negotiations of 1921, expressed the view that,

> Through the Under Secretary, an Irish Catholic, Mr. MacMahon, who is a friend of every Catholic ecclesiastic in Ireland, he [Mr Cope] got into touch with clerics who were in touch with the men who pulled the strings – Richard Mulcahy and Michael Collins.[103]

One is brought back once again to the pre-eminent influence of 'Andy' Cope. To him O'Connor attributed 'the real credit of an Irish settlement.'[104] Fr MacMahon confirmed the view of O'Connor and of many others that his father acted as an intermediary between the Castle administration and Cardinal Logue. The Cardinal, he related, was a family friend and often stayed in their Phoenix Park residence when he visited Dublin; and Cope was also a regular visitor to the house. He could not say if Cope and Cardinal Logue ever met in their home.[105] A clear example of MacMahon facilitating a meeting with Cardinal Logue is to be found as early as July 1920. A letter of P. A. Marrinan, the County Inspector of Limerick RIC, to Wylie communicated the view that 'Cardinal Logue holds the key of the situation,' and added that 'I have no doubt the Under Secretary [MacMahon] could find a way' of contacting the Cardinal.[106] The reaction of the Castle administration to this letter was swift. On 18 July Cope saw Logue and reported to Anderson that he was willing to leave the door open for further discussion, if such a course appeared necessary or helpful.[107] The grounds for future communication were securely laid and, as well as MacMahon's personal contacts with the Cardinal, Cope certainly met Logue on one more occasion at least. On Friday, 3 June 1921 Sturgis recorded, 'Andy and MacMahon spent yesterday visiting the Cardinal and urging a second meeting at once between de Valera and Craig.'[108]

Their efforts were designed to bring about a truce and they were left in no doubt that Cardinal Logue was prepared to support something less than a republic. 'The Cardinal,' it was reported, 'said definitely that not even the Extremists wanted a Republic.'[109] The visit of MacMahon and Cope to Logue may not have affected his own inherent opposition to the Republic, but the decision of a meeting of the Catholic hierarchy on 21 June 1921 not to recognise the Irish Republic could not have complemented their designs any more perfectly than if they had composed the contents of the episcopal statement themselves. De Valera visited Maynooth and made a personal appeal to the assembled bishops; he wanted them 'to give straight-out recognition to the Republic;' and he had arranged with the Dáil's Publicity Department that newspaper headlines should read, 'THE IRISH BISHOPS RECOGNISE THE REPUBLIC.'[110] The bishops' rejection of the Republic was a crushing blow for de Valera and greatly encouraged Cope in his endeavours. Other bishops were also approached. On 22 June, Cope and MacMahon were in Belfast for the King's opening of the Northern Ireland Parliament, and Sturgis recorded that Cope arrived back on the following day 'having been seeing Fogarty and two other bishops.'[111] Crucial events were happening at such a rapid rate – the meeting of the Catholic hierarchy (21 June); the opening of the Northern Ireland Parliament (22 June); the arrest of de Valera (23 June) – that Sturgis, a keen gambler, complained of being so busy that he could not take time off to bet on a horse, Ballyheron at 8-1, that he lost £50![112] Personal priorities, however, of whatever value, had to take second place to the diplomatic task at hand. The aim was to persuade the bishops to urge a peace policy on de Valera, and to get him to settle for something less than the Republic. The evidence indicates that this persuasion and pressure contributed not only to the truce, but also to the Treaty. For example, when, on 24 November 1921, it appeared that the Treaty negotiations might break down, Cope proposed going to Ireland and seeing some Church dignitaries whom he knew would support him. In fact that night he went to the Jermyn Street Hotel where the Archbishop of Tuam, Thomas Gilmartin, was staying and saw the bishop even though he was in bed. He urged him to go to Ireland and 'get busy' with Bishop Fogarty and Archbishop Byrne of Dublin.[113] Not surprisingly, on Sunday 26 November, Cope was in much better form and able to report: 'things are humming on the other side. The Bishops especially busy.'[114] Without a doubt the contact between Cope and the Catholic hierarchy played a vital part in the signing and acceptance of the Treaty; without a doubt, also, the role of James MacMahon in facilitating contacts with the bishops was of paramount importance. No wonder then, as Fr MacMahon related, that the moment that news of the signing of the Treaty was wired back to Dublin, his father, James MacMahon, should telephone Cardinal Logue and inform him of the outcome of the talks.[115] Logue and the bishops had helped to bring the Treaty about; they were also to help in securing its popular approval. What of Michael Collins in the midst of this clerical diplomacy? The recollections of Fr MacMahon provided evidence that Collins supported the initiatives of his father. When a friend of the MacMahon family became aware of a planned attack on the Under-Secretary's life, he visited Dublin and made contact with Collins. He was then able to bring James MacMahon the comforting news that the action had not been ordered by Collins, himself, and, that on his explicit instructions the attempt on his life had been stopped.[116] Granted the connection between Collins and Cope it is not to be wondered at that MacMahon, who was indispensable to Cope's plans, should benefit from the protection of Collins. What is, perhaps, surprising is the lack of recognition afforded the role of Cope in recent biographies of Collins. Pakenham concluded his study of the Treaty by acknowledging the influence of Cope but confessed that the full extent of his contribution 'must remain for the present a mystery.'[117] Using sources unavailable to Pakenham it has been possible to lift, a little, the veil of mystery surrounding the activities of Cope. The picture revealed is disturbing to the traditional image of Collins. His success was gained by an element of secret intrigue which many will find disconcerting; the justification of his stand on the grounds of realism is found to be suspect; and one is ineluctably forced to question the very basis of his commitment to the Republic. To contrast his position with that of James MacMahon is instructive. Fr John MacMahon felt that his father had contributed to a sensible resolution of the crisis of his time, and believed that Cope, whom he described as 'capable', 'honest', 'courageous' and 'good', had played an admirable part in the final settlement.[118] Such an attitude on behalf of James MacMahon would seem eminently justified: he had never accepted the Republic; and he was content to accept a further degree of Irish independence with an English connection. It accorded with his highest political aspirations. With Collins it was a different matter: he had taken an oath to the Republic. Here one touches upon the crux of the matter. It was suggested previously, and deliberately treated in some detail, that even as early as October 1917, when the Sinn Féin party adopted a new constitution, that the attitude of both Collins and Griffith towards the Republic was ambivalent. In fact, it may be argued that as they were never really committed to the Republic, they were open to a political settlement which rejected it.

It is not without significance that the republican pedigree of both Collins and Griffith after 1916 came under scrutiny in the Treaty debates; and a consideration of this issue will serve as the final analysis of the aims and ideals which divided Collins and Griffith from those who, because they stood by the Republic, became the losers in modern Irish history.

COLLINS, GRIFFITH AND THE REPUBLIC

Brugha, in particular, stressed the significance of Griffith's actions in 1917:

> I tell Mr. Griffith [he declared on 7 January 1922] that only for a certain arrangement that he made in 1917, that he would not be now in public life any more than he was in 1916. I have here the Sinn Féin Constitution as passed by the Ard-Fheis held in October, 1917; there is a clause in this resolution which took us three nights to get passed – to get Mr. Griffith to agree to it – this is the Clause. 'Sinn Féin aims at securing the international recognition of Ireland as an independent Irish Republic.' Mr. Griffith objected to that, but eventually we came to an agreement by adding this: 'having achieved that status the Irish people may by referendum freely choose their own form of Government.' These are the vital clauses in the Constitution of the Sinn Féin movement. In the Constitution we forged the weapon by which we produced the Dáil. If Mr. Griffith had not agreed to that . . . I say he would not be in public life to-day anymore than he was before 1916.[119]

Despite the clarity of Brugha's case and despite the reminder of other members of the Dáil that they had all taken an oath to the Republic, Griffith refused to admit the republican nature of either Sinn Féin or the Dáil.

> I am told [he asserted] that the people of Ireland elected us to get a Republic. They elected us in 1918 to get rid of the Parliamentary Party; they elected us in 1921 as a gesture, a proper gesture of defiance to the Black-and-Tans; they elected us, not as doctrinaire Republicans, but as men looking for freedom and independence.[120]

Michael Collins took the same view – a view that has become part of the legend of those who accepted the Treaty: they wanted freedom and independence – not an Irish Republic. When Brugha defended Count Plunkett against a vicious attack by Griffith in which he had called the Count a 'humbug', Collins refused to accept the standing conferred on Plunkett in the republican movement. Brugha praised Plunkett as

> the member for Roscommon who gathered together the various national forces that were disorganised or unorganised after Easter Week, and founded the movement that brought the Dáil into existence.[121]

Collins replied that,

I deny that the value of the work was as has been stated. At all events, that was not my opinion of the work, and neither was it my view then nor is it now that it was the Deputy for North Roscommon who called together the national forces after 1916.[122]

The centrality of the Roscommon election of 1917 is again apparent. Neither Collins nor Griffith was willing to accept the vital role of Plunkett at the time, nor were they willing to concede that the persons associated with his name – Brugha, Fr O'Flanagan and J. J. O'Kelly – had made a genuine contribution to the formation of Republican Sinn Féin and of Dáil Eireann. The historical evidence comes down in favour of Count Plunkett and his supporters. Griffith and Collins had their eyes elsewhere: Griffith on his long cherished ideal of monarchical Sinn Féin; Collins on the IRB. The IRB, which had occasioned the first differences between Collins and Brugha, played a decisive part in the passing of the Treaty. Once again the recollections of General Maguire provided a valuable insight into its influence at this time; his claim that the IRA rather than the IRB directed military operations against the British has already been noted; he also observed that, as the war progressed, increasing overtures were made to leading IRA commanders, such as himself, to join the IRB. His impressions are substantiated by other sources. James Hogan, a member of both the IRA and the IRB, acknowledged that the IRA command dictated the Irish military campaign, and concluded, 'I would say that on the eve of the Truce the IRB was semi-moribund beneath, and alive only on top or in its upper levels.'[123] This opinion is corroborated by Florence O'Donoghue for the South Munster Division. As noted earlier he gave the strength of the IRA in the counties of Cork, Kerry and Waterford as 31,000 compared to an IRB membership of 1,170, and observed that, 'since the active campaign commenced in 1919 the IRB as such had not undertaken any military activity in the South Munster Division.'[124] While it is true that many members of the Supreme Council of the IRB were also on the GHQ staff of the IRA, including Collins himself, it is also true that the chain of command emanating from the IRA was controlled by Brugha as Minister of Defence. One is left with the startling impression, in the light of the eminence accorded Collins as head of the IRB, that its specific military contribution to the war effort before the truce was minimal, and that the organisation mobilised its latent strength not to wage war, but to secure the signing of the Treaty. Throughout the Treaty talks Collins kept not only the Cabinet of Dáil Eireann informed, but also the Supreme Council of the IRB. On 12 December 1921, Seán Ó Muirthile, secretary of the Council, issued the following directive to the IRB organisation:

The Supreme Council, having due regard to the Constitution of the Organisation, has decided that the present Peace Treaty between Ireland and Great Britain should be ratified. Members of the Organisation, however, who have to take public action as representatives are given freedom of action in the matter.[125]

Ordinary members of the IRB, many of them holding important positions in the IRA, were expected to obey the directive of the Supreme Council without question. 'The constitutions of the IRB,' as O'Beirne-Ranelagh noted in his study of the organisation, 'were careful to deny democratic procedures within the organisation.'[126] Brugha was particularly incensed by the directive issued by the Supreme Council of the IRB. Contrasting the honourable mention made to the IRB in the Proclamation of Easter Week with the 'dastards' who made up the present Supreme Council, he declared, on 19 May 1922, that,

This body, the Irish Republican Brotherhood, was used to get a majority in this Dáil, and the majority of seven by which this Treaty was approved of in this Dáil could never have been got only that the Irish Republican Brotherhood was used in this way . . . In other words, the body that was used to bring the Republic into existence has been prostituted in order to disestablish the Republic.[127]

Barely seven weeks later Brugha was shot dead fighting for the Republic. Incredible as it may appear almost seventy years on, General Maguire still lives to endorse the testimony of Cathal Brugha. Maguire did join the IRB, and experienced the pressure on free choice created by their actions. As he waited in the halls of the National University rooms at Earlsfort Terrace waiting to cast his vote in the Treaty debate, he was very conscious of the directive of the Supreme Council; of the example of the leaders, such as Collins; and of the verbal encouragement of fellow IRB members to row in with them and vote for the Treaty.[128] Maguire voted against the Treaty on 7 January 1922, but the majority, by 64 votes to 57, followed the lead given by Collins and Griffith. Both men claimed that their own aims and those of their organisations would be met by the British promise of freedom and independence. The irony in the case of Collins was particularly acute: as an IRB man he professed loyalty to Pearse who had proclaimed a Provisional Government to create a Republic, while Collins became head of a Provisional Government to dismantle the Republic created by Dáil Eireann.

Many lessons may be drawn from this study of Collins in the light of his contacts with 'Andy' Cope. It is manifestly clear that no history of Ireland covering the years 1920 to 1922 can safely be written without due acknowledgement of the activities of Cope of the Castle. In the delightful words of Wheeler-Bennett, Cope of the 'rastaquouère' — adventurer type — character and the 'crepuscular' methods deserves to emerge from the twilight zone of the secret service to the broader pages of historical narrative.[129] His emergence casts shadows on the images both of Collins and the Treaty. The bravery and resourcefulness of Collins have to be balanced by a recognition of the conspiratorial methods which brought him into contact with a Castle agent, the Treaty, hailed by those who accepted it as a victory for democracy, has to be assessed in the knowledge that those who advocated it, be they from the ranks of the IRB or the Catholic clergy, were influenced by secret manoeuvres which were hardly compatible with the democratic process. If the Treaty was a victory for anyone, it was for the policy of the British administration. Having resolved in 1920 to abandon a Home Rule policy and to embark on a policy of partition, they could, in 1922, congratulate themselves that such a policy had been achieved and that both Irish Parliaments accepted the Crown of England as head of the State. In pursuit of this policy a pattern was set for the resolution of other imperial problems: partition was to be proposed, if special interests warranted it; and, from among the emerging native population, men had to be chosen with whom the British could, in plain language, do business. Ultimately it has to be recognised that the withdrawing imperial power has the force, unless it is defeated in the field, to influence the future of an emerging nation. The imperial power chooses the native leaders to whom it will entrust the future of the developing country. In Ireland the British found it best to do business with Collins and Griffith.

Traditional Irish histories, especially those written by advocates of the Treaty, record that Collins and Griffith were justified in their enterprises and successful in their endeavours. They dwell on the measure of independence which Ireland received; they tend to ignore the imperial structure into which Ireland was accommodated; they rarely mention the name of 'Andy' Cope; and they regularly deride Brugha, Count Plunkett, Fr O'Flanagan, Stack, J. J. O'Kelly, Mary MacSwiney and other opponents of the Treaty as die-hard obscurantists. By focussing on the activities of Cope and their implications for Collins and the pro-Treaty party, this study reveals that those who lost out in the passing of the Treaty merit far more sympathetic treatment than they have received. The same conclusion may also be drawn from their dealings with de Valera.

6

De Valera and the Republic: the Break with Sinn Féin

The scope of this study is such that, as with Collins, it is only possible to focus on one charge made against de Valera by those republicans who did not join Fianna Fáil. They maintained that de Valera, while professing loyalty to the Republic and acting as head of the republican government, was secretly planning to enter the Free State in the most effective and opportune manner. In many ways the allegation bears a striking similarity to that made against Collins, namely that while publicly acting as a committed member of the Republican Dáil, he was privately planning to accept a new political order that contained something less than the Republic. Many of the issues that arose between de Valera and his opponents were debated at meetings of the Republican Second Dáil Eireann. Although some reports of these meetings appeared in *An Phoblacht* and some other records do exist of its transactions, the O'Kelly collection of documents contains, what I believe to be, the only bound record of the meetings of the Second Dáil. J. Bowyer Bell in his excellent study of the IRA lamented the paucity of manuscript source material and noted that 'the records of the Second Dáil have disappeared entirely.'[1] To find the minutes of the Republican Dáil in the Mortimer O'Kelly collection was to uncover a long sought after source of information. They provide invaluable detail concerning the aims and methods of de Valera both before and immediately after the founding of Fianna Fáil. The story begins with the announcement of de Valera on 25 October 1922, at the height of the Civil War, that he had established a republican government in opposition to the Provisional Government and the soon to

139

be created Free State.[2] De Valera was appointed President of the
Republic and, in turn, appointed a Council of State made up of
twelve deputies. Later, on 13 November, he announced his Cabinet.
In large part de Valera's action was prompted by the initiative of
the IRA. Following a meeting of the army executive on 16 and 17
October, it was proposed that 'this executive calls upon the former
President of Dáil Eireann to form a government which will preserve
the continuity of the Republic.'[3] The army's action was prompted
by two considerations: firstly, Joe McGarrity, representing a section
of Clan na Gael, had urged that American support would be more
forthcoming if it could be directed to some republican authority;
and, secondly, a response was required to the pastoral of the Catholic bishops which condemned the violence of the anti-Treaty forces.
The statement of the hierarchy, made known on 10 October and
read in all churches on 22 October, forcibly declared that 'in the
absence of any legitimate authority' the forces opposed to the
Treaty were guilty of 'murder and assassination.'[4] By announcing
the formation of a republican government on 25 October, de Valera
was not only providing a response to the hierarchy's condemnation,
but also he was aligning himself with the policy advocated by the
IRA and by McGarrity in America. The 'legitimate authority' derived
from de Valera's unilateral declaration of defiance was not entirely
lacking in legal credibility, at least in republican eyes. It was claimed
that the Provisional Government by adjourning the Second Dáil
meeting until 30 June 1922, and then by postponing the meeting
indefinitely, had failed to allow the Second Dáil to dissolve itself
in a proper manner. It was further claimed that the meeting of the
Parliament of 9 September lacked the republican mandate which
could only be conferred by the proper dissolution of the Second
Dáil. In short, the anti-Treaty republicans maintained that the Free
State Parliament derived its validity from the British Parliament,
while they retained the legitimacy conferred by the Republican
Dáil Eireann — the truce source of lawful authority in Ireland. So
argued the republicans. The legal standing of the Second Dáil was
the foundation stone on which de Valera constructed his republican government and from which he drew his own title to the
presidency of the Republic. Herein lies the value of the minutes of
the Second Dáil: they reveal the anxieties and aspirations of de
Valera as he tried to implement his policy in the most sacred republican institution of the post-Treaty era.

De Valera not only adopted the symbolic trappings of a republic
by using notepaper with the heading 'Dáil Eireann Government of
the Republic', but also he attempted to introduce a legislative pro-

gramme which denied the legitimacy of the Free State. One such piece of legislation, issued under the names of de Valera, as President of the Republic, and by Patrick Ruttledge, as Minister of Home Affairs, decreed on 17 November 1922, that the

> resolution passed by Dáil Eireann on 7 January 1922 purporting to approve of the instrument entitled 'Articles of Agreement for a treaty between Great Britain and Ireland' . . . be hereby rescinded and revoked . . . and that any act purporting to be done thereunder is void and of no effect.[5]

At a stroke the Treaty was undone! The Republic still lived in the assembly of the Second Dáil and de Valera committed himself to making the reborn republic a viable reality. Regularly he referred to the Provisional Government as 'an unconstitutional and usurping junta.' Motivated by ideas such as these many followed de Valera in opposition to the Free State which had come formally into existence on 6 December 1922. Many died in the Civil War and the reprisal executions — 77 in all throughout the course of the war — notably, or notoriously, the executions of Rory O'Connor, Liam Mellows, Richard Barrett and Joe McKelvey on 8 December 1922 hardened the resolve of the survivors to be true to the principles for which their comrades had died. The death of these leading republicans did, however, taken in conjunction with the earlier deaths of Brugha, Boland and Childers and that of Liam Lynch at the end of the war, weaken the republican voice at the highest level. To some extent the emergence of Mary MacSwiney, while not compensating for the tremendous loss of these able men, did enhance the republican cause. In the early days of 1917 Mary MacSwiney had manifested signs of sympathy with the approach of Count Plunkett, and, following the death of her brother Terence on hunger strike, she became a dedicated republican. Not only did she carry the mantle of her dead brother, but also in a highly successful tour of America and in an impassioned speech against the Treaty she had shown herself to possess great ability and considerable powers of persuasion. She used these qualities unsparingly in defence of the Republic. The armed battle for the Republic, however, ended in failure. On 27 April 1923, Frank Aiken, the new Chief-of-Staff of the IRA, and de Valera, as head of the Republican Government, ordered the suspension of all offensive operations. This was followed by a further order on 24 May to dump arms. De Valera informed 'the Soldiers of the Republic, Legion of the Rearguard,' that

> Military victory must be allowed to rest for the moment with those

who have destroyed the Republic . . . Other means must be sought to safeguard the nation's right.[6]

These 'other means' were discussed at meetings of the Second Dáil.

DE VALERA AND THE SECOND DÁIL AFTER THE CIVIL WAR

Unfortunately the views of de Valera immediately after the Civil War are not to be found in the minutes of the Second Dáil because he was arrested at Ennis on 15 August 1923 as he prepared to contest the Clare election. Unfortunately, too, he was arrested before he could give voice to his post-Civil War policy. Ironically, in the light of his calculated co-operation with Eoin MacNeill to win the Clare election of 1917, he won the seat in 1923 with MacNeill as his opponent. The Angelus bell that had summoned advanced nationalists to unite in 1917 now served as a tocsin to warn Irishmen of the division over the ideals of Faith and Fatherland. De Valera remained in prison until 16 July 1924. During that time there were five meetings of the Second Dáil. The first meeting took place on 28 December 1923. Only thirteen deputies attended this meeting. The small assembly did not betoken any dramatic falling away in the republican position. Rather it emphasised the dangers under which the anti-Treaty party expressed their opposition. Many republicans were, like de Valera, in prison; many engaged in hunger strikes; and some died in the process. Fear of arrest and imprisonment made it impossible to conduct an open republican meeting. Confusion and doubts, however, did exist in the republican ranks; not only had they lost the guidance of their leader; but also they had lost the August election, gaining only 44 seats to the Government's 63. Three recurring themes were discussed at the early meetings of the Second Dáil: the attitude to be adopted to the Free State; the legitimacy of their own organisation; and the details of a practical policy which they could present to the people. Such questions as whether they should pay income tax; whether they should pay a dog tax or a licence for a motor car were debated in the light of the recognition conferred on the Free State administration by such payments. Eventually it was decided that, as they could not protect the people from the enforcement of such measures, they should adopt the same attitude as that taken to the English Government after 1919 – to comply with the law, but to deny its legitimacy. The question of the legal standing of the Second Dáil was frankly discussed at a meeting on 15 January 1924. Countess Markievicz maintained that it was mere pretence and play-acting to pose as the Government of the Republic.

It was nonsense [she asserted] to call ourselves a Government when the people have turned us down. We have the majority against us and until we have the majority of the people with us again we are not a Government.[7]

This pragmatic and honest appraisal of the political situation evoked a critical response from most of the other members present – a response in which they sought to give justification to the concept of a republican government. Count Plunkett declared, 'The question of the majority did not arise. We had a Government apart from the majority. The present F.S. Government was set up by England.' David Kent defended the stand of the Second Dáil by declaring that 'the Second Dáil represented all Ireland, and had not yet been dissolved;' while Mary MacSwiney 'denied that the right of the majority extended to the surrender of the independence of the Nation.' This last sentiment also found expression in the statement of Dr Kathleen Lynn that 'no generation can surrender the independence of the country.'[8] By stressing the idea of nationality and by focussing on the unbroken republican link with the Republic proclaimed in 1916 and popularly approved in 1919, the Second Dáil found reason to justify itself. It was proposed and passed unanimously that the assembly 'heartily approve of the Republican Cabinet appointed by President de Valera, which Cabinet is to continue as the Government of the Republic.'[9] Unity was preserved by distinguishing between the existence of the Government and its capacity to function. It was agreed that, in the circumstances, little legislative activity could take place. Policy matters were, however, debated and Mary MacSwiney presented detailed proposals on the practical implementation of the Democratic Programme. Countess Markievicz, as might be expected, granted her proven social concern, spoke in favour of the programme; but, more surprisingly, many other deputies were also anxious to draw up a policy of social and economic reform. Confirmation is given to the view expressed earlier that not only republicanism, but also a social commitment lost out in the vote on the Treaty. By July 1924, therefore, when de Valera was released from prison, he was free, if he wished, to take up his position as President of the Republic using the Second Dáil as the source of his lawful authority; or he might endeavour to change the direction of the Second Dáil. The decisions taken in his absence had been made by a small group of people – the average number at any one meeting was no more than fifteen; and, contrary to the assertion of some writers, no policy of abstention from the Free State Parliament had been explicitly formulated by the Second Dáil. Such a policy was, of course, tacitly implied by the denial of the legitimacy of the Free State institutions. Room for manoeuvre would, however, have appeared to exist as some fifty five leading republicans, enjoying a new freedom of mobility, began their meeting at 23 Suffolk Street on 7 August.

De Valera did not waver in the slightest from the course he had adopted in October 1922. He acted as if the Civil War had not been fought – or won! He was happy to accept the title of President of the Republic; he upheld the role of the Second Dáil as 'the *de jure* Government and Legislature;' and he referred to the Free State Government as 'the present Junta.'[10] Having justified his course of action from 1922 onwards, including the cease-fire, de Valera then proposed that,

> We, the surviving faithful members of the Second Dáil, hereby approve of the Acts of the members of the Second Dáil, who, in October, 1922, set up the Emergency Government of the Republic with the concurrence of the Army.[11]

Not only did de Valera justify his actions retrospectively, but also he acted to make an effective reality of a new government. He appointed a new ministry composed of Austin Stack, responsible for Home Affairs and Finance; Art O'Connor, responsible for Economic Affairs and Local Government; Frank Aiken, Minister of Defence; Patrick Ruttledge and Robert Barton as ministers without portfolio; and he, himself, was responsible for Foreign Affairs. Seán T. O'Kelly acted as Chairman of the Second Dáil. Every effort was made to set up a viable alternative government with proper regard to its constitutional validity. The minutes reveal that while deputies, including de Valera, stressed that their legitimacy derived from the non-dissolution of the Second Dáil, they also created a broader based assembly made up of all republican deputies. This was called Comhairle Na d-Teachtaí. Membership of this body was precisely defined. Those eligible were:

1. The surviving members of the Second Dáil who remained faithful to the Republic.
2. Republican deputies elected in June 1922.
3. Republican deputies elected in August 1923.
4. Any other Republican deputies who may be hereafter elected during the existence of the Emergency Government.[12]

By this procedure the republican assembly was able to renew itself: membership of the Second Dáil elected in 1921 provided republican legitimacy; membership of the Comhairle Na d-Teachtaí provided for ongoing republican government. Count Plunkett was appointed chairman of a committee to draft standing orders for this new assembly and on 29 August 1924 he informed de Valera that, with the assistance of Brian O'Higgins and Tom Derrig, he had completed his task.[13] The standing orders witness to an intention to observe parliamentary procedures, and also testify to de Valera's willingness to take his part in this new republican order which challenged the Free State. This refashioning of the Second Dáil went hand in hand with the revival of the Republican Sinn Féin party. By the beginning of June 1924 there were 1,000 branches of Sinn Féin throughout Ireland – a rapid and spectacular increase following the fragmentation of the organisation after the Treaty.[14] The IRA also, under the direction of Aiken as Chief-of-Staff, was linked harmoniously with the political wing of the republican movement. Everything seemed set fair for a renewal of republican faith and fervour. De Valera gave every indication of being totally committed to the republican cause as formulated by himself and his colleagues in the Second Dáil; but almost immediately his commitment became hedged around with first caution, then qualification, and finally compromise.

Questions concerning the possibility of entering the Free State Parliament had been raised at the Sinn Féin Ard-Fheis in November 1924. De Valera was not able to answer them. He was in prison in Belfast throughout almost the entire month of November, having been arrested while campaigning in the Northern Ireland elections. On 11 December 1924, however, he was present at a large gathering of Comhairle Na d-Teachtaí when the questions were posed again. Deputies were keen to have a clear message to put before the Free State electorate: should they, or should they not, enter Leinster House, if they secured a majority in any forthcoming election? De Valera replied:

> The Oath was a barrier to entering those buildings. Other clauses were equally objectionable. He was not prepared to state his personal view, much would depend on the size of our majority.[15]

This answer, while recognising the oath as an obstacle, left much room for manoeuvre. The by-election results of 11 March 1925 had a dramatic effect on de Valera and caused him to embrace the flexibility of manoeuvre permitted him by his December statement. Nine seats were contested in the rarely adverted to, but significant, March elections: the republicans won only two, and these they secured in second position. De Valera, though shocked and disappointed, did not share his feelings with the republican deputies as a body, but a year later he did confide his views to Joe McGarrity.

> Since the nine Bye-elections [he wrote], I have been convinced that the programme on which we were working would not win the people in the present conditions. It was too high, and too sweeping. The oath, on the other hand, is a definite objective within reasonable striking distance.[16]

After the election defeats de Valera focussed on the problem of the oath. For him the debate was no longer to be continued on an academic plane: principle was to be tempered by the demands of practical realities.

DE VALERA AND THE OATH: SECRET NEGOTIATIONS

On 18 March 1925, one week after the disastrous election results, de Valera addressed a meeting of Comhairle Na d-Teachtaí. Rumours had been circulating that some republican deputies were prepared to take the oath and to enter the Free State Parliament. Faced by these whisperings de Valera declared that,

> He believed the time had come when this rumour was hampering the cause. The question of entering with the Oath must be definitely closed. But the question is what if the Oath were removed? Even if we had a majority vote to-morrow and we wanted to take control we could not get in without taking the Oath. The thing would be to concentrate upon the removal of the Oath.[17]

Later, in the same meeting, de Valera added that 'he did not believe that any Republican representative could go up there and take the Oath even for the sake of taking over control.' After further discussion, in which Mrs Clarke, David Kent and Austin Stack were prominent, a vote was taken on the principle of going into the Free State 'Dáil' at present. 'On a show of hands the majority were in favour of the principle of abstention.'[18] This was the first explicit policy decision of the Second Dáil in favour of abstention: it was made in regard to the specific circumstances of 1925; and it was made, interestingly enough, in the absence of Mary MacSwiney who was in America working for the republican interest. Contrary to many common assumptions the principle of abstention was adopted under the presidency of de Valera and MacSwiney was not directly involved. On 22 April de Valera and forty-four other republican deputies gave public expression to their views on the oath and the Free State Parliament. The statement read:

> We the undersigned do not recognise the legitimacy of either the 'Free State' or 'Northern' Parliaments.
> The rumour, therefore, sedulously propagated, despite repeated official denials, that we, or any of us, propose (or at any time contem-

plated) entering the Free State Parliament and taking the oath of allegiance to the British King, is without foundation.[19]

De Valera denied, therefore, not only the propriety of taking an oath to the King of England, but also the very legitimacy of the Free State Parliament itself. As de Valera had made clear in December 1924, other clauses in the Free State constitution 'were equally objectionable' to the oath. To most of the deputies it appeared illogical and contradictory to contemplate the taking of an oath to an assembly whose lawfulness one denied on many other grounds. It also seemed illogical to many of them to accept the 'objectionable' clauses in the Free State constitution, even if the oath were removed. De Valera thought otherwise. His observation to the republican deputies on 18 March 1925 that 'the thing would be to concentrate upon the removal of the Oath' served as a marker to his new policy.

De Valera's new departure was first formulated at a standing committee of Sinn Féin on 7 May 1925 which resolved unanimously, but privately, that,

> The president may act on the assumption that the question of Republicans entering the Free State 'Parliament' if the oath were removed, is an open question, to be decided on its merits when the question arises as a practical issue.[20]

This Sinn Féin resolution was raised by de Valera at a meeting of Comhairle Na d-Teachtaí on 22 June 1925 and a discussion ensued. Unfortunately the full minutes of that meeting were not recorded. However, during the debate David Kent mentioned a new initiative on the part of the Free State which must have alarmed de Valera. Kent reported that,

> he heard that the F.S. were in touch with Dr Mannix and that it was possible they would try to use him as an intermediary.[21]

In fact, whatever about the Free State's approaches to Mannix, de Valera had visited him secretly in Rome shortly before the June meeting of Comhairle Na d-Teachtaí. Any danger to the republican position through the mediation of Mannix was caused not merely by intrigue on the part of the Free State but by de Valera himself. From the moment in 1917 when de Valera had committed himself to a political career he had been acutely conscious of the power of the Catholic Church and had endeavoured to harness the Church's influence in his own interests. The condemnation in October 1922 by the Catholic hierarchy of the anti-Treaty side had gravely weakened the republican movement, and, as de Valera prepared for a new beginning, he badly wanted the support of the Church. Above all he wanted the advice and approval of the three leading Catholic churchmen who had been loyal to him and to the Republic: Archbishop Mannix of Melbourne; Mgr Hagan, Rector of the Irish College in Rome; and the Very Reverend Fr Peter Magennis, head of the Carmelite Order, who was also based in Rome. Mannix was the single most prominent Catholic ecclesiastic to defend de Valera's stand against the formal condemnation of the Catholic Bishops: Hagan, continuing the policy of his predecessor, Mgr O'Riordain, defended the republican position at the Vatican after the Treaty; and Magennis, who, as President of the Friends of Irish Freedom, had welcomed and assisted de Valera in America in 1919, also continued to support him after the Treaty. De Valera and his closest colleague, Seán T. O'Kelly, enjoyed links of friendship with these three men built up through personal contact in Ireland, Rome and America. In May 1925 all three churchmen were in Rome — Mannix having arrived there with a group of pilgrims from Australia on 28 May. De Valera decided to meet them. Disguised as a priest he secretly left Ireland and reached Rome. He was accompanied by Seán MacBride who acted as secretary and interpreter. MacBride later recalled that,

> Both Monsignor Hagan and Monsignor Magennis were enthusiastic that the meeting should take place . . . they also contacted Archbishop Mannix and found him only too willing to meet Mr de Valera secretly in the Irish College.[22]

Private talks took place between de Valera and Mannix, and further discussions occurred between de Valera and all three churchmen. MacBride felt that,

> It was really in these meetings that the whole plan of campaign for the future policy of Fianna Fáil and the dismantling of the Treaty was taken.[23]

Details of these meetings are hard to come by and unfortunately there is a discrepancy between the account of Dermot Keogh, the historian of this episode, and his prime source Seán MacBride. Keogh, claiming to follow MacBride, puts the meetings in early 1926; MacBride, in his own account, maintains that Archbishop Mannix was in Rome with an Australian pilgrimage, thus making a date in the summer of 1925 necessary.[24] A letter from Hagan to de Valera on 31 May 1925, and described by Keogh as 'an authoritative document', proposed new initiatives. The document, Keogh asserts, 'provided both a theological and historical explanation of how to enter the Dáil;' whilst Seán MacBride was even more explicit about the outcome of the meetings – 'The whole policy of entering the Dáil,' he wrote, 'by taking the oath as an "empty formula", and of proceeding to dismantle the constitution of the Free State and Treaty was taken.'[25] All the indications are that de Valera was initiating this new departure and that both Hagan and Mannix, in particular, encouraged him on his new course. Both men visited Ireland in the summer of 1925 to assist de Valera: Mannix arrived on 29 June and stayed until 31 October; Hagan was also in the country for the latter part of this period. Seán T. O'Kelly also returned to Ireland from America. O'Kelly was fully supportive of de Valera's new approach and, as the republican representative in America and formal head of the American Association for the Recognition of the Irish Republic (AARIR), he exercised considerable influence. The letters of Seán T. O'Kelly to Mary MacSwiney, still working in America on the republican mission, reveal that in the month of September Mgr Hagan was staying with the O'Kelly family in Stephen's Green, and that regular contacts were made with de Valera and Archbishop Mannix.[26] Another side to the talks was revealed in a letter of Dr Patrick McCartan to Joe McGarrity. McCartan, a leading IRB man in 1916 – he had been on the Supreme Council – and active in many spheres of the nationalist cause after the Rising, had taken the Treaty side. He informed McGarrity that with the knowledge and approval of both de Valera and Cosgrave, head of the Free State Government, he had had two interviews with Mannix. His role was that of an intermediary. The fears expressed in June 1925 by David Kent were well justified. Mary MacSwiney certainly drew that conclusion. She bluntly told de Valera that 'it looks as if the Free Staters believe you have sent Dr. Mannix out to prepare the way for a surrender on our part.'[27] She then passed on a warning from Joe McGarrity:

> No steps towards a settlement [he said] should be made by you or other leaders without consulting the rank and file. Such action had led to trouble before and would lead to it again.[28]

De Valera did not heed this request. The rank and file – as well as leading figures in the Second Dáil and Sinn Féin – were left in the dark as, in secret consultation with leading Catholic clerics and his representative in America, de Valera formulated his new policy. While this policy was taking definitive shape, it should be noted that in the summer of 1925, the exact date is not known, another journey abroad was made on behalf of de Valera.

This mission was made with another policy in mind and indicates that until the very last de Valera was keeping all options open; or, as appears more likely, attempting to retain his control over all republican groupings. In July 1925 Lemass, as Minister of Defence, and Aiken, as Chief-of-Staff of the IRA, obviously acting with de Valera's approval, countenanced an IRA mission to Russia. Gerry Boland, a member of the Dáil and one of the deputies closest to de Valera, departed on this mission together with Seán Russell, quartermaster general of the Army.[29] One of their objectives was to study the use of military aeroplanes in warfare situations. Their interest was clearly not simply theoretical. Nothing came of their visit, however, although de Valera did meet an agent named Marino in Ireland. Confirmation that de Valera was still supporting the military options of the IRA after the Civil War is further revealed in a letter of Lemass and Aiken to Seán T. O'Kelly on 2 July 1925. They wrote on behalf of the Dáil Eireann ministry of which de Valera was President and urged O'Kelly, as American envoy, to raise more money for the Army.

> We are endeavouring [they said] to maintain the Army as an effective force, capable of being brought into immediate action should the occasion arise that would justify or necessitate its use.[30]

In the previous year just over £11,000 donated from America had been used to support the IRA. De Valera remained identified with this policy until November 1925 when he decided to announce publicly his new departure based on removal of the oath. The phase of secret negotiation had ended; the period of open confrontation was about to begin.

DE VALERA AND THE OATH: OPEN CONFRONTATION

Matters came to a head as republicans prepared for the opening of the Sinn Féin Ard-Fheis on 17 November 1925. Some of the motions on the agenda openly opposed the approach to the oath which de Valera had been pursuing in secret. Rumours of a new departure had clearly been circulating in republican circles. De Valera was forced to fight for his policy in public, if it was to have any chance of success. He took the initiative at a large gathering of Comhairle Na d-Teachtaí – about fifty members – on 15 November. The deputies were warned that there was a danger of the meeting being raided by Free State forces. De Valera opened the proceedings by immediately raising the question of the oath. He made his own position very clear: 'he thought the time had come to close the present chapter and begin anew.'[31] J. J. O'Kelly, as chairman, was reluctant to allow discussion on any proposal that was prepared to accept the Free State institutions, and there were attempts to post-pone the debate on the oath. De Valera insisted, however. He said that 'he would not allow himself to be re-elected at the Ard Fheis without knowing where he stood.'[32] Finally, presumably to over-come O'Kelly's objection, it was proposed by Seán McEntee and seconded by Mary MacSwiney that they convene the following day as Cumann Na Phoblachta, a republican organisation set up by de Valera soon after the Treaty, and discuss the oath in that assembly. De Valera opened the meeting on Monday, 16 November by dealing directly with the motion, submitted by the Cahirciveen branch, that was to be debated at the Sinn Féin Ard-Fheis. The motion was an open challenge to his own policy. It read:

> Owing to the insidious rumours that Republicans will enter the 'Free State Parliament' if the Oath be removed, we call on Sinn Féin to get a definite statement from the Government that they will adhere to the policy of Cathal Brugha, Erskine Childers, and their fellow martyrs, and enter only an Irish Republican Parliament for all Ireland.[33]

The republican ideal of Brugha was to be opposed to that of de Valera. Naturally de Valera was unhappy with the Cahirciveen pro-posal and told the assembled deputies that 'if held as a matter of dogma by the Ard Fheis he could not conscientiously carry on.'[34] The threat of resignation led to a compromise proposal devised by Mary MacSwiney and Countess Markievicz. Arguments among Dáil deputies gave way to debate among Sinn Féin members — many individuals were members of both associations — as the Sinn Féin Ard-Fheis opened on the following day. For three days the discussions continued in the Town Hall at Rathmines. Ultimately a compromise was arrived at, which postponed a final decision. It was agreed that,

> No change be made in the policy of the Sinn Féin organisation at this Ard Fheis; but it is agreed that no subject is barred from the whole organisation or part of it with the exception of the acceptance of allegi-ance to a foreign King and the Partition of Ireland.[35]

By not endorsing the Cahirciveen resolution the way was open for de Valera to pursue this policy. It was evident, however, that once the policy issue was open to debate, it would result in serious con-flict. Indeed some sections of the republican movement had already moved to counter the initiative of de Valera.

On the very morning of the meeting of Comhairle Na d-Teachtaí, 15 November, at which de Valera introduced his new proposal, the IRA acted. Seán Lemass, as Minister of Defence, was summoned to a meeting of the Army Convention. The grave message that he was instructed to bring back to the republican deputies was that the army 'had withdrawn allegiance from the Republican Government and had set up the Army Council as the Supreme Governing Body.'[36] Frank Aiken was also dismissed from his position as Chief-of-Staff, largely through the influence of George Plunkett. The army wished to have no truck with de Valera's policy on the oath. This had been made clear to him personally when he attended the first day of the Army Convention on 14 November.[37] With the mention of the name of George Plunkett, one is given a pointer to the group of republicans who emerged as the most prominent opponents of de Valera: they were Count Plunkett, who could hardly have been unaware of his son's action, Fr O'Flanagan and J. J. O'Kelly. All three men were committed to the ideals of Cathal Brugha and had been associated with the North Roscommon by-election. They were joined by Mary MacSwiney. Prior to de Valera's shift in policy they had worked loyally for him and for the Republic. Fr O'Flanagan had left Ireland for America in November 1921 to work in the republican cause with the full approval and recommendation of de Valera. He remained in America until the early months of 1925. While in America he co-operated most effectively with J. J. O'Kelly who was sent to the States in 1922 as the representative of the Republic. Together, again at the request of de Valera, they went in 1923 to Australia where they defended the republican position until they were imprisoned. On their release and deportation they returned to America where O'Kelly became republican envoy in September 1923. From that time until his recall in October 1924 they worked together to rebuild the strife torn AARIR and to raise funds for the republicans in Ireland. Both tasks were tackled with considerable success. On O'Kelly's return to Ireland he was appointed chairman of the Second Dáil by de Valera in December 1924. While O'Kelly and Fr O'Flanagan were actively engaged for the Republic abroad, Count Plunkett and Mary MacSwiney had played prominent parts in defending and developing the republican movement in Ireland. The return of O'Kelly from America was followed almost immediately by Mary MacSwiney's departure to the States – she was there from January to late October 1925.[38] Her return, coinciding almost exactly with de Valera's publicly declared policy on the oath, marked the start of the alliance which challenged de Valera's new departure most strongly. Before the Sinn Féin Ard-Fheis of November 1925, Mary MacSwiney had warned de Valera in writing of the dangers involved in his new policy; and J. J. O'Kelly had not only forestalled any discussions of it in the Second Dáil, but also he had been involved secretly in the formulation of the Cahirciveen resolution. After the Ard-Fheis most members of the Second Dáil and of Sinn Féin, while little thinking that a split in the republican movement was likely, realised that a period of open argument would be necessary before reconciliation could, they hoped, be achieved. Looking back over the years from 1922 to 1925 it seemed incredible to republicans like Count Plunkett, Fr O'Flanagan, J. J. O'Kelly and Mary MacSwiney that de Valera, having supported the legitimacy of the Second Dáil in opposition to the Free State, could ever envisage entering the Free State Parliament. On reflection, however, some actions of de Valera during those years did raise their suspicions.

Two incidents involving J. J. O'Kelly merit attention: firstly, at the August 1923 election, while O'Kelly was in prison in Australia, his seat at Louth was allocated to Frank Aiken; and, secondly, in July 1924, he was informed that he was being recalled as republican envoy to the States and that Seán T. O'Kelly would be his replacement. Of the first incident J. J. O'Kelly wrote to de Valera at the time acquiescing in the decision but noting that 'my defeat, on account of my position, will give temporary justification to those who oppose our mission.'[39] Later he viewed the loss of his seat in a different light and wrote,

> One of the memorable achievements of that Election was to have my constituency in Louth annexed in the interest of Mr de Valera's pliant instrument, Frank Aiken, while I was a prisoner at Botany Bay, a proceeding without parallel in the history of Irish elections.[40]

The burden of O'Kelly's complaint was that de Valera had given Aiken his safe seat at Louth in order to increase the standing of Aiken in the republican movement. The second incident was of similar import: de Valera was placing his own man in America who could be relied on to use American money and influence in the interests of de Valera, himself. Fr O'Flanagan saw the recall of O'Kelly in that light. He was later reported as saying that,

> He and J. J. O'Kelly had been made tools of by de Valera for working up an Organisation in America for the followers of de Valera's policy to profit by. As soon as he and Sceilg had gotten things well under way in the U.S.A. a slick little politician was sent over.[41]

In such a fashion Fr O'Flanagan described Seán T. O'Kelly. Fr O'Flanagan was also critical of de Valera's dealings with Archbishop Mannix in 1925. He declared that,

De Valera had, it seemed, gone to Europe to meet Mannix several years
ago but he had heard of it only a few months ago. After the visit, over
came Archbishop Mannix to Ireland and here also he was made a tool
of for working de Valera's plans; and he had joined others in welcoming the Archbishop.[42]

Fr O'Flanagan's remarks confirm the story of Dermot Keogh and
Seán MacBride that de Valera secretly visited Mannix in Rome. The
complaint of those republicans who contested the new departure
of de Valera was that they had been used and deceived: that while
they were working for the Republic, de Valera was placing men of
proven loyalty to himself in key positions of power so that his own
particular brand of republicanism might be achieved. In the dénoue-
ment of the crisis in 1926 de Valera, himself, admitted that from
1923 onwards he was saying one thing in the Second Dáil, while
planning for another eventuality. De Valera's revelation about his
true intentions was made at the culmination of a series of actions
which split Sinn Féin and the Second Dáil, and ended in the creation
of the Fianna Fáil party. These events will now be considered.

DE VALERA AND THE SPLIT IN SINN FÉIN

The issues that had been raised at the November 1925 meetings of
the Second Dáil and of Sinn Féin clarified the matters dividing the
protagonists, and crystalised the alignment of personalities around
the central object of controversy — the oath. However, if the editorial of *An Phoblacht* may be taken as representing the mood in
the Sinn Féin party, it appeared that differences had been resolved;
and that the divisive question of the oath was a thing of the past.
On 27 November 1925 the editor wrote of the suggestion to take
the oath under protest and then drive out the Free State authorities,
that,

> The answer has been given at the Ard Fheis to all such specious plead-
> ing. The acceptance of allegiance to England or the partition of Ireland
> is incompatible with membership of Sinn Féin.[43]

Certainly those republicans who had opposed de Valera in the
November debates acted as though the oath was an issue of the past.
They played a prominent part in the call from the Rathmines
Cumann to formulate a national, economic, and cultural plan for
the future.[44] Fr O'Flanagan, still Vice-President of Sinn Féin, was
appointed chairman of a sub-committee to draft a new national
programme. J. J. O'Kelly was secretary of the committee. The project was the considered response by the Standing Committee of

Sinn Féin to the problems facing the republican movement in 1925. Although de Valera was President of Sinn Féin, 'he never once showed the slightest interest in it,' maintained O'Kelly.[45] De Valera was only concerned with bringing his own plans to fruition: for him the issue of the oath was not yet dead. He showed his hand after a striking, but brief, display of republican unity on 10 December 1925 when all elected deputies met in the Rotunda to protest at the Free State's acceptance of the findings of the Boundary Commission.[46] On 6 January 1926 de Valera reverted to the policy he had first aired in November 1925 and he declared at a meeting of the Ranelagh Sinn Féin Cumann that, if the oath were removed, he would be prepared to enter the Free State Dáil.[47] Within the space of a month de Valera put forward his revived policy on the oath in a motion to be debated at an extraordinary Ard-Fheis. The proposal, as announced on 2 February 1926, read that,

> Once the admission oaths of the Twenty-six-County assemblies are removed, it becomes a question not of principle, but of policy whether or not Republican representatives should attend these assemblies.[48]

De Valera did not embark on this course of confrontation without some preparation. At home Seán Lemass, one of his most trusted supporters, continued a series of articles in *An Phoblacht*, begun in September 1925, in which he called for changes in Sinn Féin. On 22 January 1926 Lemass declared that,

> There are some who would have us sit by the roadside and debate abstruse points about a 'de jure' this and a 'de facto' that, but the reality we want is away in the distance — and we cannot get there unless we move.[49]

He developed this pragmatic approach further on 29 January when he asserted that immediate objectives were required; that they should be realisable in a short time; and that the oath 'is the most obvious one, but there are others.'[50] Lemass said all that de Valera wished to say, and he said it well. The case for a change in policy was being made at home with clarity and conviction. Abroad too de Valera did not take anything for granted. Seán T. O'Kelly was already working for de Valera's interest as republican envoy in America, but in January 1926 Frank Aiken also arrived in the States on a special mission for de Valera. His aim was to retain for de Valera the financial support of the military element in America, especially that connected with Joe McGarrity.[51] As a former Chief-of-Staff of the IRA he was ideally suited for his task. If the monetary power of America appeared safely harnessed to de Valera's side, so too did the moral power of those Catholic churchmen who favoured the anti-Treaty side. De Valera could still rely on Hagan in Rome and Mannix in Melbourne. As de Valera, therefore, prepared for the extraordinary Ard-Fheis, due to take place on 9 March 1926, he did so with confidence. He had seized the initiative from his opponents and he had laid his plans well. From a position of disadvantage his opponents prepared to challenge de Valera's new designs.

The Standing Committee of Sinn Féin was totally unaware of de Valera's proposals. Although President of the organisation, de Valera had neither co-operated with their programme of reform, agreed to in November 1925, nor consulted them about the revival of his policy on the oath. The committee, therefore, immediately disowned de Valera's proposals: they were, it stated, the 'personal responsibility' of the President; and they were 'not to be regarded as being made on behalf of the Standing Committee.'[52] An alternative proposal of Fr O'Flanagan, made in his capacity as vice-president of Sinn Féin, was appended to these disclaimers.

It is incompatible [the motion read] with the fundamental principles of Sinn Féin as it is injurious to the honour of Ireland, to send representatives into an usurping Legislature set up by English law in Ireland.[53]

Five hundred delegates gathered in the Rotunda on 9 March and discussed the rival motions. It was not until after lunch on 10 March that de Valera and Fr O'Flanagan made their final speeches. The vote was taken and Fr O'Flanagan's amendment, which was seconded by J. J. O'Kelly, was carried by 223 votes to 218. Although this amendment was later defeated as a substantive motion by 179 votes to 177, de Valera conceded that his new departure had been defeated, but only as a matter of policy. On 11 March 1926 he announced to the Ard-Fheis that he was resigning the presidency of Sinn Féin. It was against this background that de Valera broke with Sinn Féin and founded Fianna Fáil. Later he was to claim that it was reasonable to ignore the majority decision against his motion, because 'even if a majority had been secured for it, the minority would nevertheless refuse to accept the majority decision.'[54] This subtle and rather tortuous explanation for his conduct, which, if applied generally, would destroy the normal democratic process, has received a sympathetic hearing from many historians.[55] In fact there are good reasons to be critical of de Valera. He was, above all, and despite all his pretensions to be arguing over a matter of policy, concerned with changing the 'fundamental principles' of an organisation – a point explicitly stressed in Fr O'Flanagan's proposal. In the case of Sinn Féin the principle involved was a constitutive element in the composition of the society – a raison d'être of the association itself. To abandon the principle was to change the very nature of the organisation: to form, indeed, a new party. For de Valera to blame members of Sinn Féin for being loyal to the principles of their party rather than being prepared to embrace the new policies of his own was churlish in the extreme. Moreover, Mary MacSwiney had made it clear to de Valera that, if she and her followers were in a small minority, they would 'drop quietly out and devote ourselves to educational work. There would be nothing gained', she added, 'by starting an opposition party.'[56] In her mind fidelity to the principles of Sinn Féin was preferable to the fragmentation of the party: the same priorities did not motivate the policy of de Valera. MacSwiney shrewdly noted, however, that a fifty-fifty division would be 'the most dangerous position for the cause.' The burden of MacSwiney's criticism of de Valera's new departure was that it threatened 'a quite unnecessary division on a hypothetical situation which to my mind will never become actual.'[57] It was not her policy, she maintained, which was unrealistic; it was that of de Valera. The Free State would never change its commitment to the oath. Contemporary newspapers accepted MacSwiney's opinion. The *Irish Times* observed that neither Parliament had the slightest intention of abolishing their admission oaths; and the *Tribune* commented on de Valera's proposal that it 'is very sane, very late, and very futile.'[58] Far better, MacSwiney argued, to confront the Free State with a united and renewed republican movement rather than to accept a programme which was based on a hypothetical absurdity. In March 1926 de Valera's policy could reasonably be so described: it offered no more hope, possibly even less, than that of Sinn Féin. His policy only became realistic when he proposed accepting the oath as an 'empty formula.' The indications are that de Valera was secretly planning such a departure from as early as 1925. De Valera was no fool. He must have been aware that the oath would never be removed. If it were, he would have had no problem in entering the Free State Dáil. He would have had no need to consult with Mannix, Hagan and Magennis in the summer of 1925. The solution he received from them was not, as has been noted, concerned with any hypothetical removal of the oath; it envisaged the taking of the oath as an 'empty formula.' Shrewd politician as he was, de Valera must have known that to present the republican movement with a new policy based on taking the oath as an empty formula would have been political suicide. The first tentative step away from the Republic was best made by rallying a group of supporters around the hypothetical removal of the oath.

Further reason to be critical of de Valera is to be found in his attitude towards other articles in the Treaty. Already it was becoming part of republican folklore that there were eleven clauses in the Treaty that recognised the English King, thus making acceptance of the Free State impossible, even if the oath were removed. A republican pamphlet of the time spelt out the message. It proclaimed:

> Mr Kevin O'Higgins says: 'the following Articles in the Free State Constitution are vital and must not be altered,' namely:
> Article 12. Parliament shall consist of the King and two Houses.
> Article 17. Every member of Parliament must take the oath of allegiance to the King.
> Article 24. Parliament shall be summoned and dissolved by the representative of the King.[59]

The other eight articles in the Constitution were listed and the pamphlet concluded, 'Can you say anything about the Free State more damning than this?' While Mary MacSwiney regularly highlighted these Articles, and did so in her January letter to de Valera, he put them firmly out of his mind. The message of de Valera was that there was only one issue — the oath. When he was defeated on that issue on 10 March 1926 he did not immediately announce the formation of Fianna Fáil. Nor, contrary to many common assumptions, did de Valera's opponents in Sinn Féin force him into the wilderness. Before the Ard-Fheis ended, Fr O'Flanagan proposed that the Assembly should express its feelings of admiration for President de Valera — a proposal that was graciously seconded by Mary MacSwiney. Then Mary MacSwiney, as senior Vice-President of Sinn Féin, took the chair as the two rival groups appointed committees to discuss the future of Sinn Féin. It was agreed that,

> The joint committees be given full powers, on behalf of the Sinn Féin organisation, to deal with all matters arising out of the present situation, and to make all necessary arrangements for co-operation.[60]

Co-operation, therefore, was the intention of de Valera's opponents within the Sinn Féin movement. The oft painted picture of extremists, such as Mary MacSwiney, Fr O'Flanagan and J. J. O'Kelly, denying de Valera the freedom to put his realistic policies into practice is seen in a different perspective. In their efforts to preserve the republican ideal they were reacting responsibly to a policy which de Valera had devised in secret, having captured the republican movement in America and having received the blessing of leading Catholic churchmen. A policy, moreover, which from the very outset, despite protestations to the contrary, was prepared to take republicans into the Free State Dáil. Under close scrutiny it is the methods and motives of de Valera on which a shadow of suspicion is cast. The shadow becomes even darker when one examines the manner in which he parted company with his colleagues in the Second Dáil.

7

De Valera and the Republic: the Break with the Second Dáil

DE VALERA AND THE FOUNDING OF FIANNA FÁIL

On 28 March 1926 Comhairle Na d-Teachtaí met to discuss the new situation created by de Valera's resignation from the presidency of Sinn Féin. Forty-six members were present at the meeting. They were informed immediately by Art O'Connor, the chairman of the joint committees of Sinn Féin, that 'it was found that no co-operation was possible on the proposal to enter the "Free State Parliament" in the event of the oath being removed.'[1] In order to clarify the position of the Second Dáil Mary MacSwiney proposed that,

> The entry of any member of Dáil Eireann into the Free State Parliament or any Parliament set up by British law in Ireland is inconsistent with the policy advocated by the Republican Teachtaidhe and candidates since 1922.[2]

During the debate on this motion de Valera admitted that before he was arrested in Ennis in August 1923, he was prepared, in his election address, to propose the possibility of entering the Free State. 'If I had a chance in Ennis,' he declared, 'I would have said I was willing to go in.'[3] De Valera had intimated to Mary MacSwiney at the time of the 1923 elections that he was prepared to be flexible in regard to entering the Free State. 'If the oath goes,' he wrote, 'policy will have to be decided by the members elected;' but his subsequent actions, deriding the legitimacy of the Free State, appeared to rule out any arrangement with it.[4] As a result de Valera's admission shocked most of the assembled deputies. It meant that for three years de Valera had been presiding over a republican Dáil and a republican Sinn Féin while contemplating entry into the Free

State. Count Plunkett was the first to give voice to his feelings. He was amazed and saddened by de Valera's disclosure.

> If the Oath is abolished [he said defiantly] the facts it represents are the same. The Oath is the seal of the document. As long as you accept any portion of English control the absence of the Oath makes no difference. When I was elected in 1917 I was not to enter the British Parliament under any conditions. I see no difference between the Free State Parliament and British.[5]

Count Plunkett then read the republican oath and, referring directly to de Valera's proposal, declared bitterly, but with determination,

> I am going to keep that Oath. Those who set up the Treaty agreed to carry out English authority. They have set up a mock temple of liberty, and this new proposal is an attempted surrender of the Republic. Be we many or few, we go on — Ireland will maintain the struggle as she has done for ten years.[6]

Having reminded de Valera of the principles underlying the republican oath, Count Plunkett called for an end to discussion and the taking of a vote. By 26 votes to 15 the Dáil approved of Mary Mac-Swiney's proposal. A substantial majority of Dáil deputies was, therefore, opposed to de Valera's new policy. Despite this clear indication of the Assembly's views, de Valera was reluctant to accept the majority verdict against his policy. Instead he insisted that a vote of confidence should be taken which forced deputies to choose more precisely for or against himself. Presumably, by introducing this personal element into the debate, he hoped to sway people in his favour. To an extent he was successful. The proposal by Mary MacSwiney 'that this assembly does not approve of the policy outlined by the President' was passed, but only by 19 votes to 18.[7] During the course of this debate de Valera revealed some interesting facts about his new policy and manifested absolute autocratic tendencies which do much to justify the stand of his opponents. He spoke as if he were going to enter the Free State Dáil, even if the oath were still in place. He asserted boldly that,

> The day in which you can prevent the Institution being run as a British one, you have won. You go in as a majority to convert it into a National Institution.[8]

De Valera was also prepared to renew the Civil War, if he could win it. 'If able to assert majority rule by arms you put them out of course,' he calmly stated, as if such a proposition were self evident.[9] With a strange irony he then proposed to his dissident followers the same course of action as Collins had suggested to him during the

Treaty debates. Collins had proposed that, while de Valera remained in the Dáil with his party, he, Collins, would accept the Treaty and the obloquy of the masses, as they took the first step towards the Republic. They would join forces again later. De Valera, having fought the Civil War in protest against such a procedure, now put the same proposal to members of the Second Dáil.

> I am prepared [he said] to take the risks and go after the people. If I go into the bog on the bog road or other hard ground I'll take the risks and expect to find you on the High Road when I come out.[10]

Count Plunkett immediately responded to this suggestion. He complained of de Valera's lack of leadership during the past year.

> It was open to the President [he declared] to have a vigorous Cabinet to discuss matters of policy, and they in turn to discuss these matters with Comhairle Na d-Teachtaí ... It was in the power of the President to have inaugurated a programme big and noble, but no, he comes along later, holds a series of meetings — says you don't want a Cabinet, but a Committee — ultimately the only remedy is to go into the Free State Parliament. I do not question the President's sincerity, but the fact is that people are discussing becoming the fag end of British power here.[11]

The criticism by Count Plunkett raises an issue not often adverted to: the damage done by de Valera to Sinn Féin and the Second Dáil by his attitude from March 1925 to March 1926. Instead of stimulating badly needed policy initiatives in the social and economic order, and instead of taking advantage of the political instability in the Free State caused by the Boundary Commission and the Army Mutiny of 1924, de Valera had his mind set on other things. He was concerned not on how to advance the standing and reputation of anti-Treaty republicans in regard to the Free State; but on how best to enter the very Free State whose legitimacy he publicly denied. If his record over the past year in particular provided grounds for criticism, so too did his answers to his critics in the Republican Dáil as they continued to question him about his future policy.

Members of the Second Dáil were anxious to have more specific information about de Valera's policy. He was unwilling to provide it. From the first signs of deviation from the republican position, David Kent had been quick to question de Valera's intentions. Kent had a distinguished pedigree in the nationalist movement going back to a period of imprisonment in the days of the Land League; and he had been wounded in 1916 while his brother had been executed. He bluntly asked de Valera whether he was going to enter the Free State Parliament: he 'wanted to know,' he insisted, 'if the President was going to go in or not.'[12] De Valera refused to reply. When

Laurence Brady asked 'would the President be prepared to go in there leading a party of 10?' de Valera replied, 'I cannot say what I would do in all the circumstances.'[13] M. P. Colivet, a deputy from Limerick and a former Minister of the Republican Dáil, then put the question, 'How long will it be till the details are put before us?' 'Probably not till the actual time of entry,' de Valera replied; and added, 'Count Plunkett and others will say I am accepting things.' To this reply Count Plunkett quietly said, 'We will.'[14] Many other questions were put to de Valera and he was extremely reluctant to give answers that limited his future conduct in any way. Finally Colivet asked, 'Can you give us no help for the immediate future?' 'I cannot give you more information now,' was the reply of de Valera. In some frustration Colivet concluded, 'It looks as if the President wants *carte blanche* to develop his policy in public. We have not the policy before us in any shape or form.'[15] De Valera responded with some indignation and declared, 'I did not come here asking you to approve of the policy, and if you disapprove it as outlined vote against it.' It was in these circumstances, faced by the authoritarian diktat of de Valera, that the vote was cast and de Valera defeated by 19 votes to 18.[16] Neither his manner nor his methods were designed to win friends: he had determined on his new approach; and he was confident that in private conversations he had won to his side some significant allies. For the rest, they could take it or leave it. Efforts were still made, however, by his adversaries to preserve unity in the ranks. On 29 March the Comhairle Na d-Teachtaí reassembled and Art O'Connor was elected temporary chairman of an Advisory Council until the next meeting. Mary MacSwiney proposed that the Council, composed of four representatives from Comhairle Na d-Teachtaí, two from Sinn Féin, two from the Army and two from Cumann na mBan should serve as the focal point of unity until further decisions were made. She allowed considerable latitude to de Valera: the arrangement, she said, was not to bind 'the minority party to inaction in their policy.'[17] Privately Mary MacSwiney also voiced her concern that something should be done for de Valera's financial situation now that he no longer qualified for the salaried post of President.[18] This sympathetic concern on the part of MacSwiney will come as a surprise to those who depict her as a heartless harridan.

If Mary MacSwiney had hoped that de Valera might postpone an irrevocable decision which would bring about an end of republican unity she was mistaken. On 13 April 1926 de Valera ended all speculation about his future plans by announcing that 'we are ourselves forming a new organisation'; on 17 April, in a further interview to the press, he announced that the party was to be called Fianna Fáil and he outlined its aims; and on 16 May the inaugural meeting of Fianna Fáil was held in La Scala Theatre in Dublin.[19] In his speech to his supporters at the La Scala meeting de Valera dwelt at length on the national and theological implications of the oath. He maintained that it was his policy to enter the Free State only if the oath were removed. His rallying cry – that 'we should unite to smash the oath' – was simple and direct, and well constructed to win support.[20] The duty of republicans was to cast aside anything that impeded their participation in the national advance. De Valera wanted his following to be like a young man: 'honest and courageous, but without set prejudices or any commitment of his past to hamper him.'[21] The principles so highly valued by other republicans were to be laid aside as the quest for power assumed paramount importance. Inevitably de Valera's opponents suffered from more direct criticism on the part of de Valera. Although they rejected his policy, he maintained, 'there is no substitute republican policy in the field.'[22] Not a whisper was to be heard of de Valera's own major responsibility for failing to produce such a policy; nor, did he mention that he had positively obstructed the Sinn Féin committee appointed to construct a new national programme. On the matter of principle de Valera asserted that his opponents accused him of betraying republican principles, but 'wherein they are contrary has nowhere been set out or explained.'[23] In such a fashion he ignored the specific reminder of Count Plunkett as to the nature of his republican oath; the detailed itemisation by Mary MacSwiney of the eleven other clauses in the Treaty contrary to the republican ideal; and the vocal protests of many that he was about to enter a Free State Dáil whose legitimacy he had consistently denied. De Valera's speech was an admirable exercise in propaganda: his case was presented in a clear and compelling manner; that of his opponents was ridiculed by a combination of distortion and omission. Inevitably when Comhairle Na d-Teachtaí met on Saturday 22 May 1926 there were many issued to be discussed; not the least of which was de Valera's position as President of the Republic.

DE VALERA AND HIS POSITION AS PRESIDENT OF THE REPUBLIC

The meeting of Comhairle Na d-Teachtaí of 22 and 23 May 1926 began with Art O'Connor reading a statement from the Ard Comhairle of Sinn Féin. This body had met earlier and decided that it was no longer possible to co-operate with de Valera and his new party. The statement read:

All Teachtaí 'um Dáil Eireann who are prepared to accept the new policy of entering either of the foreign controlled partition 'Parliaments' in Ireland, if the Oath of Allegiance is removed, are hereby called upon to resign their seats to Ceann Comhairle, Dáil Eireann, and to notify the Hon. Secs. Sinn Féin of their resignations as they no longer represent the Organisation which nominated them and secured their elections.[24]

The resolution of Sinn Féin spelt out the logical implications of the split – if de Valera wished to embark on a new departure, he must take the consequences. The members of the republican Dáil, however, were still prepared to seek some form of co-operation. Two main issues presented themselves as obstacles to unity: the election of a new president; and the relationship of Fianna Fáil with the government of Dáil Eireann. The debate began on Sunday, 23 May. In the course of the debate, de Valera, possibly to prevent Art O'Connor assuming the position of President of the Republic, denied that he, himself, had ever been the President of the Republic since his resignation in January 1922 after the acceptance of the Treaty. This claim on his part was absolutely incredible. It ran counter to many public proclamations and to the expressed purpose of the Second Dáil as regularly recorded in the minutes. David Kent, who emerged as a leading opponent of de Valera's plans, pointed out that such a contention could not be sustained: he asserted that de Valera had assumed the title of President of the Republic in October 1922; that he had issued the cease fire order of April 1923 as President of the Republic; that an acting President had been appointed during de Valera's time in prison; and that meetings of the Cabinet and of the Dáil had taken place with an acknowledged President or vice-President of the Republic in attendance.

> Are we now going to be told [he concluded] that all the time we were wrong in calling it Dáil Eireann, and that Mr. de Valera was not President of the Republic at all?[25]

The reply of de Valera, granted the public record and the minutes of the Republican Dáil, was quite amazing. He stated:

> I was not President of the Republic from the time I resigned that position when the Treaty was passed. I do not know that I ever formally accepted the position. I was elected Head of the Emergency Government and I have always maintained that position as such . . . I would not have accepted the position as President of the Republic on this account. I was prepared to act as Head of the Revolutionary Government for the time being.[26]

Faced by this total denial of the values that had motivated him in his struggle against the Treaty, David Kent replied sadly, 'I now only want to say that for the past two or three years we were only sitting here on false pretences.'[27] As the debate continued, often acrimoniously, the intention of de Valera became clearer. He wanted Fianna Fáil to retain some contact and influence inside Comhairle Na d-Teachtaí, if at all possible. He was prepared, he said, 'to propose Art O'Connor as Chief Executive provided that some arrangement as to a Coalition Cabinet could be come to.'[28] While he was reluctant to see anyone occupying the position of President, he was happy to appoint a Chief Executive who would operate through a Standing Committee or an Advisory Council which contained Fianna Fáil participants. The proposal clearly cut the ground from under the feet of all deputies who had worked so hard for the Republican Government under a President, since the Treaty, and it diminished the standing of Dáil Eireann. This was immediately recognised by Dr J. A. Madden, a representative of the Army, who had been elected for Mayo in 1924, and by Tom Maguire. Madden believed in the Irish Republic and did not want any misunderstanding. He 'wanted a President elected,' he declared, 'and not any camouflage.'[29] The Assembly adjourned and, when it met again in the evening, Art O'Connor put the terms of coalition to de Valera. The following guarantees were requested from Fianna Fáil:

> 1. That the members of Fianna Fáil give a guarantee that they will not enter any foreign-controlled Parliament under an Oath-bound Ministry.
>
> 2. That in the event of getting a majority they will call the representatives of all Ireland, scrap the Free State constitution, and frame an Irish one.
>
> 3. That this Assembly is recognised as the Government of the Republic, and that the Oath of Allegiance to the Republic be taken as decreed by the First Dáil.[30]

De Valera refused to accept a coalition based on these terms. While they did set bounds to his ambitions, they were compatible with the Fianna Fáil manifesto. One is left with the feeling that the first guarantee was the real obstacle: de Valera privately planned to enter the Free State Dáil with or without the oath; and for him to pledge himself to the strict Fianna Fáil policy on the oath would be to place a limit on his secret designs. If the failure to accept the terms of coalition reflects badly on the motives of de Valera, his statements in the subsequent debate on the position of the President reflects even more gravely on his character. The issue centred on the status of Art O'Connor who had been chosen to replace de

Valera: was he to be the Chairman of an Advisory Council? Or was
he to be President of Dáil Eireann and President of the Republic?
Mary MacSwiney's proposal made a decision on the issue inevitable.

> I nominate [she said] Art O'Conchubair [O'Connor] as President of the
> Republic of Ireland and Proímh Aire of Dáil Eireann and Comhairle Na
> d-Teachtaí.[31]

De Valera opposed the motion. 'He could not personally take part
in the election,' he stated, 'and neither did he consider this Assembly
Dáil Eireann.'[32] Technically he was correct in his judgement of the
Assembly. A view endorsed by J. J. O'Kelly, as Chairman, who ruled
that a meeting of Dáil Eireann, rather than Comhairle Na d-Teachtaí,
was necessary to vote on the position of President. It should be
noted, however, that in the past de Valera had treated Dáil Eireann
and Comhairle Na d-Teachtaí as one and the same institution when
it was implementing his policies. In the ensuing debate on the nature
of the Assembly two diverse views became manifest: on the one
hand there were those like Countess Markievicz, Seán Lemass and
Seán MacEntee who regarded the Second Dáil as a symbol which
offered no real prospects for the future; and, on the other hand,
there were those like J. J. O'Kelly, Count Plunkett and David
Kent who valued its *de jure* claim and hoped for a *de facto* reality
in the future. The former supported de Valera; the latter supported
Mary MacSwiney. Confusion existed in the minds of the delegates
as to their status. A point well made by M. P. Colivet who said that,

> It seemed to him that there was [sic] not two members of that Assembly
> to whom Dáil Eireann and Comhairle Na d-Teachtaí had the same mean-
> ing.[33]

It was not, however, theoretical differences concerning the status
of the republican assemblies that occasioned de Valera's opposition.
The grounds of his hostility derived from extremely practical considerations. His opponents were 'going to set up a one-party Executive;' and, he complained bitterly, 'he was not going to sit in it.'[34]
The Second Dáil, he maintained, rather than he, de Valera, was to
blame for excluding the Fianna Fáil party from its executive body.
The onus of responsibility clearly lay with de Valera: his actions
had given rise to the problem; and he had rejected the terms of coalition which had been offered. When, finally, voting took place
on Mary MacSwiney's proposal for the presidency, it was approved
and Art O'Connor was elected President of the Republic. Twenty-
two deputies voted for O'Connor, and de Valera's supporters —
fifteen in all — followed his example and did not register a vote.[35]

O'Connor then nominated his executive: it was made up of Austin Stack, Mary MacSwiney, Count Plunkett and J. J. O'Kelly. A parting of the ways seemed inevitable. Two parties with two contrasting and conflicting policies had emerged. And yet de Valera did not resign from the Second Dáil as he had done from Sinn Féin. It is reasonable to ask why did de Valera remain in the Second Dáil? The answer tells us much about de Valera, and provides further evidence to be critical of the manner in which Fianna Fáil was founded. De Valera remained in the Second Dáil, in part, for reasons of money.

DE VALERA AND THE SECOND DÁIL: AMERICA AND MATTERS OF MONEY. PART 1

The first question raised by de Valera on 23 May 1926, after he had lost the presidency of the Republic and was faced by the prospect of no Fianna Fáil representation on the Dáil executive, was money. Art O'Connor outlined the plans of his new executive to which de Valera responded by asking,

> What about the question of money? There are certain overhead charges. Were the funds that were collected in America going to be distributed to Sinn Féin and the Army and was his organisation going to be cut off?[36]

Unless Fianna Fáil got a fair share of the American money, de Valera threatened, it would immediately begin its own campaign in the States. In his aggressive assertion of the claims of Fianna Fáil to funds donated to the Republic, de Valera admitted that the envoy, Seán T. O'Kelly, was acting in his interests. He had got letters, he claimed,

> from America and Australia definitely indicating that monies were being forwarded to help the idea which I had, and that they were coming directly through the Envoy.[37]

De Valera did not reveal that he was secretly attempting to win over the AARIR to his side at the expense of the Second Dáil. Not only had Seán T. O'Kelly been engaged in such an enterprise since 1924, but also de Valera, himself, had contacted leading members of the AARIR directly he had founded Fianna Fáil. Most notably he made contact with John J. Hearn, Treasurer of the organisation, on 29 April. Hearn had been friendly with de Valera since his first tour of America; he had been one of the leading supporters who had made possible the very foundation of the AARIR in 1920; and, as Treasurer, he held a very influential position. De Valera's appeal to Hearn mirrored the appeal he was making in Ireland: support for Fianna Fáil was both practical and reasonable as no abandonment of principle was involved; all republicans were still basically united; and entry into the Free State Dáil would only come about if the oath were removed. To endorse his claim de Valera enclosed in his letter the statements he had made at the Sinn Féin Ard-Fheis and to the Comhairle Na d-Teachtaí, together with the press release containing the aims of Fianna Fáil. The highly professional and partisan message of de Valera was thus disseminated among members of the AARIR in the States.[38] Aware of the strength of his position in America, de Valera manifested no willingness to co-operate with the unsuspecting members of the Second Dáil on American money matters. Even when Art O'Connor assured him that Fianna Fáil would receive some portion of the American money, de Valera refused to promise that he would not launch a separate fund-raising mission to America. He believed that he could speak from a position of strength: events were to prove him right.

On 26 May 1926, Seán T. O'Kelly informed Mary MacSwiney, from America, that he, personally, approved of de Valera's new party and policy, and that 'the big majority of the rank and file here will favour Dev.'[39] Confirmation of this view was given to Mary MacSwiney on 16 June from the headquarters of the IRA in America. They expressed the opinion that, at the forthcoming July Convention of the AARIR, Fianna Fáil would capture the organisation and that the envoy was certainly not one to resist such a departure.[40] Any lingering doubts about the correctness of de Valera's policy in the minds of AARIR members were dispelled by the arrival in America of Archbishop Mannix. On 16 June he arrived in Chicago, a leading centre for AARIR activity, to participate in a Eucharistic Congress. The timing of his arrival could not have been improved upon, even if de Valera had planned the Archbishop's itinerary himself. Seán T. O'Kelly went to Chicago, where he dutifully attended the Eucharistic Congress and met Mannix. He then hosted a reception for Mannix in the Carnegie Hall, New York. There Mannix delivered a rousing speech in favour of de Valera, which was given a warm reception. Even the IRA, the element least favourable to de Valera's new departure, was impressed.[41] Before his departure from America, Mannix preached the same message in many other Irish centres throughout the States, notably in Boston and Philadelphia. Seán T. O'Kelly and Frank Aiken were spreading the same message: the former exercised a particular influence at the New York State Convention of the AARIR; the latter at the Ohio State Convention. It was as if a political campaign, with the blessing of the Catholic Church, were being waged on behalf of de Valera – the alliance he had made with Mannix in the summer of 1925 was reaping the richest of harvests. When Art O'Connor arrived in America on 15 July 1926 to put the case for the Second Dáil, he was far too late and could offer far too little.

> The recent visit of the Archbishop [O'Connor observed] was more than a godsend to them: its influence on the places he spoke cannot be estimated. The conjunction of a Catholic Congress and a Convention with a useful interval between for receptions of a very distinguished Churchman is a new trial I suppose for our Catholic souls.[42]

If Mannix made his presence felt in favour of de Valera, Art O'Connor, as President of the Republic, failed to make a stand on behalf of the Second Dáil. Quite clearly the task was too much for him: most loyal members of the AARIR had regarded the presidency of the Republic to be embodied in de Valera since 1919; and the vast majority of them appeared scarcely aware that a vote of the Second Dáil had changed his status. For O'Connor, arriving in America unknown and unheralded, it was an invidious position. He was simply treated, he admitted later, as 'a private individual.'[43] Few could have made an impact in that situation. O'Connor made little attempt to try. Having attended a meeting of the Resolutions Committee of the AARIR with Seán T. O'Kelly, O'Connor was convinced that he could do nothing to change the minds of the delegates and so decided to put off the battle for another day.

> At the Convention itself [he admitted] I did not attempt to influence the delegates one way or the other in the attitude they were likely to adopt upon certain resolutions which were to be brought before them.[44]

Faced by resolutions which ended the Envoy's role as effective head of the AARIR and terminated the Second Dáil's links with the organisation, O'Connor simply registered his protest in restrained terms at the proposed changes. He explained to Mary MacSwiney that,

> I tried to take what I represented clean out of the House in which it was no longer welcome. It was all very unpleasant but I was heartened by the faith of a few: 25 or so solid against the changes in the orientation of the organisation and wanted to keep it back of where it had been for years. The other 125 or so would not be cheated of their holiday and they went thro' with their policy to the bitter end even to the extent of eliminating all reference to the Envoy from the Constitution. So the break is complete.[45]

The victory of de Valera was almost absolute. At a stroke he had cut off the vital money supply to the Government of the Republic – for the year 1924 a sum of £28,000 had been collected – and siphoned off the main sources of revenue into Fianna Fáil channels. Both groups of anti-Treaty republicans made plans to take account of this final break. In Ireland those opposed to de Valera elected J. J. O'Kelly as President of Sinn Féin – Mary MacSwiney and Fr O'Flanagan being elected vice-presidents – at the Sinn Féin Ard-Fheis on 31 October 1926; while de Valera gave further momentum to Fianna Fáil at the first Ard-Fheis of the party on 24 November. In America the Second Dáil attempted to regain ground by appointing, on 6 October 1926, John J. Hearn, still loyal to their position, as envoy; while de Valera left Frank Aiken in the States to consolidate his influence in the Army and in the AARIR.[46] In the midst of these clear signs of demarcation and open confrontation it is surprising to find de Valera and his colleagues at a meeting of Comhairle Na d-Teachtaí on 18 and 19 December 1926. Why, it is again reasonable to ask, should de Valera retain links with an organisation to the policy of which he was totally opposed? The money motive would again appear to provide an answer: money with, as before, an American connection. A legal decision was imminent on the Bonds donated by Americans to the Government of the Irish Republic and de Valera could not afford to let that money pass him by.

DE VALERA AND THE SECOND DÁIL: AMERICA AND MATTERS OF MONEY. PART 2

The American Bonds case, combining both complex issues of law and finance, merits a book in its own right. The interests of the Second Dáil deputies, as they assembled in December 1926, centred precisely on $2,500,000 on deposit in America. This sum formed part of the $6,500,000 raised by the two Dáil Eireann External Loans in America thanks to the donations of about 500,000 subscribers.[47] Following the split over the Treaty a race began between the Free State authorities and the anti-Treaty republicans to lay hold of this money. Michael Collins, as Minister of Finance, sent James O'Mara, a former trustee of the External Loan, to America in March 1922; de Valera sent Stephen O'Mara, a current trustee of the Loan, to the States in April 1922. The divisions caused by the Civil War could not be better illustrated: brother not only fought brother on the field of battle, but also in the banks of America. No personal confrontation occurred between the O'Mara brothers as the mission of James was terminated by Collins in early April,

and he was replaced by Timothy Smiddy.[48] Stephen O'Mara, however, had to counter the plans put into effect by his brother. As a
trustee of the Dáil Loan, Stephen held the initiative in the contest
— he could exercise a more immediate control over the money. He
did not attempt to appropriate the money for the republican cause,
thus manifesting a certain regard for his neutral position as trustee,
but he did place the money in safe deposit boxes so that the Free
State authorities could not take possession of it.[49] On 24 July 1922
Smiddy visited the safe deposit companies — three were involved:
the Garfield, the Guaranty and the Central Union — and notified
Collins that he was alarmed at the dispositions made by Stephen
O'Mara.[50] Collins cabled back at once and advised Smiddy to 'take
proceedings immediately according to good legal opinion to safeguard [the] trust funds and securities.'[51] On 22 August 1922 Garth
Healy, who administered the financial affairs, wrote complaining
to Collins that an injunction had just been served on him, but on
that day Collins was shot.[52] The policy sanctioned by Collins,
however, and implemented by Smiddy determined the ground rules
of the contest for control of the American Bonds. How, the question
remained in 1926, could either side overcome the legal restraint
protecting the $2,500,000 in the three safe deposit boxes? Two
developments of note had taken place since August 1922: firstly,
in December 1925 the Free State had successfully argued their case
in the Irish courts for control of some of the American money in
Ireland; and, secondly, in 1925 both sides had determined to pursue their claims to the money in America through action on behalf
of the bondholders, rather than on behalf of the trustees.[53] It was
the urgency of the Free State to pursue their claim in the American
courts on behalf of the bondholders that brought about the need
for immediate action on the part of the Second Dáil.

When Comhairle Na d-Teachtaí met on 18 December 1926 the
American Bonds were a major subject of their discussions. Indeed
Countess Markievicz made a strong plea that other contentious business 'be postponed until the American thing is settled.'[54] It would
appear that on this occasion, unlike de Valera's secret negotiations
earlier concerning the AARIR, that there was a strange collusion
between de Valera and his opponents in the Second Dáil. They did
not share the same aims — there was clearly much friction between
the two groups at the meeting — but they did share the same objective in relation to the American money. Moreover, they must have
realised that a united stand was almost indispensable to their success. On the one hand the Second Dáil held unqualified title to be
the Government of the Republic; on the other hand de Valera's

testimony in the court as the man whose name was on the bond as President of the Republic was absolutely invaluable. Neither side could win in the American courts without the co-operation of the other. Finally, as the long meeting drew to a close, an arrangement was arrived at: de Valera 'gave up every right to the Office' of President and proposed the ratification of Art O'Connor in his place; Art O'Connor, in his turn, proposed that de Valera should be confirmed as a trustee of the American bonds.[55] It was agreed that in that capacity de Valera should represent the Second Dáil in the American courts. Austin Stack declared confidently that 'Mr de Valera will regard us as his principals in the course of litigation.' To this confidence de Valera replied obliquely, 'I will give an understanding here that I will safeguard the Republican position.'[56] On the face of it the Second Dáil could ask for no stronger commitment on the part of de Valera.

As the Second Dáil was making its own dispositions for the American Bonds case, Sinn Féin was also attempting to make its presence felt in America. J. J. O'Kelly, as President of Sinn Féin, asked Fr O'Flanagan to represent the Sinn Féin interest in America. Although Fr O'Flanagan saw John J. Hearn, who was chairman of the Bondholders Committee, he reported back on the dismal prospects for Sinn Féin in the States.[57] Art O'Connor was also briefly in America in 1927. He returned to Ireland, however, on 25 April without having put into effect any policy of securing the money from the bondholders for the republican position of the Second Dáil.[58] De Valera, on the other hand, arrived in America early in March and stayed until some days after the trial. With the bulk of the AARIR already solidly behind him, it was relatively easy to organise popular support in favour of Fianna Fáil. This he did. He toured America from coast to coast drumming up support for his policy. Fr O'Flanagan reported ruefully to J. J. O'Kelly that,

De Valera has had immense meetings here, at least in New York and Boston — bigger than the biggest you and I had when we were at our best here.[59]

When, on 11 May 1927, after many postponements of the court case, Judge Peters declared that the money should be returned to the original subscribers, de Valera fulfilled his promise to 'safeguard the republican position' by urging all bondholders to transfer their financial donations to the Fianna Fáil party. He thus cut the ground from under the feet of the Second Dáil republican movement whose interests he was formally representing. The naïvety, or blatant irresponsibility, of Art O'Connor and the Second Dáil was greeted with incredulity by their few supporters in America. Una Ford, editor of the *Monitor*, could not believe that de Valera could be sent by the Second Dáil as their sole representative to the court.

> His coming here as such [she exclaimed] gave him, or rather those back of him ... a clear field to work for the securing of those bond returns to aid Fianna Fáil. They not only did this the more successfully by ask-ing resubscriptions 'for the purpose for which the Bonds were originally subscribed' (such an appeal was of course a flagrant cheat) but because of the wording of that appeal they secured bonds from those who intended them for no other purpose than the original one stated on the Bonds. Thus was the whole field of resubscription of the bonds money secured at one sweep by Fianna Fáil. THAT THERE REMAINED ANY HERE WHO REFUSED TO BE DECEIVED BY THE DE VALERA APPEAL AND WHO HAVE THEREFORE THEIR BONDS STILL TO RESUB-SCRIBE TO YOU is in no way thanks to any action taken by Dáil Eireann.[60]

Una Ford acknowledged that some difficulty existed for the Second Dáil in its choice of representative to attend the New York court, but she protested strongly at the culpability of Art O'Connor and others in abandoning America to de Valera and his supporters. Her concluding verdict on the bonds case gives the view, rarely recorded, of those republicans in America who opposed de Valera.

> It is well to put on record here [she stated] the sad and tremendous fact in favour of Fianna Fáil that Bondholders' minds were so worked upon here for some years by defeatist publicity that the saving of their Bonds from the 'Free State' became the whole issue, and the transition of turn-ing them then to an ex-president (whom some believed still president) of the Irish Republic was of easy gradation. It was a miracle after that, we repeat, to salvage anything for THE REPUBLIC.[61]

The major portion of the bond money was transferred either directly to the Fianna Fáil party or, some years later, to the founding of the *Irish Press* – the process by which the de Valera family came to assume a majority share holding in the *Irish Press* has not, as yet, been revealed. De Valera had won the battle for the bonds: not only had he defeated the Free State, but also he had overcome the claims of his apparently gullible colleagues in the Second Dáil. The Dáil met on 10 December 1927 and expressed 'general disapproval of Mr. de Valera's action in asking that the returned American bonds be handed over to Fianna Fáil, instead of urging, as Trustee for the Republic, that they be applied to their original purpose.'[62] An executive statement was also issued; but it was all too late. De Valera, having acquired an unassailable control of American money and influence, left the Second Dáil. He had no further need of it. The time for talking of common republican fronts had also ended. Within days of the American court verdict, on 14 May 1927, de Valera replied to Mary MacSwiney on the possibility of Fianna Fáil and Sinn Féin coming to some sort of agreement.

> Knowing your attitude on this question [he informed her], and being as convinced that I am right as you are that you are right, I feel that we can only agree to differ.[63]

The time for talking was over. In his subsequent actions de Valera strongly opposed any initiatives from Sinn Féin and the Second Dáil which contrasted in any way with the brand of republicanism as expounded in the Fianna Fáil party. With the departure of de Valera from the Second Dáil one can take stock of the major allegation made against him by his adversaries in the republican ranks which initiated this study, namely that de Valera, while retaining membership of republican organisations, was secretly planning to enter the Free State.

DE VALERA AND FIANNA FÁIL AGAINST THE SECOND DÁIL, SINN FÉIN AND THE IRA

The purpose of this survey of anti-Treaty republicans between the years 1922 and 1927 was to comprehend as completely as possible the qualities of those republicans who claimed to be the true heirs of Pearse and 1916. Most books portray de Valera and Fianna Fáil as the rightful claimants to the Pearse inheritance: their opponents in the republican ranks are derided as die-hard obscurantists. The contrast which is painted between the two rival groups could not be more complete: on the one hand, de Valera, acting with realism and integrity, led a majority of like-minded followers into the path of constitutional politics; on the other hand, Mary MacSwiney – she is usually chosen as the archetype of his republican adversaries – marshalled a small group of supporters in stubborn resistance to any form of change. This resistance is often characterised as being marked with fascist and ultra-right-wing Catholic tendencies. The minutes of the Second Dáil make it evident that such a picture is no longer tenable. It is too facile and too partisan. The minutes do not bring into question the manifest success of de Valera, but they do depict his opponents in a far more favourable light than they have been accorded by historians. Inevitably the record of the Second Dáil also generates many questions about the methods adopted by de Valera with attendant reflections on his character.

Only the most purblind supporter of de Valera will not be disturbed by the image of de Valera which now appears. To the most damning charge of his republican opponents that from 1923 onwards he was presiding over a republican government while planning its deposition, de Valera acknowledged his guilt on 28 March 1926 when he admitted that he was 'willing to go in' to the Free State as far back as August 1923. His actions between 1923 and 1926 betray a duality that must have been difficult to live with: on the one hand, he saw entry into the Free State as a viable alternative and secretly combined with major influences in the Catholic Church and with republicans in America to attain his objective; on the other hand, he issued decrees which denied the legitimacy of the Free State and supported the IRA in its efforts to overthrow it. While engaged in this covert activity to subvert the original aims of Sinn Féin and the Second Dáil, de Valera also intervened in order to frustrate the attempts of others to formulate an alternative republican programme. The actions of de Valera after he had been deposed as President on 28 March 1926 reflect equally badly on his character. He denied that he was ever President of the Republic after January 1921; he refused to provide an outline of his future policy so that a common front might be preserved; and he remained in the Second Dáil only as long as was necessary to acquire control of republican money in America. During most of these years de Valera was, of course, President of the Second Dáil and drew a salary as President of the Republic whose very authority he was underming. In political terms his actions are best described as Machiavellian: power at any price was to be the guiding principle. Strangely this judgement, usually pronounced with connotations of disparagement, would have been greeted with some approval by de Valera. He was a self-confessed advocate of the tactics of Machiavelli. When Richard Mulcahy met him in early 1917, de Valera remarked,

> You are a young man going in for politics. I will give you two pieces of advice — study economics and read the 'Prince.'[64]

Dr Patrick McCartan also noted that de Valera was often seen with a copy of *The Prince* during his first tour of America. Supporters of de Valera may well follow their leader and see a Machiavellian policy as something to be commended; his opponents may well have a different view on the matter. Whether one condones or condemns de Valera's methods, there can be little doubt that Machiavellian is a fitting epithet for them not only in the years of Fianna Fáil's foundation, but also in the years when he led Fianna Fáil into office.

When, in May 1927, de Valera had the American money in his

hands, his policy had still not brought him into the corridors of power. For that a further change of policy was necessary. The oath, as he must have known all along, was not removed. He then presented his followers with the policy of taking it as an empty formula. This policy was made known to the public on 11 August 1927. The strength of de Valera's character is shown by the fact that not one of the 42 Fianna Fáil deputies demurred from pronouncing the oath to be 'an empty political formula.'[65] The conspiratorial nature of the decision made in the secret conclaves of the few, also, no doubt, tended to forge that special unity which is the preserve of all secret societies. Ironically, de Valera, having criticised Collins for working through the secrecy of the IRB, resorted to the same tactics to achieve his final goal. Archbishop Mannix, an invaluable influence to the last, immediately defended de Valera's action on the oath: 'There was no perjury,' Mannix declared publicly, 'where there was no falsehood.'[66] It was all so simple that one is forced to ask why it was never proposed before: why fight the Civil War at all, if such a solution was acceptable? Here one encounters the real-politik that was part of de Valera's make up. Realist that he was, de Valera must have known that such a proposal made in the immediate aftermath of the Treaty or of the Civil War would have lost him both credibility and support. The indications are, however, that this was the course to which Mannix and Hagan directed de Valera in 1925 and from that time onwards was carefully fostered by him. Those who had subscribed to the removal of the oath as a policy and had committed themselves to de Valera could not, it was calculated, easily retreat from the course they had adopted and return to the Sinn Féin fold. The only Fianna Fáil deputy who might have resisted the 'empty formula' development with any chance of disturbing the unity in the party was Countess Markievicz and she died on 15 July 1927. The absence of protest has created the impression that from March 1926 de Valera rallied around himself a body of republicans on a realistic new departure that was consistently pursued. The full implications of the dramatic change in policy in 1927 have not been adequately adverted to: either de Valera was not realistic in 1926; or, as seems more likely, being totally realistic, he led Fianna Fáil to power on a path he could never proclaim publicly until a point of no return had been reached.

If some supposition is involved in discerning the innermost intentions of de Valera in these years, no such doubts exist about dispelling some of the myths that have grown up about the foundation of Fianna Fáil. Regularly it is recorded that de Valera led a majority of republicans into the Free State when the split was made with the

Second Dáil and with Sinn Féin. The minutes of the Second Dáil tell a different story. The republican deputies in the Second Dáil voted by a significant majority of 26 votes to 15 to reject de Valera's policy on 28 March 1926. The policy they rejected, it cannot be stressed enough, was that which was based on entering the Free State if the oath were removed. If the 'empty formula' policy had been put to the deputies at that stage, it would certainly have been defeated by an even bigger majority. Another myth that requires dispelling concerns the quality of the republicans who followed de Valera – regularly they are referred to as the most capable in the movement, while their opponents are dismissed as of inferior calibre. The names and records of those who resisted de Valera's initiative gives the lie to such a contention. Of the older members of the Second Dáil who opposed de Valera the namesof Count Plunkett, Professor Stockley, Mary MacSwiney, J. J. O'Kelly, Judge Crowley and Brian O'Higgins give witness immediately to a level of intellectual ability that was not to be found in the ranks of Fianna Fáil. As well as Mary MacSwiney other women such as Mrs Kate O'Callaghan, widow of the murdered mayor of Limerick, Dr Ada English and Mrs Cathal Brugha were also people of competence and ideas. Among the other men the names of Austin Stack, M. P. Colivet and Tom Maguire illustrate the proven administrative ability and younger talent that might have flourished in other circumstances. In the ranks of Comhairle Na d-Teachtaí and Sinn Féin other able people were to be found. To mention Peadar O'Donnell, Dr Madden and Dr Kathleen Lynn is to prove the point. Given the opportunity, there is no reason to believe that this body of people would, at the very least, have performed any worse than the Fianna Fáil party that came to power in 1932. Seen in this context both the character of de Valera and the foundation of Fianna Fáil are seen in a less favourable light. Their attainment of power was achieved by the adoption of dubious means and, their opponents would say, at a terrible price – compromise of the republican ideal. Fianna Fáil might describe itself, as it still does today, at the insistence of Seán Lemass, as 'The Republican Party', but in its abandonment of the strict republican position such a label served a propagandist, rather than a truly descriptive, purpose. Similarly, Lemass might describe Fianna Fáil as they entered the Free State Dáil as 'a slightly constitutional party', while failing to observe that the complementary statement that they were a slightly republican party was equally true.[67] Such an epithet – the slightly republican party – would appear a fitting description for Fianna Fáil in the light of de Valera's dealing with Sinn Féin and the Second Dáil. The battle for republican legitimacy assumed a new dimension with the founding of Fianna Fáil. Not only politicians but also historians have rallied to the Fianna Fáil side in proclaiming its republican credentials while disparaging those of the remnant who remained in the Second Dáil and Sinn Féin. This tendency is illustrated in the otherwise excellent article by Peter Pyne on Sinn Féin during the years 1923 to 1926, which has had a formative impact.

Pyne argued that there were four Sinn Féin parties: the Monarchical Sinn Féin of Arthur Griffith (1905-1917); the Nationalist Sinn Féin party (1917-1922); the Republican Sinn Féin party (1923-1926); and Fundamentalist Sinn Féin party from 1926 to the present day. He records that in 1926 'a new republican organisation,' Fianna Fáil, was founded. Of those that remained in Sinn Féin, Pyne wrote,

> The small extremist organisation that continued to bear the name Sinn Féin in the post-schism era differed radically from its predecessor in so many respects that it is deserving of the title the fourth or fundamentalist Sinn Féin party.[68]

In such a fashion the claim of de Valera and Fianna Fáil to be the true republicans is justified and the claim of his opponents is dismissed. With this legerdemain Pyne has reversed the judicial opinion of Judge Kingsmill Moore which was delivered in 1948 at the conclusion of the Sinn Féin Funds case. Somewhat surprisingly one finds that the distinctions made in the evolution of the Sinn Féin party are not those of Pyne himself, but those of Kingsmill Moore – with, however, a significant difference. Of the third phase of Sinn Féin development, that of the Republican Sinn Féin party, the judge stated that,

> The third and last [phase] extends from 1923 to the present day. For the first three years of the third period Mr. de Valera was supreme, but after he severed his connection in 1926 control passed to various persons among whom Father O'Flanagan, Mr. O'Kelly, Austin Stack, Judge Art O'Connor and Mrs Buckley were prominent.[69]

For Judge Kingsmill Moore it was de Valera who had broken with the republican ideal of Sinn Féin, and those who had remained in the organisation who had preserved it intact. Speaking of those who had retained their Sinn Féin membership, the judge declared,

> They appeared to me perfectly sincere, believing not only in the righteousness but also in the rightness of their claim. Moreover they adduced considerable evidence to show that they faithfully represent one approach to the Irish Republic which was prevalent in the Sinn Féin of 1917-1922,

the approach typified in Cathal Brugha amongst others and which I have termed transcendental . . . it would appear that all the required steps were taken to preserve the continuity of the organisation and that present day Sinn Féin is legally the same organisation as that which was born in 1923.[70]

In terms of republican pedigree it was not, as Pyne and others maintain, the Sinn Féin party, to which most members of the Second Dáil subscribed, that 'differed radically from its predecessor,' but it was the new republican party of Fianna Fáil. The judicial and judicious verdict of Judge Kingsmill Moore cannot be improved on. It expresses a genuine historical reality which most historians have been slow to recognise. Not only did de Valera abandon the pristine faith of pure republicanism – the heritage embodied in Pearse and Brugha – when he established Fianna Fáil in 1926, but also when he attained power in 1932 his actions were frequently hostile to the republican aspirations of those he had worked with from 1922 to 1926. Once in power, de Valera inevitably fell a victim to the divided loyalties that his Machiavellian tactics had brought about. As President of the Republic and in the courts of America de Valera had publicly denied the legitimate title of the Free State to govern – it was the 'usurping government.' When he became Head of that Free State Government, all doubts as to its legitimacy were cast aside. Lawful power in the de Valera dispensation appeared to reside in the body to which de Valera belonged. Although major measures were passed to introduce a republican dimension into the Free State, notably changes in regard to the oath, the Governor General, and in 1937 the Constitution itself, the refusal to recognise the republican credentials of those who had remained loyal to Sinn Féin and the Second Dáil created disturbing tensions. This conflict for the mantle of republican authenticity was manifested most clearly in de Valera's dealing with the IRA.

In 1936 de Valera presided over an administration that rigorously opposed the IRA, on 18 June declaring it an unlawful association, and placed many of its members in prison. The contrast with his policy in 1925 could not be more striking: in the summer of that year he was seeking money for the IRA in America; he was sending men on a military mission to Russia; and he drew up a recruiting poster to attract young men into the IRA. Seán Lemass and Frank Aiken informed Seán T. O'Kelly of this last project in their letter of 2 July 1925.

It is hoped [they stated] to induce into the Army young men who have grown to manhood since the termination of the Civil War.[71]

Commenting on this letter in the 1930s, Judge Crowley, author of the illuminating pamphlet on de Valera's actions entitled, *Step by Step from the Republic back into the Empire*, observed that,

A month previously [6 June 1925] the 'Treasonable Offences Act, 1925,' had been passed by the Free State Parliament. Section 6 made it a criminal offence, punishable with five years penal servitude, to be a member of the IRA, or to maintain or assist the IRA with money or by any other means. Mr de Valera told the young men of the country to defy that Act and join the IRA. Thousands of them did so . . . practically all those now in Arbour Hill did so. But Mr de Valera did not tell them that he intended, himself, a few years later, to swear Allegiance to the King, to become his Prime Minister, to prosecute these young IRA men before a tribunal of Free State soldiers, and to send them to penal servitude.[72]

In this betrayal of the young men he had encouraged to join the IRA, one encounters in heightened clarity one of the dilemmas that resulted from de Valera's embrace of Machiavellianism. Judge Crowley suggested with some bitterness that instead of Gerry Boland, as acting Minister for Justice, being responsible for the inmates of Arbour Hill, he, along with de Valera, Lemass, Aiken and Seán T. O'Kelly, who had all assisted the IRA after the passing of the 1925 Treason Act, should face criminal charges. His letter of protest to the *Irish Independent* was returned unpublished. The letter is important, however. It illustrates the inherent tension in the Fianna Fáil party, both in the 1930s and even today, which derived from its original commitment to the post-Treaty IRA; and its subsequent suppression of the same IRA on the grounds that it continued to proclaim the full republican programme formerly advocated by their Chief – de Valera. The clash between de Valera and the IRA also provides guidelines as to the manner in which de Valera dealt with other republican organisations. If he was willing to suppress the IRA, he could not be expected to view too kindly the Second Dáil and Sinn Féin who continued to support. it. The reaction of the Second Dáil to the attacks upon it by de Valera brought about a decisive development in the evolution of the republican tradition.

Following the departure of de Valera in 1927, the Second Dáil experienced a lack of firm leadership owing to the weakness of Art O'Connor. Plagued by self doubt as to his own future career, O'Connor relinquished the presidency in December 1927 and eventually broke completely with his colleagues by practicing law in the Free State. No further presidential appointments were made. J. J. O'Kelly, as Chairman, played a major part in directing the future activities of the organisation and was assisted by Mary MacSwiney. The connecting bonds between the Second Dáil and Sinn Féin remained strong as attempts were made to create a new republican party which might challenge de Valera. All attempts failed. Overtures to the IRA and to Cumann na mBan proved either ineffective or short-lived. Such societies as Comhairle na Poblachta, Saor Eire and the Republican Congress, which had short lives between 1929 and 1935, provide examples of such failures, as does the Councils of the Irish Republic founded in America by Seán O'Deorain. It was against this background, with the conflict between de Valera and IRA ever increasing, that the Second Dáil decided to act. In 1938 they resolved to delegate their authority to the Army Council of the IRA. When Dáil Eireann had been threatened by English military activities in the Spring of 1921, it had been agreed that, if the Republic were in danger, the Dáil should transfer its trust to the IRA. It was in this spirit that the delegation of power was made on 8 December 1938 – the anniversary of the executions in captivity of Mellows, O'Connor, Barrett and McKelvey. The declaration read:

> In consequence of armed opposition ordered and sustained by England, and the defection of elected representatives of the people over the period since the Republican Proclamation of Easter 1916 was ratified, three years later, by the newly inaugurated Government of the Irish Republic, we hereby delegate the authority reposed in us to the Army Council, in the spirit of the decision taken by Dáil Eireann in the Spring of 1921, and later endorsed by the Second Dáil . . .
>
> Confident, in delegating this sacred trust to the Army of the Republic that, in their every action towards its consummation they will be inspired by the high ideals and the chivalry of our martyred comrades, we, as Executive Council of Dáil Eireann, Government of the Republic, append our names.[73]

The signatories were J. J. O'Kelly, Count Plunkett, Mary MacSwiney, Professor William Stockley, Charles Murphy, Brian O'Higgins and Thomas Maguire. Fr O'Flanagan's attitude to this particular action is not known; but to the very last, notably as President of Sinn Féin in 1934, he contested the claims of de Valera and Fianna Fáil to be the republican party. The finding that the men – Fr O'Flanagan, Count Plunkett and J. J. O'Kelly – who first declared for Pearse and the Republic at Roscommon in 1917, were to the last aligned with the republican tradition of Sinn Féin and the IRA, rather than with that of Collins or de Valera, will be dismissed by some as a meaningless coincidence. Others, having regard also to the methods employed by Collins and de Valera to achieve power, will perhaps suffer some disquiet and a spirit of inquiry may be stimulated.

The IRA in 1938 certainly appreciated the advantage of being associated with the Second Dáil republican tradition. A typed letter in the O'Kelly collection gives the reply of the Army: 'we accept this authority', it states, 'in the name of the Army of the Republic, in the spirit in which it is tendered.'[74] The letter was signed on behalf of the Army Council by Stephen Hayes, President, and by Patrick Fleming, Secretary. The signing of this document brings to a close a chapter in the struggle for the title of republican authenticity. The demarcation lines drawn by this new alignment of forces basically remain the same today. Although divisions have occurred in Fianna Fáil, Sinn Féin and the IRA, the basic distinction in anti-Treaty republicanism remains the same. Fianna Fáil, on the one hand, following the aspiration of de Valera, claims to uphold the republican position in a constitutional manner; the IRA and Sinn Féin, on the other hand, following the spirit of de Valera's opponents, claim to be fighting for the full republican ideal which de Valera laid aside in his quest for power. Clearly this interpretation of the past has implications for the present and, in a concluding chapter, these consequences will be considered in the light of all the findings of this study.

Conclusion

'We do not want in Ireland the absence of history, we do want a larger study of its truth.'[1] Such was the view expressed by Alice Stopford Green, the historian, at the turn of the century in the midst of her controversy with Sir Horace Plunkett. Her judgement provides an appropriate conclusion to this study. Indeed, her observation may well lay claim to be of perennial value – not only in Ireland, but in other countries as well. If, to adjust the words of Eddie MacAteer, we wish to become 'prisoners of good history', a larger study of the truth is essential. In this regard two significant findings have emerged from this research into the unknown papers of J. J. O'Kelly and many other unpublished manuscript sources: firstly, in the period before 1916, the treatment by recent cultural historians of Pearse and the Irish-Ireland movement is impaired and misleading; and, secondly, in the period after 1916 the historical trend in favour of Collins and de Valera can only be justified by an admission that history has been written by the winners. Inevitably these historical conclusions have political implications. Rather than attempt to spell out the details of these implications, it appears preferable, in conclusion, to dwell on the historical dimension of the findings that have emerged.

Pearse presents a major challenge of interpretation. He wrote of himself, 'the most curious part of the story is that no one knows which is the true Pearse.'[2] This confession of internal complexity and the clear record of striking changes of direction in his short life have not prevented modern historians from uniting in a common condemnation of his actions. Shades of grey, which might have been expected, are rarely traced; of signs of sympathy, there are none. Lyons, Brown, O'Farrell, MacDonagh and Garvin all agree that Pearse was wrong to engage in a blood sacrifice in order to secure a united and independent Ireland. Their point of view was given concise expression by John Bowman in a recent article. Bowman referred to the writings of Fr Francis Shaw, which have been considered in this work, and wrote,

> Shaw asserted that Pearse's view 'moulds the broad course of Irish history to a narrow pre-conceived pattern; it tells a story which is false and without foundation.'[3]

Apparently sympathetic to this judgement, Bowman added that the view of Pearse 'was also dangerous.' In political terms Bowman noted that there had been a healthy critique of the Pearse tradition with the result that 'Pearse's imprimatur is no longer holy writ for all the South's politicians.'[4] There can be no doubt that Bowman is correct both in his assessment of modern historical interpretation concerning Pearse and in its political consequences. The findings of this study, however, challenge the contemporary historical portrayal of Pearse, and logic indicates that fresh political approaches may be in order.

The condemnation of Pearse in modern times has largely been brought about by arraigning him on false pretences. Regularly it is asked what right did Pearse have to pursue his revolutionary ambitions when the constitutional process was about to bring an answer to Ireland's problems? Only when one begins to question the suppositions behind such a charge is it possible to begin a defence of Pearse. In this work I have suggested that the first step to be taken to secure a fair reappraisal of Pearse is to put the question – why did a Home Rule reformer become a revolutionary? In answering that question one finds a justification for Pearse's actions: he acted in 1916 because he did not believe in England's promises about Home Rule and wished to preserve a united Ireland. Historical evidence supports his stand. Three events merit special attention: Asquith's refusal in 1914 to impose Home Rule on Ulster; Lloyd George's secret promise to Carson in 1916 that parts of Ulster would be excluded from any Home Rule Act; and England's secret treaty with Italy on 26 April 1915 excluding the Pope from the Peace Conference – an indication that not all small nations, notably Ireland, rightly struggling to be free were to be treated equally. The words of Carson explicitly identifying the Tory party as the main cause of Ireland's problems bear repetition: 'I was only a puppet,' he said, 'and so was Ulster, and so was Ireland in the political game that was to get the Conservative Party into power.' The role of Carson, the Tory Party and English imperialism should figure largely in any appraisal of the 1916 Rising: that they do not do so is inexplicable. However, they take pride of place in the work of the French historian Louis Paul Dubois, rightly described by Lyons as a 'shrewd French observer' for his magisterial study of *Contemporary Ireland* (1907).[5] For Dubois the issue was crystal clear: Ulster resistance to the law of Home Rule, and the English Government's co-operation with it, was plain 'anarchy' – 'c'est l'anarchie.'[6] A more explicit rejection of the cultural exposé of Lyons would be hard to find. British policy in Ireland, Dubois maintained, was a denial of democracy and was determined by Tory Party interests. A denial of democracy because,

> To separate Ulster or a part of Ulster from Ireland is to divide the indivisible – to mutilate a living body. . . . To refuse autonomy to Ireland because Ulster does not want it is a strange abuse of the theory of the right of minorities, and a clear violation of the constitutional principle of majority rule. Has liberty been refused to Bohemia or Poland because there are dissenting minorities in those countries?[7]

Having posed that question, Dubois asserted that the Tory Party was responsible for the Ulster problem.

> We know [he writes] that the Ulster question is an artificial creation of England. L'Ulster politique est made in London. If it is anti-national, it is because the collusion of Tories and the Orangemen have rendered it so, and the path of progress for Ireland is closed.[8]

By focussing on internal factors recent cultural historians have neglected a basic historic reality, firmly stressed by Dubois and admitted by Carson, that political developments in Ulster were 'made in London.' If, following the pattern of modern cultural interpretations, one is happy to accept the secret provisions underlying British policy; and, if one accepts that the democratic principle may take second place to the ethic of imperialism – even in Ulster in 1916 it should be recalled that there were 17 Home Rule MPs as opposed to 16 Unionists – then Pearse will stand condemned. If, on the other hand, one is disturbed by the hidden designs of British policy; if one rejects the supra-national claims of imperialism; if one accepts the historical evidence against the 'two nation' theory as applied to Ireland; and, finally, if one values the democratic process, then the mystical sacrifice of Pearse will be understood and, possibly, accepted as an unhappy necessity. Instead of blaming Pearse for the 1916 Rising, one will pose a different question: what right did Tory Unionists and Carson have to combine in order to subvert the national and democratic request for reform along Home

Rule lines? Reform which, it is worth recalling, still accepted the claims of the King of England to be King of Ireland. The answer to that question had, and has, political implications.

If blame may be apportioned to the British administration for the failure to grant Home Rule, so too responsibility must be taken for the final political settlement which redrew the map of Ireland – the Northern Ireland Act of 1920 and the Anglo-Irish Treaty of 1921. This dual settlement was an undoubted success for British diplomacy: it not only frustrated the visionary aspirations of Pearse, but also it negated the ideals which had inspired the revival in Irish national consciousness since the turn of the century. Contrary to the views of most cultural commentators this revival in the Gaelic League and in the Catholic Church did not presage any revolutionary intent, but, rather looked forward to a future in which Catholics and Protestants would participate in a renewed and reformed Ireland following the passage of Home Rule. As late as 1913, in the midst of the Home Rule crisis, Douglas Hyde at a meeting of Protestants in Dublin – a gathering which included Yeats – declared that there was no basis for the religious fears raised by the Protestants in the north against Home Rule. Indeed Hyde testified to the 'sense of fair play, the justice, the toleration, and the entire absence of religious bigotry on the part of my Catholic fellow countrymen.[9] Admittedly the anti-modernist legislation of the Roman Catholic Church, notably the *Ne Temere* decree of 1908 concerning marriage, was already threatening any signs of religious accord; but all hopes of unity and reconciliation were ended by the English political settlement which copper-fastened partition and created a permanent Roman Catholic/Protestant divide. This north/south division was matched by the emergence of equally divisive barriers in the Free State after the signing of the Treaty and the Civil War. The whole spectrum of life was affected: not only the political, but also the civil, the social and the cultural. Burgeoning intellectual societies and literary publications which had promised so much in the early years of the century were devastated. National ideals gave way to the factions of political parties. Eoin MacNeill, writing his memoirs at the end of his life, was acutely aware that the mood of renewal and of national revival occasioned by the first meeting of the Gaelic League in 1893 had been lost.

> Anyone looking around in Ireland at the present day [he wrote] can see that the standard of patriotism for young and old has drifted back to what it was before 1893. Patriotic duty consists now in voting for the right party or organising the party vote ... nowadays one might think that Ireland is only a political entity.[10]

Emphasis on the party system inevitably militates against the national good and the proclamation of ideals. Sadly in Ireland the deleterious consequences of such a condition have been compounded by several factors. Firstly, while many of those who joined the Treaty party (represented by the modern party of Fine Gael) and the Fianna Fáil party were motivated by the highest ideals, many others were weaned from the full republican position by the offer of jobs and pensions. At the outset, therefore, the composition of the two parties was made up of supporters of very mixed calibre. Secondly, as is generally recognised in Ireland and has been scientifically quantified by Al Cohan in his study of *The Irish Political Elite*, these early founders of the major political parties in the state have perpetuated their control of the parliamentary machine by transfering their power to members of their families on an extremely localised base.[11] In such a situation the enunciation of ideals and the national good has had to give second best to local issues, and to candidates so rooted in their home base that concern for higher principles is often limited. Such a political development could not have been envisaged when the Free State was established in 1922, but MacNeill's vision of a harmonious Gaelic unity was almost inevitably bound to suffer as many eminent men who supported the new state had little love for Irish-Ireland ideals. Reflection on the lives of three men — Cardinal Logue, Tim Healy and James Campbell — is instructive.

Cardinal Logue, in a nominal capacity, had been Professor of Irish at Maynooth before the appointment of Fr Eoghan O'Growney. The latter's energetic and dedicated labours had inspired the foundation of the Gaelic League in 1893. Logue passively supported the League but manifested no zeal for its enterprises, although a native Irish speaker. He was also resolutely opposed to Sinn Féin. That Logue survived to support the Free State marked a success for the old order in which it was natural, as in the bishop's pastoral of October 1922, to condemn republicans. The appointment of Tim Healy as Governor General was also a success for the old order, and not without symbolic significance. Not only was it a recognition of the Westminster party system in opposition to Sinn Féin abstentionism, but also it was a recognition for the Irish politician who was renowned for betraying Parnell. The national ideals of Parnell as well as Pearse were rejected in the appointment of Healy — British policy could not have devised a more fitting symbol of its triumph. The appointment of Sir James Campbell, Baron Glenavy, as chairman of the Free State Senate, was of similar significance. He opposed everything for which Pearse stood. Before 1916 he had joined forces with Carson to defend illegality in opposition to Home Rule; and, immediatley after the Rising, he declared that he 'wouldn't be satisfied unless 40 of them were shot.'[12] Moreover, he made this statement in his capacity as Attorney General, when faced by a request for clemency from William Wylie, the prosecuting counsel. If the support of Logue and Healy for the Free State conveys a certain symbolic significance, the appointment of Campbell gave expression to a precise political reality. It was a clear sign that Britain had secured her political objectives with the creation of the Free State. The dedicated followers of Pearse protested: what right did England have, they asked, to carve a political entity from the heart of Ulster in opposition to the wishes of the majority of the Irish people? The answer to that question, as with the question on Home Rule, had, and has, political implications.

Political implications are also raised by a consideration of the Irish dimension of the historical process after 1916. If Pearse has had a bad press from historians in recent years, so too have those republicans who opposed both Collins and de Valera. The findings of this study confer on the republican tradition associated with Cathal Brugha a level of recognition that has hitherto been denied it. Intellectually and culturally it was fashioned, even before the 1916 Rising, by an awareness of a distinctly Irish historical perspective and by a thorough involvement in the Irish language movement. Following the Rising and the executions, resistance to English rule was fostered by an appeal — rational, practical, and emotional — to Irishmen to secure their national independence, and develop their individual identity in a separatist Irish state. The primacy of the group in asserting the principles of Pearse at Roscommon in 1917 cannot be contested. Nor can it be denied that the group — notably Brugha, Count Plunkett, Fr O'Flanagan and J. J. O'Kelly — played a major part in both shaping the character of Republican Sinn Féin in October 1917, and in defining the republican and social principles of Dáil Eireann in January 1919. Despite the fact that their contribution was vital and invaluable — that Sinn Féin and Dáil Eireann would have been significantly different institutions without their input — their role in creating a republican party is rarely mentioned. True they lost out to Collins over the Treaty and to de Valera over the founding of Fianna Fáil, but the circumstances of their defeats indicate that they lost out on the battlefields of power politics rather than in an open competition over policies and ideals. That Collins did not have a price on his head and was in touch with Cope of the Castle prior to the Treaty, raises many questions about his personal image, his probity, and the majority he

managed to gather around himself with the help of the secret influence of the IRB. That de Valera secretly planned entry into the
Free State, conducting negotiations to that purpose in Rome and
in America, while retaining the title of President of the Republic
raises similar questions about his personal image, his probity, and
the manner in which he entered the Free State with the Fianna Fáil
party. A contrast between the utterances of de Valera and his opponents in the Second Dáil is illuminating. His opponents stressed
the value of integrity which was enshrined in the keeping of the
oath. An attitude embodied in the statement of Professor Stockley
that, 'if you can do nothing, that is no excuse for doing wrong.'[13]
De Valera's statements, in contrast, were clearly Machiavellian: the
Free State was both an illegal usurper and a lawful alternative; the
oath was both a grave obstacle and a meaningless ritual; he was, and
he was not, the President of the Republic. Chameleon-like he
changed his principles to suit the circumstances. Any evaluation
of the manner in which he founded Fianna Fáil and entered the
Free State should frankly acknowledge that he attained power by
walking in the path of *The Prince*.

Historical revisionism, in the style of modern Russia, where Stalin
and even Lenin are subject to impartial scrutiny, is clearly needed.
Such a need is well illustrated by the recent book of Roy Foster,
Modern Ireland, 1600-1972, which has been acclaimed as indispensable reading for anyone wishing to understand contemporary
Ireland. Of the Brugha republican tradition it says nothing: Brugha,
himself, merits only one brief mention in the text; Count Plunkett
two, in which he is described as 'incompetent' and 'a disastrous
leader;' Fr O'Flanagan, J. J. O'Kelly and Mary MacSwiney do not
receive any recognition at all.[14] Admittedly the book is a survey
covering a long period, but to focus on Griffith, Collins and de
Valera alone as the heirs of the Pearse tradition is to tell only one
side of the story. The author may reply, with some justification,
that he is simply reflecting current historical interpretations and
their balance of emphasis. In that he may well be correct; but that
is to say, that he, like they, is writing history from the point of
view of the winners. Correction is long overdue. The results, however unpalatable, should be faced. If the republicans of the Brugha
tradition deserve to be praised for their faithful fidelity to principle
– as the historical evidence indicates; rather, than to be condemned
for their inflexible intransigence – as their opponents would wish,
then more credibility is conferred upon the historical lineage of the
IRA and Sinn Féin. The 1938 delegation of power by the remnant
of the Second Dáil to the Army Council of the IRA assumes a new

significance. As the papacy values the line of apostolic succession, so too the IRA sees the Second Dáil's delegation of power as a direct link with the original Dáil Eireann and with Pearse's declaration of 1916 that created the Republic. In some ways it may be argued that the delegation of power by republican Dáil Eireann to the IRA in 1938 and de Valera's Constitution in 1937 marked a decisive stage in the evolution of Irish nationalism. These events may also be said to complete this study with a fitting, if rather surprising, degree of unity. The book began by tracing the contrasting attitudes inside the Gaelic League to Fr Yorke's speech upholding Sinn Féin ideals in 1899. At that time J. J. O'Kelly, representing the separatist element in the League fully approved of Fr Yorke, while Douglas Hyde, representing the more constitutional element in the League, was opposed to him. In 1938, after all the traumatic events of the intervening years, it was as if nothing had changed. O'Kelly, remaining true to his separatist sentiments, was happy as a member of Dáil Eireann to delegate power to the IRA, and Hyde, remaining true to his preference for constitutional procedures, was happy to become the first President of Ireland under de Valera's new Constitution. The former remained outside the political process; the latter took his place at its head. It is tempting to use this alignment as further evidence of the classic division of Irish nationalists into physical force and constitutional categories: O'Kelly representing the line of Tone, the Fenians, Mitchel and Pearse; Hyde representing the heritage of Grattan, O'Connell and Parnell. Such a distinction is false. O'Kelly was also an admirer of Daniel O'Connell. Not only did he write a life of O'Connell in which he highlighted his astute resistance to English rule, but also he devoted much of his time and energy to the restoration of O'Connell's home at Derrynane. While these sympathies did alienate O'Kelly from some republicans – Brian O'Higgins was especially annoyed – his scholarly presentation of the case in favour of O'Connell should serve as a warning against facile distinctions between physical force and constitutional nationalism. His book might also serve as a pointer to common ground on which all forms and forces of Irish nationalism might meet. Another caveat against the simplistic delineation of the republican remnant of 1938 as mere perpetuators of the Irish physical force tradition is provided by the presence of some distinguished Anglo-Irish women in their ranks. Two in particular remained loyal to the Republic long after de Valera had entered the Free State; Mrs Despard, sister of Lord French – Lord Lieutenant of Ireland at a critical stage of the Anglo-Irish war; and Albina Brodrick, sister of the Earl of Midleton – the leader of the Southern Unionists in the

negotiations leading up to the Treaty. It was not any abstract historical tradition that had drawn these two most unlikely of candidates into the ranks of extreme republicanism: they were motivated by what they regarded as the injustice of England's reaction
to the legitimate democratic demands of republican Sinn Féin and
of Dáil Eireann. These observations are offered in order to clarify
the motives behind those who remained loyal to the Republic in
1938. Republicans of that time were not all blind followers of the
Irish physical force tradition: the historical base for their opposition
to English rule in Ireland was far more cultivated than a mere repetition of the demands of Tone – far more learned, in fact, than
the historical dissertations of Pearse, himself; and blended into
these traditional Irish demands for independence was a request,
with a particular appeal to the English, that the rule of law should
be upheld and that justice should be administered in Ireland. Believing that acceptance of the Free State meant a compromise of these
ideals, members of Sinn Féin and the IRA remained outside the
constitutional system in 1938. Possibly it may be argued that by
their present methods the IRA have so distanced themselves from
the character of the republicanism of Pearse and Brugha that they
have forfeited the right to use their names. In that regard it should
be noted that the delegation of power in 1938 presumed that the
IRA, 'in their every action' to secure the Republic, 'will be inspired
by the high ideals and the chivalry of our martyred comrades.'
How far, it is reasonable to ask, would the martyrs of 1916 and the
seventy-seven men put to death in the Civil War period have approved
of present IRA methods? Has the IRA, it may be asked, broken
faith with its historic roots? A prophetic insight into this question
appears in the writings of Francis Stuart, himself a republican prisoner during the Civil War.

> Once the process of division had started, H [Stuart] foresaw it continu-
> ing, and subdivisions taking place, especially on the republican side, per-
> haps creating small enclaves of what he looked on as true revolutionaries
> whose aim had less to do with Irish independence than in casting doubt
> on traditional values and judgements.[15]

The original intention of the republican movement would, Stuart
predicted, be lost sight of as split after split obscured the pristine
purity of purpose. Clearly in any process of self appraisal the IRA
has reason to consider critically whether its actions have impaired
the integrity of its cause. However, the IRA is not the only nationalist organisation which needs to engage in self appraisal. By not
naming Pearse in the Forum report or endorsing his aims, both

Fianna Fáil and Fine Gael have distanced themselves from his message. Both parties need to examine themselves as to the genuineness of their commitment to the full nationalist and republican aspirations of Pearse; and to assess the extent to which their party structures perpetuate the priorities of party at the expense of the national good. To attempt to draw more explicit political implications on the part of either the English or Irish protagonists in the sad saga of modern Irish history would be both pretentious and tendentious. Historical conclusions are more properly the subject of this study and they have been made with particular reference to the persons of Pearse, Brugha, Collins and de Valera. The evidence indicates that both Patrick Pearse and the followers of Cathal Brugha – those who have lost out in the struggle for political power – merit rehabilitation as the standard bearers of a lost republican ideal.

It is fitting to conclude with an historical observation of a general character. It is this: the historical base of the New Ireland Forum is both incomplete and inadequate. Plausible words and a mask of impartiality cannot conceal the fact that it is both partial and partisan. In consequence, the Anglo-Irish Agreement is inherently deficient and defective. There is an old philosophical dictum to the effect that 'from nothing, nothing comes.' Such an expression perfectly describes the historical introduction to the Forum Report. While it would be simplistic to suggest that the adoption of a sounder historical approach would, of its own, produce more realistic political policies – many other factors in the more recent past manifestly require that they be taken into consideration – the acceptance of a false historical perspective has undoubtedly contributed to a condition of crisis and confrontation. The findings of this study strongly suggest that all the parties to the New Ireland Forum, including the Christian churches, the major political parties, and the two sovereign governments who signed the Anglo-Irish Agreement, should honestly appraise their own responsibility for the Anglo-Irish problem instead of seeing it as something outside themselves. Regrettably the indications are that the power politics which created the problem are still the dominant factor determining its evolution today. Sadly the motto chosen for the Forum by its chairman – 'I raise up my eyes,' presumably a version of the psalm, 'To you, O Lord, I have lifted up my eyes' – has met with no response. As one reflects on the tragic events of the past twenty years one is forcibly reminded of the words of Seán O'Casey, expressed through the character of Mrs Boyle in *Juno and the Paycock*, that 'these things have nothin' to do with the Will of God. Ah, what can God do agen the stupidity o' men!' With spiritual considerations in mind, the prayer of Mrs

Boyle, expressed by O'Casey in Roman Catholic imagery but conveying the words of the prophet Ezekiel, is extremely apposite. Lamenting the killing of her son, she pleads: 'Sacred Heart o' Jesus, take away our hearts o' stone, and give us hearts o' flesh! Take away this murderin' hate, an' give us Thine eternal love'.

For those of religious conviction these sentiments call for a response; for those without any religious commitment the enigmatic prediction of Francis Stuart, which terminated his own personal odyssey in a prison cell, may strike some chord of feeling. Stuart wrote that,

> He did begin to see the silence that he had entered as the deep divide between the past and what was still to come. Whatever it was that was at the other end there was no way of telling. It might be a howl of final despair or the profound silence might be broken by certain words that he didn't yet know how to listen for.[16]

The choice is ours: do we continue to tread the path of powerful self-interest until we encounter the 'howl of final despair'? or do we allow truths as yet unknown — reflections of the Truth that sets us free — to lead us through the 'profound silence' and into the way of peace?

Bibliography

PRIMARY SOURCES

MANUSCRIPT SOURCES: INSTITUTIONAL ARCHIVES AND PUBLIC RECORDS

1. **Dublin Diocesan Archives (DDA)**
   Walsh, Archbishop William J., Papers

2. **House of Lords Record Office**
   Lloyd George Papers (LGP)

3. **Limerick Diocesan Archives (LDA)**
   O'Dwyer, Bishop Edward Thomas, Papers

4. **National Library of Ireland (NLI)**
   Celtic Literary Society Minutes 19934
   Corrigan Papers 24379, 24380
   Devoy, John, Papers 18100
   Duffy, Gavan, Papers 5581
   Gaelic League Minutes 9800
   Green, Alice Stopford, Papers 9932
   Hearn, John, Papers 15987, 15988, 15989
   MacNeill, Eoin, Papers 10882
   O'Brien, William, Papers 15653
   Plunkett, Count G.N., Papers 11383

5. **Public Records Office England (PROE)**
   Cabinet Office (CAB) 24/123, 24/125, 24/126
   Colonial Office (CO) Papers under the broad heading CO/903-906 contain the records from Dublin Castle on nationalist organisations both before and after 1916. Some items are closed for 75 or even 100 years.
   Anderson, Sir John, Papers CO/904/188
   Defence of the Realm Regulations CO/904/169
   Press Censorship Files (1917-18) CO/904/166

Press Censorship Files (1918-19) CO/904/167
Seditious Literature CO/904/161
Sinn Féin activities CO/904/23

Personal Papers
Sturgis, Mark, Diary 30/59
Wylie, William E., Papers 30/89

6. **Public Records Office Ireland (PROI)**
   Sinn Féin Funds Case material: J.J.O'Kelly evidence (39, 40); Pádraig
   O'Caoimh evidence (41); verdicts of Judge Kingsmill Moore on 26
   October and 19 November 1948.

7. **State Paper Office (SPO), Dublin Castle**
   Cabinet and Ministry Minutes DE 1/2, 3 Oct. 1919 to 3 Sept. 1920; DE 1/3,
   30 Sept. 1920 to 2 Dec. 1921; DE 1/4, 11 Jan. 1922 to 21 April 1922.
   Dáil Eireann Papers DE 2/514, DE 2/251.
   Dublin Metropolitan Police: miscellaneous files, 1916 and 1917
   Press censorship records 1916-1917 and 1917-1919

8. **Trinity College Dublin Archives (TCDA)**
   Dillon, Dr Thomas, memoir 3738

9. **University College Dublin Archives (UCDA)**
   MacNeill, Eoin, Papers LA 1/G, LA 1/G 371
   MacSwiney, Mary, Papers P48a/43, P48a/121, P48a/124, P48a/136
   Mulcahy, R.J., Papers P7/D/5, P7/D/6, P7/D/36, P7/D/39, P7/D/96,
   P7a/209

10. **University College Dublin, Folklore Department**
    Douglas Hyde memoir

MANUSCRIPT SOURCES: PRIVATE PAPERS

O'Kelly, Mortimer, collection (M. O'K):
Minute books of the Society for the Preservation of the Irish Language,
1876-1941; Minute book of the Gaelic League, 12 June 1906 to 5 June 1912;
Minute book of the Second Dáil, Dec. 1923 to Dec. 1926 (SDM); collection of
letters, part of typed statement of Fr Michael O'Flanagan to his bishop, 6 April
1925; material relating to America and to the American bonds.

PUBLISHED SOURCES

Official publications: England:
Hansard; Royal Commission on the Rebellion in Ireland. *Report of the Com-
mission* (London, 1916); Royal Commission on the Rebellion in Ireland.
Minutes of evidence and appendix of documents (London, 1916).

Official publications: Ireland:
Dáil Eireann. *Minutes of Proceedings of the First Parliament of the Republic*

of Ireland, 1919-1921 (Dublin, 1921); Dáil Eireann. *Official Report for the period 16 August 1921 to 26 August 1921 and 28 February 1922 to 8 June 1922* (Dublin, 1922); Dáil Eireann. *Official Report. Debate on the Treaty between Great Britain and Ireland signed in London on 6 December 1921* (Dublin, 1922); *The Public General Acts passed by the Oireachtas of Saorstát Eireann during the year 1925* (Dublin, 1926).

CONTEMPORARY JOURNALS AND NEWSPAPERS (I.E. PUBLISHED BEFORE 1939)

An Claidheamh Soluis (ACS), An Phoblacht, Archivium Hibernicum, Banba, Catholic Bulletin (CB), Freeman's Journal, New Ireland, Sinn Féin, Studies, The Peasant and Irish Ireland, The Irish Ecclesiastical Record, The Gaelic American (NY), *The Irish Press* (Philadelphia), *The Irish World* (NY), *The New York Times, The Irish Times, The Irish Nation, The Irishman, The United Irishman, The National Volunteer, Nationality, The Plain People, The Tablet, The Westminster Gazette, The Wolfe Tone Weekly, The Wolfe Tone Annual.*

MODERN JOURNALS AND NEWSPAPERS
(Material published after 1939. Some were also used as contemporary publications)

The Sunday Independent, The Irish Times, The Sligo Champion, The Sunday Tribune, The Irish Press, The Sunday Times, Eire-Ireland, Studies, The Crane Bag, The Irish Sword, Irish Historical Studies (IHS), Studia Hibernica, Anglo-Irish Studies, The Capuchin Annual, University Review

INTERVIEWS WITH PEOPLE WHO EITHER HAD CONTEMPORARY EXPERIENCE OF EVENTS UP TO 1938, OR HAD DOCUMENTARY MATERIAL RELATING TO THEM

Mortimer O'Kelly, Fr John MacMahon, General Thomas Maguire, Leon Ó Broin, Fr Liam Breen, Abbot Sylvester Mooney, Fr Seán Ó Catháin, Fr Fergal McGrath, Fr Bernard O'Dea, Eoin O'Keeffe, Br Peadar O'Loinsigh, Clare Ring, Maire Brugha, Sheila Humphries, Sophie Mallin, Nora O'Sullivan, Mary O'Mara and Mgr Andrew Coffey

CONVERSATIONS OR CORRESPONDENCE WITH PEOPLE WHO PROVIDED VALUABLE INFORMATION AND ASSISTANCE:
Abbot Gregory Freeman, Gerry Cronin, Brian Kennedy, Pat Callan, Fr Denis Costello, Michael Gill, Breda Governey, Fergus Kelly, Fr P. B. MacCionnaith, Fr Edward O'Callaghan, Proinsias Ó Conluain, Brian Ó Cuiv, Fr Peter O'Dwyer, Aindrias Ó Muimhneacháin, Fr Kieran O'Shea, Pádraig Oliver O'Snodaigh, Daniel O'Sullivan, Donnchadh Ó Suilleabháin, Fr Anthony Gaughan, Fr Mark Tierney, Fr Henry O'Shea, Brian Murphy, Máire Brennan, Nollaig Ó Gadhra, Kevin Etchingham

SECONDARY SOURCES

Aubert, R. (ed.), *The Christian Centuries, Vol. V. The Church in a Secularised Society* (London, 1978)

Béaslaí, P., *Michael Collins and the Making of a New Ireland, Vols. 1 & 2* (Dublin, 1926)

Bell, J. Bowyer, *The Secret Army* (London, 1972. First pub. 1970)

Bew, Paul, *Conflict and Conciliation in Ireland 1890-1910* (Oxford, 1987)

Birrell, A., *Things Past Redress* (London, 1937)

Blythe, E., 'Hyde in Conflict' in Seán Ó Tuama (ed.), *The Gaelic League Idea* (Cork and Dublin, 1972)

Bowman, J., 'Shooting down old heroes and romantic dreams', *The Sunday Times*, 23 Oct. 1988

Breatnach, L., *An Pluinceadach* (Dublin, 1971)

Brennan, R., *Allegiance* (Dublin, 1950)

Bromage, M. C., *De Valera and the March of a Nation* (London, 1956)

Brown, T., *Ireland, A Social and Cultural History, 1922-1979* (London, 1982. First pub. 1981)

Buckland, P., *Irish Unionism, Two. Ulster Unionism and the Origins of Northern Ireland, 1886-1922* (Dublin, 1973)

Chesterton, G. K., *Irish Impressions* (London, 1919)

Coffey, Rev. P., 'Belgium's New Cardinal: A sketch of his life and work', *Irish Ecclesiastical Record*, July 1907

Coffey, Rev. P., 'James Connolly's Campaign against Capitalism', *CB*, April to Aug. 1920

Coffey, Rev. P., 'Economic Ideals and Policies for the Wage Earning Masses', *CB*, Feb. 1921

Cohan, A., *The Irish Political Elite* (Dublin, 1972)

Colum, P., *Arthur Griffith* (Dublin, 1959)

Comyn, D. (ed.), *Geoffrey Keating, The History of Ireland Vol. 1* (London, 1902)

Corish, P. J., *The Irish Catholic Experience, A Historical Survey* (Dublin, 1985)

Cronin, S., *The McGarrity Papers, Revelations of the Irish Revolutionary Movement in Ireland and America 1900-1940* (Tralee, 1972)

Daly, D., *The Young Douglas Hyde. The Dawn of the Irish Revolution and Renaissance, 1874-1893* (Dublin, 1974)

Davis, R., *Arthur Griffith and Non-Violent Sinn Féin* (Dublin, 1974)

Davis, R., 'The Advocacy of Passive Resistance in Ireland, 1916-1922', *Anglo-Irish Studies*, 111, 1977

Dillon, G. Plunkett, 'The North Roscommon Election', *Capuchin Annual*, 1967

Dillon, T., 'Birth of the New Sinn Féin and the Ard Fheis, 1917', *Capuchin Annual*, 1967

Dillon, T., 'Ireland, 1865-1921', *University Review*, 111, 8, N.D.

Dubois, L. P., *Contemporary Ireland* (Dublin, 1911. First pub. Paris, 1907)

Dubois, L. P., *Le Drame Irlandais et L'Irlande Nouvelle* (Paris, 1927)

Edwards, R. Dudley, *Patrick Pearse. The Triumph of Failure* (London, 1979. First pub. 1977)

Fallon, C. H., *Soul of Fire: A Biography of Mary MacSwiney* (Cork and Dublin, 1986)

Fanning, R., *Independent Ireland* (Dublin, 1983)

Farrell, B., *The Founding of Dáil Eireann. Parliament and Nation Building. Studies in Irish Political Culture* (Dublin, 1971)

Fathers of the Society of Jesus (compiled by), *A Page of Irish History, Story of University College, Dublin, 1883-1909* (Dublin and Cork, 1930)

Fay, W. G., and Catherine Carswell, *The Fays of the Abbey Theatre, An Autobiographical Record* (London, 1935)

Fogarty, Bishop, *The Great Bishop of Limerick* (Dublin, 1917)

Forester, M., *Michael Collins − the Lost Leader* (London, 1972. First pub. 1971)

Foster, R. F., *Modern Ireland 1600-1972* (London, 1988)

Fottrell, M. A., 'The Angelus', *CB*, Nov. 1918

Gallagher, T. (T. P. O'Neill, ed.), *The Anglo-Irish Treaty* (London, 1965)

Garvin, T., *Nationalist Revolutionaries in Ireland, 1858-1928* (Oxford, 1987)

Gaughan, J. A., *Memoirs of Constable Jeremiah Mee, R.I.C.* (Dublin, 1975)

Gaughan, J. A., *Austin Stack, Portrait of a Separatist* (Dublin, 1977)

Gwynn, D., *Life of John Redmond* (London, 1932)

Hally, Col. P. J., 'The Easter Rising in Dublin: The Military Aspects', *The Irish Sword*, VII, 29, Winter 1966 and VIII, 30, Summer 1967

Healy, T. M., *Letters and Leaders of My Day, II* (London, 1928)

Horgan, J. J. (compiled by), *The Complete Grammar of Anarchy* (London, 1919)

Hyde, D., *The Gaelic League and Politics* (Dublin, N.D.)

Hyde, D., *Mise agus an Conradh* (Dublin, 1937)

Jedin, H. (ed.), *History of the Church, Vol. X. The Church in the Modern Age* (New York, 1981. First pub. 1979)

Jones, T. (ed. Keith Middlemas), *Whitehall Diary, Vol. III. Ireland from 1918-1923* (London, 1971)

Kearney, R., 'Between Politics and Literature: the Irish Cultural Journal', *The Crane Bag*, 7, 2

Kee, R., *The Green Flag, A History of Irish Nationalism* (London, 1972)

Keogh, D., *The Vatican, the Bishops and Irish Politics, 1919-1939* (Cambridge, 1986)

Laffan, M., 'The Unification of Sinn Féin in 1917', *IHS*, XVII, 67, March 1971

Laffan, M., *The Partition of Ireland, 1911-1925* (Dublin, 1983)

Lavelle, P., *James O'Mara, A Staunch Sinn Féiner, 1873-1948* (Dublin, 1961)

Lawlor, S., *Britain and Ireland, 1914-1923* (Dublin, 1983)

Leslie, S., *Cardinal Gasquet* (London, 1953)

Longford, the Earl of, and O'Neill, T. P., *Eamon de Valera* (Dublin, 1970)

Lyons, F. S. L., *Ireland since the Famine, 1850 to the Present* (London, 1971)

Lyons, F. S. L., *Culture and Anarchy in Ireland, 1890-1939* (Oxford, 1982. First pub. 1979)

Macardle, D., *The Irish Republic* (Dublin, 1951)

McColgan, J., *British Policy and the Irish Administration, 1920-1922* (London, 1983)

Macready, Gen. C. N. F., *Annals of an Active Life, 1* (London, N.D.)

MacDonagh, O., *States of Mind, A Study of Anglo-Irish Conflict 1780-1980* (London, 1983)

MacEoinn, U., *Survivors* (Dublin, 1980)

MacFinn, P.E., *An tAthair Mícheál P. Ó hIceadha* (Dublin, 1974)

McInerney, M., 'Gerry Boland's Story', *The Irish Times*, 11 Oct. 1968

Mansergh, N., *The Irish Question, 1841-1921* (London, 1965)

Martin, F. X. (ed.), *Leaders and Men of the Easter Rising: Dublin 1916* (London, 1967)

Martin, F. X., '1916 – Myth, Fact, and Mystery', *Studia Hibernica*, 7, 1967

Martin, F.X., 'MacNeill and the Foundation of the Irish Volunteers', in Martin F. X. and Byrne, F. J. (eds) *The Scholar Revolutionary, Eoin MacNeill, 1867-1945, and the Making of the New Ireland* (Shannon, 1973)

Miller, David W., *Church, State and Nation in Ireland 1898-1921* (Dublin, 1973)

Moynihan, M. (ed.), *Speeches and Statements by Eamon de Valera 1917-1973* (Dublin, 1980)

Mulcahy, R., 'The Irish Volunteer Convention, 27 October 1917', *Capuchin Annual*, 1967

Murphy, B., 'The Canon of Irish Cultural History: some Questions', *Studies* 77, no. 305, Spring 1988

Murphy, B., 'Father Yorke's "Turning of the Tide" (1899): the strictly cultural Nationalism of the early Gaelic League', *Eire-Ireland*, Spring 1988

Murphy, R., 'Walter Long and the making of the Government of Ireland Act, 1919-'20', *IHS*, XXV, no. 97, May 1986

Neligan, D., *The Spy in the Castle* (London, 1968)

O'Beirne-Ranelagh, J., 'The IRB from the Treaty to 1924', *IHS*, XX, no. 77, March 1976

O'Brien, C. C., '1891-1916', in Conor Cruise O'Brien (ed.), *The Shaping of Modern Ireland* (Dublin, 1970. First pub. 1960)

Ó Broin, L., 'The Gaelic League and the Chair of Irish at Maynooth', *Studies*, LII, no. 208, Winter 1963

Ó Broin, L., *Revolutionary. Underground, the Story of the Irish Republican Brotherhood, 1858-1924* (Dublin, 1976)

Ó Broin, L., *No Man's Man. A biographical memoir of Joseph Brennan – Civil Servant and first Governor of the Bank of Ireland* (Dublin, 1983)

O'Callaghan, Edward P., *Bishop Edward Thomas O'Dwyer and the course of Irish Politics, 1870-1917* (UCG, 1976. Unpublished MA thesis)

O'Casey, S., *Autographies 1* (London, 1980. *Drums Under the Windows*. First pub. 1945)

O'Conluain, P. and O'Ceileachair, D., *An Duinnineach* (Dublin, 1958)

O'Connor, Sir J., *A History of Ireland, 1798-1924, II* (London, 1925)

O'Donoghue, F., *No Other Law, the Story of Liam Lynch and the Irish Republican Army, 1916-1923* (Dublin, 1954)

O'Donoghue, F., 'Re-organisation of the Irish Volunteers, 1916-1917', *Capuchin Annual*, 1967

O'Farrell, Padraic, *The Seán MacEoin Story* (Dublin and Cork, 1981)

O'Farrell, Patrick. *Ireland's English Question* (London, 1971)

O'Fearail, Pádraig, *The Story of Conradh na Gaeilge, A History of the Gaelic League* (Dublin, 1975)

O'Flanagan, Fr M., 'The Roscommon Election', *CB*, March 1917

O'Flanagan, Fr M., 'Colonial Home Rule', *CB*, Sept. 1917

O'Flanagan, Fr M., *The Strength of Sinn Féin* (Dublin, 1934)

Ó hAilin, T., 'Irish Revival Movements', in Brian Ó Cuiv (ed.), *A View of the Irish Language* (Dublin, 1969)

O'Hegarty, P. S., *A History of Ireland Under the Union, 1801-1922* (London, 1952)

O'Kelly, J.J. (Sceilg), 'Arthur Griffith: some reminiscences', *CB*, Sept. 1922

O'Kelly, J. J., 'Michael Collins: an attempt to appreciate his complex personality', *CB*, Oct. 1922

O'Kelly, J. J., *The National Outlook* (Dublin, 1936)

O'Kelly, J. J., *Stepping Stones* (Dublin, 1939)

O'Kelly, J. J., *Fr Michael O'Flanagan, Sceilg's Graveside Oration* (Dublin, 1942)

O'Kelly, J. J., *Cathal Brugha* (Dublin, 1942)

O'Kelly, J. J., *A Trinity of Martyrs* (Dublin, N.D.)

Ó Luing, S., *I Die in a good cause, A study of Thomas Ashe idealist and revolutionary* (Dublin, 1970)

O'Neill, Thomas P., 'In search of a Political Path: Irish Republicanism 1922-1927', *Historical Studies* X (Galway, 1976)

O'Riordain, Rev. M., *Catholicity and Progress in Ireland* (London, 1905)

Ó Suilleabháin, D., *An Piarsach agus Conradh na Gaeilge* (Dublin, 1981)

Pakenham, F., *Peace by Ordeal* (London, 1935)

Pearse, P. H., *From a Hermitage* (Dublin, 1915)

Plunkett, Count G. N., 'At the Foot of the Cross', *Studies*, March 1917

Plunkett, Sir H., *Ireland in the New Century* (London, 1905. First pub. 1904)

Pyne, P., 'The New Irish State and the Decline of the Republican Sinn Féin Party, 1923-1926', *Eire-Ireland* XI, 3, 1976

Ryan, W.P., *The Pope's Green Island* (London, 1912)

Shaw, Francis, 'The Canon of Irish History – a Challenge', *Studies* LXI, no. 242, Summer 1972

Snoddy, O., 'Three by-elections of 1917', *Capuchin Annual*, 1967

Stewart, A. T. Q., *The Ulster Crisis, Resistance to Home Rule, 1912-1914* (London, 1979. First pub. 1967)

Stewart, A. T. Q., *Edward Carson* (Dublin, 1981)

Stewart, F., *Black List, Section H* (London, 1982. First pub. 1971)

Talbot, H., *Michael Collins' Own Story* (London, N.D.)

Taylor, A. J. P., *Essays in English History* (London, 1976)

Tierney, M., 'A survey of the Reports of French Consuls in Ireland, 1814-1929', in Liam Swords (ed.), *The Irish-French Connection 1578-1978* (Paris, 1978)

Towey, T., 'The Reaction of the British Government to the 1922 Collins-de Valera Pact', *IHS* XXII, no. 85, March 1980

Townshend, C., *The British Campaign in Ireland 1919-1921. The Development of Political and Military Policies* (Oxford, 1975)
Wheeler-Bennett, J. W., *John Anderson, Viscount Waverley* (London, 1962)

Footnotes

INTRODUCTION

1. A. J. P. Taylor, *Essays in English History* (London, 1976) p. 217.
2. *Sunday Independent*, 8 Aug. 1982, p. 7.
3. F. X. Martin (ed.), *Leaders and men of the Easter Rising: Dublin 1916* (London, 1967) p. XI; see also F. X. Martin, '1916 — Myth, fact and mystery', *Studia Hibernia*, 7, 1967, pp 7-126.

Chapter 1. PEARSE THE REFORMER

(1)   Pearse: reformer or revolutionary?
1. Patrick O'Farrell, *Ireland's English Question* (London, 1971) p. 229.
2. F. S. L. Lyons, *Culture and Anarchy in Ireland, 1890-1939* (Oxford, 1982. First pub. 1979) p. 27.
3. Oliver McDonagh, *States of Mind, A Study of Anglo-Irish Conflict, 1780-1980* (London, 1983) p. 116.
4. *Ibid.* p. 86.
5. *Ibid.* p. 112.
6. Terence Brown, *Ireland, A Social and Cultural History, 1922-1979* (London, 1981) p. 47.
7. Tom Garvin, *Nationalist Revolutionaries in Ireland, 1858-1928* (Oxford, 1987) p. 33 and p. 78.
8. Lyons, *op. cit.* p. 90; Garvin, *op. cit.* p. 99.
9. Francis Shaw, 'The Canon of Irish History – A Challenge', *Studies*, LXI, 242, Summer, 1972, p. 136 quoting Pearse, 'The Coming Revolution', pp 91-93.
10. Ruth Dudley Edwards, *Patrick Pearse. The Triumph of Failure* (London, 1979. First pub. 1977) p. 178.
11. Garvin, *op. cit.* p. 92.

(2)   Pearse and Fr Yorke
12. Brian Murphy, 'Fr Peter Yorke's "Turning of the Tide" (1899): the strictly cultural Nationalism of the early Gaelic League', *Eire-Ireland*, Spring 1988, p. 38; Anon., 'The Passing of Fr Yorke', *CB*, XV, 8, Aug. 1925, pp 788-805.
13. *The United Irishman*, 9 Sept. 1899, p. 5.
14. Douglas Hyde, *Mise Agus an Conradh* (Dublin, 1937), pp 72, 73.
15. Dominic Daly, *The Young Douglas Hyde* (Dublin, 1974) p. 120.
16. Padraic Colum, *Arthur Griffith* (Dublin, 1959), p. 32.
17. UCDA, MacNeill Papers, Memoir, LA/G/371 pp. 55.
18. Dáil Eireann, *Minutes of the Proceedings of the First Parliament of the Republic of Ireland, 1919-1921* (Dublin, 1921) 9 May 1919, p. 82.
19. David Comyn (ed.), Geoffrey Keating: the History of Ireland, 1 (London, 1902) p. 5.

(3)   Pearse, the Gaelic League and Sinn Féin
20. Leon Ó Broin, *Revolutionary Underground, the Story of the Irish Republican Brotherhood 1858-1924* (Dublin, 1976) pp 118, 119.
21. NLI, Minutes of the Celtic Literary Society, 19934, part 1, 6 Oct. 1899.
22. UCD, Folklore Department, Hyde Memoir.
23. *The United Irishman*, 3 March 1906.
24. *An Claidheamh Soluis (ACS)*, 15 Dec. 1917.
25. PROI, Sinn Féin Funds Case, (32), p. 3.
26. *Ibid.* p. 6.
27. Richard Davis, *Arthur Griffith and Non-Violent Sinn Féin* (Dublin, 1974) p. 82 and pp 81-86.

28. PROI, Sinn Féin Funds Case, (32), p. 5.

29. Douglas Hyde, *The Gaelic League and Politics* (Dublin, nd) p. 3 from a speech made in Cork, 15 Dec. 1914.

30. *The National Volunteer*, 20 Nov. 1914.

(4)   'Footpads, South Sea islanders' and the IRB

31. *The Freeman's Journal*, 25 May 1903.

32. UCD, Hyde Memoir; Edwards, *op. cit.* p. 88.

33. *The Freeman's Journal*, 25 May 1903.

34. *ACS*, 12 Dec. 1908.

35. Seán O'Casey, *Autobiographies 1* (London, 1980. First pub. 1963) p. 403; Leon Ó Broin, 'The Gaelic League and the Chair of Irish at Maynooth', *Studies*, Winter 1963 for a more measured view of Fr O'Hickey.

36. UCDA, Mulcahy Papers, P7/D/5, p. 7.

37. J. J. O'Kelly, *Cathal Brugha* (Dublin, 1942) p. 14; Proinsias Ó Conluain and Donncha Ó Ceileacháir, *An Duinnineach* (Dublin, 1958) p. 221.

38. Ó Conluain, *op. cit.* pp 221, 222.

39. NLI, Gaelic League Minutes, 9800, 13 May 1902.

40. Pádraig Eric MacFinn, *An tAthair Micéal Ó hIceadha* (Dublin, 1974) pp. 51, 52.

41. *Banba*, Abran 1903, p. 180; see NLI, Gaelic League Minutes, 9800, 17 and 24 Sept. and 8 Oct. 1901 for confirmation of MacNeill's influence against O'Donoghue.

42. Edwards, *op. cit.* p. 57.

43. *Banba*, Abran 1903, p. 180.

44. Garvin, *op. cit*, p. 92.

45. *Banba*, Meitheamh 1903, p. 221. Translated from the Irish, 'Níl puinn maitheasa san leabhrán seo.'

46. *Banba*, July 1903, p. 247.

(5)   Pearse and the Keating branch

47. *ACS*, 4 April 1908 for a letter of J. J. O'Kelly giving his version of events, and a letter in reply by Douglas Hyde justifying himself.

48. UCD, Hyde Memoir.

49. *The Peasant and Irish Ireland*, 11 April 1908.

50. Mortimer O'Kelly Papers (M. O'K), Gaelic League Minutes, 14 Jan. 1908.

51. *ACS*, 11 April 1908; *ACS*, 21 March 1908; *ACS*, 23 May 1908.

52. Ó Conluain, *op. cit.* pp 193, 194; *ACS*, 23 May 1908 and Edwards, *op. cit.* p. 87 for the allegation of Pearse; and W. P. Ryan, *The Pope's Green Island* (London, 1912) p. 134.

53. *ACS*, 30 May 1908.

54. Edwards, *op. cit.* p. 85; Donnchadh Ó Suilleabháin, *An Piarsach agus Conradh na Gaeilge* (Dublin, 1981) p. 109; Garvin, *op. cit.* pp 92, 93. Garvin states that Pearse became editor of *ACS* in 1902; in fact his editorship began in 1903.

55. Mortimer O'Kelly Papers (M. O'K), Gaelic League Minutes, 8 Aug. 1908.

56. John Sweetman to Eoin MacNeill, 25 June 1909, NLI, MacNeill Papers, 10882.

57. Richard Kearney, 'Between Politics and Literature: the Irish Cultural Journal', *The Crane Bag*, 7, 2, The Forum Issue, p. 166.

58. *Ibid*. p. 165.

59. Ó Conluain, *op. cit*. p. 162; Tomás Ó hAilin, 'Irish Revival Movements', in Brian Ó Cuiv (ed.), *A View of the Irish Language* (Dublin, 1969) p. 97.

60. W. G. Fay and Catherine Carswell, *The Fays of the Abbey Theatre, an autobiographical record* (London, 1935) p. 114.

61. J. J. O'Kelly (Sceilg), 'Arthur Griffith: some reminiscences', *CB*, XII, 9, Sept. 1922, p. 560; *Banba*, May 1902, pp 89-92.

(6)   The Keating branch and the 1916 Rising

62. UCDA, Mulcahy Papers, P7/D/6 p. 2.

63. *Ibid*. P7a/209, p. 18.

64. Ó Conluain, *op. cit*. p. 150; Ó Broin, *Revolutionary Underground*, p. 148.

65. Ó Broin, *Revolutionary Underground*, p. 169 quoting Bulmer Hobson, *The Irish Times*, 6 May 1961.

Chapter 2. PEARSE THE REVOLUTIONARY

(1)   Pearse, the IRB and Carson

1. Garvin, *op. cit*. p. 55 and p. 47.

2. Edwards, *op. cit*. p. 239, Seán Cronin, *The McGarrity Papers* (Tralee, 1972) p. 58 dates the letter as 2 Sept. 1915.

3. J. J. Horgan (compiled by), *The Complete Grammar of Anarchy* (London, 1919) pp. 26, 27.

4. *Ibid*. p. 26.

5. *Ibid*. p. 33; Robert Kee, *The Green Flag, A History of Irish Nationalism* (London, 1972) p. 528.

6. Eoin MacNeill to John J. Horgan, 16 Dec. 1913, in John J. Horgan, *Parnell to Pearse, some recollections and reflections* (Dublin, 1948) pp 228, 229.

7. UCDA, Eoin MacNeill Papers, LA 1/G371 p. 76.

8. F. X. Martin, 'MacNeill and the Foundation of the Irish Volunteers', in F. X. Martin and F. J. Byrne (ed.), *The Scholar revolutionary, Eoin MacNeill 1867-1945, and the Making of the new Ireland* (Shannon, 1973) p. 101.

9. Augustine Birrell, *Things Past Redress* (London, 1937) p. 220.

10. Michael Laffan, *The Partition of Ireland, 1911-1925* (Dublin, 1983) p. 58.

11. Hyde, *The Gaelic League*, p. 3.

12. Denis Gwynn, *The Life of John Redmond* (London, 1932), p. 380.

13. *CB*, IV, 10, Oct. 1914, p. 639.

(2) Pearse and the IRB prepare for the Rising

14. Ó Broin, *Revolutionary Underground*, p. 164.
15. Earnan de Blaghd, 'Hyde in Conflict', in Seán Ó Túama (ed.), *The Gaelic League Idea* (Cork and Dublin, 1972) p. 36.
16. UCD, Folklore Dept., Hyde Memoir.
17. J. J. O'Kelly, *Cathal Brugha* p. 4.
18. Edwards, *op. cit.* pp 236, 237.
19. *Ibid.* p. 238.
20. P. S. O'Hegarty, *A History of Ireland under the Union, 1801-1922* (London, 1952) p. 700.
21. P. H. Pearse, *From a Hermitage* (Dublin, 1915) pp. 11, 12.
22. *New Ireland*, 15 April 1916.
23. Edwards, *op. cit.* pp 261, 262.
24. *Ibid.* pp 241, 242.
25. Ó Broin, *Revolutionary Underground*, p. 161 and pp 165-168.
26. Colonel P. J. Hally, 'The Easter Rising in Dublin. The Military Aspects', *The Irish Sword*, Winter 1966, p. 315.
27. F. X. Martin, '1916 — Myth, Fact and Mystery', *Studia Hibernica*, 7, 1967, p. 108.

(3) 1916: Imperial considerations

28. Lyons, *op. cit.* p. 177.
29. Nicholas Mansergh, *The Irish Question, 1841-1921* (London, 1965) p.191 quoting Lord Salisbury, *The Quarterly Review*, 312, 1883, p. 584; Kee, *op. cit.* p. 420 quoting *The Times*, 5 April 1893; *Ibid.* p. 469 quoting Robert Blake, *The Unknown the Prime Minister* (London, 1955) p. 130.
30. Mark Tierney, 'A Survey of the Reports of French Consuls in Ireland 1814-1929', in Liam Swords (ed.), *The Irish-French Connection 1578-1978* (Paris, 1978) p. 134.

(4) 1916: the 'two-nation' theory

31. *The Freeman's Journal*, 20 June 1916; *The Irish Times*, 7 Oct. 1983, p. 8 for the submission of Biggs-Davison where the speech is wrongly dated as 20 June 1910.
32. J. J. O'Kelly, *Fr Michael O'Flanagan, Sceilg's Graveside Oration* (Dublin, 1942) pp 1-4; J. Anthony Gaughan, *Memoirs of Constable Jeremiah Mee, R.I.C.* (Dublin, 1975) pp 55, 56; *The Sligo Champion, Sesquicentenary 1836-1986*, p. 57.
33. M. O'K, Fr O'Flanagan's personal statement to his Bishop, 6 April 1925.
34. *The Freeman's Journal*, 8 Sept. 1917, p. 6; Paul Bew, *Conflict and Conciliation in Ireland 1890-1910* (Oxford, 1987) pp 218, 219.
35. Kee, *op. cit.* p. 473 and pp 626, 627 for analysis of the 1918 election.
36. A. T. Q. Stewart, *The Ulster Crisis, Resistance to Home Rule, 1912-1914* (London, 1979. First pub. 1967) p. 49 and p. 68; Patrick Buckland, *Irish Unionism Two. Ulster Unionism and the origins of Northern Ireland 1886-1922* (Dublin, 1973) p. 93 and frontpiece for map of Parliamentary representation.

37. A. S. Green to *The Westminster Gazette*, 13 May 1912 in NLI, A. S. Green Papers, 9932.

38. Kee, *op. cit.* p. 480 quoting Denis Gwynn, *Life of John Redmond* (London, 1931) p. 232.

39. *The Freeman's Journal*, 9 June 1920.

40. *The Irish Times*, 7 Oct. 1983, p. 8.

41. Sir Horace Plunkett, *Ireland in the New Century* (London, 1905). First pub. 1904); Mgr. M. O'Riordain, *Catholicity and Progress in Ireland* (London, 1905).

42. Brian Murphy, 'The Canon of Irish History: some Questions', *Studies*, 77, 305, Spring 1988, pp 76-78.

43. *Ibid.* pp 69-75.

(5)   Pearse: right or wrong?

44. *Sunday Tribune*, 30 March 1986.

45. Kee, *op. cit.* p. 583; Richard Murphy, 'Walter Long and the Making of the Government of Ireland Act, 1919-20', *IHS*, XXV, 97, May 1986, pp 87, 88.

46. Hubert Jedin (ed.), *History of the Church, X. The Church in the Modern Age* (New York, 1981. First pub. 1979) pp 40, 41; Roger Aubert (ed.), *The Christian Centuries, Vol. V. The Church in a Secularised Society* (London, 1978) p. 541.

47. Shane Leslie, *Cardinal Gasquet* (London, 1953) p. 238.

48. G. K. Chesterton, *Irish Impressions* (London, 1919) p. 41.

49. Francis Shaw, 'The Canon of Irish History', p. 145.

50. *CB*, May-June 1916, VI, 5 and 6, p. 246. The May issue was suppressed; it is to be found, in part, in the bound volumes for 1938.

(6)   Pearse and the New Ireland Forum

51. *The Irish Times*, 3 May 1984, p. 10 section 3.5.

52. A. T. Q. Stewart, *Edward Carson* (Dublin, 1981) p. 125.

53. Ireland Today. Bulletin of the Department of Foreign Affairs, Special Issue, Nov. 1985, p. 4, article 1(a).

54. *The Irish Times*, 3 May 1984, p. 10, section 3.1.

55. *Ibid.* sections 3.14 and 3.20.

56. Conor Cruise O'Brien, '1891-1916', in Conor Cruise O'Brien (ed.), *The Shaping of Modern Ireland* (Dublin, 1970. First pub. 1960) p. 23.

Chapter 3. THE EMERGENCE OF A REPUBLICAN MOVEMENT AFTER 1916

(1)   Ireland after the Rising of 1916

1. Leon Ó Broin, 'Joseph Brennan and the Administration of Ireland (1912-1922)', Private Paper, p. 13; Leon Ó Broin, *No Man's Man* (Dublin, 1983) for an invaluable study of the life of Joseph Brennan.

2. PROE, CO 904/23/2 for Proclamations after the Rising.

3. SPO, CSO, Press Censorship Records 1917-1919, Blue Cards, 47 (new),

20 Aug. 1919; James Carty, *Bibliography of Irish History, 1919-1921* (Dublin, 1936), p. XVII.

4. PROE, CO, 904/161/3 for the Police report on the distribution of anti-recruiting and seditious literature in 1915; SPO, CSO, Press Censor's Office, White Cards, no. 70.

5. Lord Decies to Attorney General, 5 Sept. 1916, SPO, CSO, Press Censorship Records, White Cards 1916-1917, no. 54. James Campbell was the Attorney General.

6. Note from the Chief Secretary's Office, 16 Nov. 1917, initialled W. P. B., PROE, CO, 904/161/10.

7. *CB*, VII, 4, April 1917, p. 202.

8. O'Farrell, *op. cit.* p. 285; Lyons, *op. cit.* p. 101; Garvin, *op. cit.* p. 76.

9. Garvin, *op. cit.* p. 76.

10. Richard Davis, 'The Advocacy of Passive Resistance in Ireland, 1916-1922', *Anglo-Irish Studies*, 111, 1977, p. 38.

11. *The Freeman's Journal*, 22 June 1916, p. 7.

12. David Miller, *Church, State and Nation in Ireland 1898-1921* (Dublin, 1973) pp 329, 330.

13. UCDA, Mulcahy Papers, P7a/209, p. 51.

14. UCD, Folklore Dept., Hyde Memoir.

15. UCDA, Mulcahy Papers, P7a/209, p. 50; Ó Broin, *Revolutionary Underground*, p. 175.

16. *Ibid.* P7/D/36, p. 2; and P7a/209, p. 52.

17. *Ibid.* P7a/209, p. 52.

18. Ó Broin, *Revolutionary Underground*, p. 179.

19. *CB*, IX, 8, Aug. 1919, p. 410, Brian Farrell, *The Founding of Dáil Eireann, Parliament and Nation Building. Studies in Irish Political Culture 2* (Dublin, 1971) p. 11; Michael Laffan, 'The Unification of Sinn Féin, *IHS*, XVII, 67, March 1971, p. 354.

20. *Ibid.* p. 411. This unsigned article entitled, 'Report of the Irish National Aid and Volunteer Dependents Fund', pp 410-436, was written by J. J. O'Kelly in his capacity as Treasurer of the Society.

21. NLI, Devoy Papers, 18100, Report of John Archdeacon Murphy, p. 4.

22. J. J. O'Kelly, 'Michael Collins: an attempt to appreciate his complex personality', *CB*, XII, 10, Oct. 1922, p. 627.

23. Miller, *op. cit.* pp 342, 343; *The Irish Nation League. Objects and Provisional Constitution* (Dublin, 1916) pp 3-8.

24. Lawrence Ginnell to Stephen M. O'Mara, 16 Aug. 1916, Private Papers.

25. *Ibid*, Lawrence Ginnell to Bishop O'Dwyer, 11 Aug. 1916, Limerick Diocesan Archives, Bishop O'Dwyer Papers quoted in Edward P. O'Callaghan, *Bishop Edward Thomas O'Dwyer and the Course of Irish Politics 1870-1917* (Unpublished MA Thesis, UCG, 1977) pp 359, 360.

26. *The Irish Times*, 11 Sept. 1916, p. 3; PROI, Sinn Féin Funds Case, (39), p. 35; George Murnaghan to A. B. Walsh, Dublin Diocesan Archives, A. B. Walsh Papers, 385/7.

27. *The Irish Nation League*, objects 1, 2, 3 and 5.

28. *The Irish Nation*, 15 July 1916, p. 5.
29. *Ibid*. 19 Aug. 1916, p. 3 for offer of co-operation; 16 Sept. 1916 for rejection of union.
30. *The Irishman*, 16 Sept. 1916.
31. *Ibid*. 4 Nov. 1916.
32. *Ibid*. 16 Sept. 1916; 14 Oct. 1916.
33. *Ibid*. 4 Nov. 1916.
34. *Ibid*. 25 Nov. 1916.
35. *Ibid*. 18 Nov. 1916 supplement.
36. *The Irish Nation*, 2 Dec. 1916; 25 Nov. 1916 for the letter of Pim to Frank Healy, the O'Brienite candidate.
37. Pim to Lord Decies, 2 Oct. 1916, SPO, CSO, White Cards 1916-1917 (9).
38. *Ibid*. Lord Decies to Under-Secretary, 7 Dec. 1916.

(2)   Count Plunkett and the North Roscommon by-election
39. PROI, Sinn Féin Funds Case, (39), pp 12, 13; Farrell, *op. cit*. p. 12.
40. M. O'K, Statement by Fr O'Flanagan, pp 4-8.
41. *Ibid*. Minute books of the Society of the Preservation of the Irish Language (SPIL), V and VI.
42. Count Plunkett to J. J. O'Kelly, 7 Jan. 1917, *Ibid*.
43. *CB*, VII, 1, Jan. 1917, pp 53-57.
44. Geraldine Plunkett Dillon, 'The North Roscommon Election', *Capuchin Annual*, 1967, p. 338.
45. Labhras Breathnach, *An Pluinceadach* (Dublin, 1971) pp 49, 50.
46. *Ibid*. pp 50, 51; *The Wolfe Tone Annual* (Dublin, 1935) p. 45 and *Ibid*. (Dublin, 1946) pp 75, 76 gives Count Plunkett's statement. He says he was 'commissioned by the Executive of the Irish Volunteers'.
47. J. J. O'Kelly, 'Arthur Griffith: some reminiscences', *CB*, XII, 9, Sept. 1922, pp 563, 564.
48. Louis Walsh, 'The Campaign in North Roscommon', *Nationality*, 14 April 1917, pp 5, 6; Fr Michael O'Flanagan, 'The Roscommon Election', *CB*, VII, 3, March 1917, pp 146-151.
49. *CB*, VII, 1, Jan. 1917, pp 53-57.
50. Gavan Duffy to F. O'Connor, 10 April 1917, NLI, Gavan Duffy Papers, 5581(117).
51. PROE, CO 904/23/3 for 'The Sinn Féin Movement', p. 4 and pp 1-20 for Count Plunkett's address and other speeches.

(3)   Count Plunkett and his Convention of April 1917
52. Trinity College, Dublin, Archives, (TCDA) Dr Thomas Dillon Memoir, 3738, p. 1.
53. Fathers of the Society of Jesus, *A Page of Irish History: Story of University College Dublin 1883-1909* (Dublin and Cork, 1930) p. 491.
54. NLI, William O'Brien Papers, 15653(3).
55. F. O'Connor to Gavan Duffy, 25 March 1917, NLI, Gavan Duffy Papers, 5581(101); Laffan, 'The Unification of Sinn Féin', p. 359.

56. J. J. O'Kelly, *Stepping Stones* (Dublin, 1934) p. 4, PROI, Sinn Féin Funds Case, (39), p. 16.

57. Capt R. J. H. Shaw to Lord Decies, 26 Nov. 1917, SPO, CSO, Press Censorship Records, Blue Cards 1917-1919 (1 old).

58. *Nationality*, 31 March 1917.

59. Hon. Sec of Irish Nation League to Count Plunkett, 24 March 1917, NLI, Gavan Duffy Papers, 5581(99).

60. *Nationality*, 24 Feb. 1917.

61. J. J. O'Kelly to Gavan Duffy, 30 March 1917, NLI, Gavan Duffy Papers, 5581(105).

62. *Ibid.*

63. Gavan Duffy to F. O'Connor, 10 April 1917, *Ibid.*, 5581(117).

64. TCDA, Dr Thomas Dillon Memoir, 3738, p. 11; Thomas Dillon, 'Ireland, 1865-1921', *University Review*, 111, 8, p. 82.

65. Dillon, 'Ireland, 1865-1921', p. 83.

66. *Nationality*, 28 April 1917.

67. NLI, Count Plunkett Papers, 11383(1).

68. *CB*, VII, 5, May 1917, p. 278 quoting the *Evening Herald*.

69. Dillon, 'Ireland, 1865-1921', p. 83.

70. TCDA, Dillon Memoir, p. 2.

71. *CB*, VII, 5, May 1917, p. 279.

72. Laffan, 'The Unification of Sinn Féin', pp 367, 368.

(4) Count Plunkett and his differences with Arthur Griffith

73. Dillon, 'Ireland, 1865-1922', p. 83.

74. Béaslaí, 1, *op. cit.*, pp 151-153.

75. Miller, *op. cit.* p. 355.

76. *Ibid.*

77. *Ibid.*

78. *The Irish Times*, 21 May 1917.

79. Report of Owen Brien, 21 May 1917, PROE, CO, 904/23/3.

80. Sinn Féin Executive of Tralee to Count Plunkett, 22 May 1917, NLI, Count Plunkett Papers, 11383(9).

81. Florence O'Donoghue, 'Re-organisation of the Irish Volunteers 1916-1917', *Capuchin Annual*, 1967, p. 382.

82. Liam de Róiste to Mansion House Committee, 2 June 1917, Private Papers.

83. Mary MacSwiney to Count Plunkett, 30 May 1917, NLI, Count Plunkett Papers, 11383(6).

84. Robert Brennan, *Allegiance* (Dublin, 1950), p. 153.

85. William O'Brien to Dr T. Dillon, 28 May 1917, NLI, William O'Brien Papers, 15653(3); NLI, Gavan Duffy Papers, 5581(160); *Nationality*, 9 June 1917, p. 1 for a tribute to F. J. O'Connor.

86. Thomas Dillon, 'Birth of the new Sinn Féin and the Ard Fheis, 1917', *Capuchin Annual*, 1967, p. 396.

87. Fr O'Flanagan, *The Strength of Sinn Féin* (Dublin, 1934) pp 5, 6.

88. TCDA, Dillon Memoir, 3738, p. 3.

89. *Nationality*, 23 June 1917, p. 5.
90. Nicholls to Duffy, 14 Sept. 1917, NLI, Gavan Duffy Papers, 5581(178); 5581(161) for the June invitation.
91. *Ibid.*

Chapter 4. THE IDEALS OF REPUBLICAN SINN FÉIN

(1)   De Valera enters the arena

1. Oliver Snoddy, 'Three by-elections of 1917', *Capuchin Annual*, 1967, p. 344 quoting the *Saturday Record*, 30 June 1917.
2. *Ibid.* p. 345.
3. *Ibid.* p. 345.
4. Seán Ó Luing, *I die in a good cause. A study of Thomas Ashe idealist and revolutionary* (Dublin, 1970) pp 129, 130; UCDA, Mulcahy Papers, P7a/209, p. 60; J. Anthony Gaughan, *Austin Stack, Portrait of a Separatist* (Dublin, 1977) p. 72.
5. *Nationality*, 14 July 1917.
6. Interview with Fr Bernard O'Dea O.S.B.
7. Bishop Fogarty, *The Great Bishop of Limerick* (Dublin, 1917) p. 16; *CB*, VII, 9, Sept. 1917, pp 587-590 for obituary of Bishop O'Dwyer.
8. O'Donoghue, 'Reorganisation of the Irish Volunteers', p. 384; General Richard Mulcahy, 'The Irish Volunteer Convention 27 October 1917', *Capuchin Annual*, 1967, p. 404.
9. *Ibid.* p. 384.
10. Ó Luing, *op. cit.* p. 187.
11. *The Irish Nation*, 6 Oct. 1917 quoting *The Freeman's Journal*, 26 Sept. 1917.
12. *CB*, VII, 12, Dec. 1917, p. 778.
13. *Ibid.* p. 776.
14. Ó Luing, *op. cit.* p. 189.
15. PROE, CO 904/166, Press Censorship Reports, Oct. 1917.

(2)   The Sinn Féin and Volunteer Conventions, October 1917

16. TCDA, Dillon Memoir, 3738, p. 4.
17. PROI, Sinn Féin Funds Case, (39), p. 22; J. J. O'Kelly, *A Trinity of Martyrs* (Dublin, n.d.) p. 40.
18. *CB*, VII, 12, Dec. 1917, pp 709, 710; PROI, Sinn Féin Funds Case, (39), p. 26 where the judge asked J. J. O'Kelly to produce the Bulletin's copy of the Sinn Féin constitution as no other was available.
19. TCDA, Dillon Memoir, 3738, p. 4.
20. Brennan, *op. cit.* p. 155.
21. *Nationality*, 3 Nov. 1917, p. 1.
22. PROE, CO 904/23/5 Police report by Owen Brien on the Sinn Féin Convention; Brennan, *op. cit.* pp 154, 155.
23. The Earl of Longford and Thomas P. O'Neill, *Eamon de Valera* (Dublin, 1970) pp 68, 69.
24. Mulcahy, 'The Irish Volunteer Convention', p. 407.

25. *Ibid*. pp 408, 409; O'Donoghue, 'Reorganisation of the Irish Volunteers', p. 384.
26. UCDA, Mulcahy Papers, P7/D/36 p. 6; P7/D/96(4) for Risteard Mulcahy (son of the General) to Béaslaí, 9 Jan. 1962, maintaining that Béaslaí's *Michael Collins and the Making of a New Ireland*, *I*, p. 175, p. 197 and p. 261 incorrectly states Brugha to be Chief-of-Staff of the Volunteers and has caused many others to make this mistake.
27. *Ibid*. P7/D/6 p. 11.
28. *Ibid*. P7/D/36 p. 5.
29. *Ibid*.
30. *Ibid*. P7a/209 p. 63; Florence O'Donoghue, *No Other Law* (Dublin, 1954) p. 189 gives the IRA strength for Cork, Kerry and Waterford in 1921 as 31,000; Townshend, *The British Campaign in Ireland 1919-1921* for all Ireland as 5,000.
31. *Ibid*. p. 64, O'Donoghue, *No Other Law*, p. 189 gives the IRB strength for Cork, Kerry and Waterford in 1921 as 1,170; Ó Broin, *Revolutionary Underground*, p. 196 gives the IRB strength for all Ireland in June 1921 as 1,617.
32. Thomas Dillon, 'Birth of the New Sinn Féin', p. 398.
33. Pádraig Ó Fearail, *The Story of Conradh na Gaeilge* (Dublin, 1975) pp 44, 45; Garvin, *op. cit.* p. 79 gives the number of branches in 1913 as c.1,000 and the impression that the League was expanding. Ó Fearail's figure for 1913 is c.500 and a graph of membership shows a marked decline.
34. PROI, Sinn Féin Funds Case, (39), pp 33, 34.

(3)   Griffith, Collins, de Valera and republican Sinn Féin
35. Review of Béaslaí, *Michael Collins*, by W. J. W. in *Studies*, XVI, 27, March 1927, pp 152-154.
36. Brennan, *op. cit.* pp 152, 153.
37. Ó Broin, *Revolutionary Underground*, p. 184.
38. Hayden Talbot, *Michael Collins' Own Story* (London, n.d.) p. 65.
39. PROE, CO 904/23/5 p. 50 of Report of Sinn Féin Convention.
40. Brennan, *op. cit.* p. 153.
41. M. A. Fottrell, 'The Angelus', *CB*, VIII, 11, Nov. 1918, p. 552.
42. *Irish Independent*, 26 Nov. 1917.
43. PROE, CO 904/166, Press Censorship report for end of Dec. 1917.
44. UCDA, MacNeill Papers, LA 1/G 371, p. 144.
45. *Irish Independent*, 24 Sept. 1917.
46. Dáil Eireann, *Official Report 1921-22*, 16 Aug. 1921, p. 9.
47. *Ibid*.

(4)   Count Plunkett, Fr O'Flanagan, Brugha, J. J. O'Kelly and republican Sinn Féin
48. Béaslaí, *op. cit.* 1, p. 79.
49. UCDA, Mulcahy Papers, P7/D/96(3).
50. J. J. O'Kelly, *A Trinity of Martyrs*, pp 102, 103; Gaughan, *Austin Stack*, p. 25.

51. Nicholls to Gavan Duffy, 4 April 1917, NLI, Gavan Duffy Papers, 5581 (114); O'Connor to Gavan Duffy, 4 April 1917, *Ibid*. 5581(115).
52. UCDA, Mulcahy Papers, P7a/209, p. 59.
53. George Noble Plunkett, 'At the Foot of the Cross', *Studies*, March 1917, p. 114.
54. Fr Michael O'Flanagan, 'Colonial Home Rule', *CB*, Sept. 1917, p. 548.
55. PROE, CO 904/23/5, p. 26.
56. Fr Michael O'Flanagan, *The Strength of Sinn Féin*, p. 6.
57. *Ibid*. p. 8.

(5)   The republican element in the First Dáil Eireann of 1919
58. UCDA, Mulcahy Papers, P7/D/5, p. 2; Ó Broin, *Revolutionary Underground*, p. 181.
59. *Ibid*. P7/D/39, p. 5; p. 14; and p. 6.
60. Béaslaí, *op. cit*. p. 225.
61. Brennan, *op. cit*. p. 202.
62. *Ibid*. p. 168.
63. Patricia Lavelle, *James O'Mara, A staunch Sinn Féiner 1873-1948* (Dublin, 1961) pp 121-132.
64. UCDA, Mulcahy Papers, P7/D/39, pp 15, 16.
65. PROE, CO 904/167/1, p. 292.
66. Dáil Eireann, *Minutes of Proceedings of the First Parliament of the Republic of Ireland, 1919-1921* (Dublin, 1921), 21 Jan. 1921, p. 16.
67. *Ibid*. p. 20.
68. *Ibid*. p. 23.
69. Thom's Irish Who's Who (Dublin, 1923) p. 41; Fr Peter Coffey, 'Belgium's new Cardinal: a sketch of his life work', *IER*, July 1907, pp 30-43; Patrick J. Corish, *The Irish Catholic Experience. A Historical Survey* (Dublin, 1985) p. 240.
70. Miller, *op. cit*. p. 444, 445; Brian Farrell, *op. cit*., pp 57-61 for Seán T. O'Kelly's role in the drafting of the Programme.
71. Fr Peter Coffey, 'James Connolly's Campaign against Capitalism', *CB*, April-Aug. 1920.
72. PROE, CO 904/167/2, p. 418 of Press Censorship reports for Jan. 1919.

Chapter 5. COLLINS AND THE REPUBLIC
(1)   Collins and Cope

1. Dáil Eireann, *Official Report, Debate on the Treaty between Great Britain and Ireland* (Dublin, n.d.) 22 Dec. 1921, p. 133.
2. M. Collins to Seán T. O'Kelly, 28 April 1922, SPO, DE 2/514.
3. Seán T. O'Kelly to M. Collins, 1 May 1922, *Ibid*.
4. M. Collins to Seán T. O'Kelly, 2 May 1922, *Ibid*.
5. Richard Murphy, 'Walter Long', p. 87.
6. Townshend, *op. cit*. pp 78-81; J. W. Wheeler-Bennett, *John Anderson, Viscount Waverley* (London, 1962) p. 48; John McColgan, *British Policy and the Irish Administration, 1920-22* (London, 1983) pp 4-21; Murphy, 'Walter Long', pp 88, 89.
7. Wheeler-Bennett, *op. cit*. p. 60.

8. *Ibid*. p. 60.

9. Uinseann MacEoinn, *Survivors* (Dublin, 1980) pp 321, 322 for the recollection of Tony Woods who was involved in the incident.

10. General Sir C. N. F. Macready, *Annals of an Active Life, II* (London, n.d.) p. 493 and p. 491.

11. Thomas Jones (K. Middlemas ed.), *Whitehall Diary, III: Ireland 1918-1925* (London, 1971) p. 74.

12. The Parliamentary Debates, 5th series, vol. 56, 5 March 1924, c.535, 536.

13. General Macready to Lloyd George, 1 May 1920, Lloyd George Papers (LGP), F/36/2/13.

14. Lord French to Lloyd George, 27 July 1920, LGP, F/48/6/37.

(2) Collins and peace initiatives

15. Wheeler-Bennett, *op. cit.* p. 72; Frank Gallagher (T. P. O'Neill ed.), *The Anglo-Irish Treaty* (London, 1965) pp 19, 20.

16. PROE, William Wylie Papers, 30/89/1, p. 16.

17. *Ibid*. pp 18-20.

18. Corrigan Papers, NLI, 24379, 24380.

19. Recollection of Mrs Máire Brennan of her father, Andrew Byrne, who worked at Corrigan's all his life and who knew Collins.

20. Gallagher's account records that both Griffith and Anderson were in Corrigan's office but did not meet; Wheeler-Bennett gives the view of Wylie that a personal meeting did take place. As Wylie was present it would appear reasonable to accept his account.

21. Wheeler-Bennett, *op. cit.* p. 72.

22. SPO, DE 2/251 extracts from *The Irish Times*, 15, 16 and 17 Nov. 1965, Gallagher, *op. cit.* p. 20.

23. *Ibid. The Irish Times*, 16 Nov. 1965.

24. Macready to Anderson, 2 Nov. 1920, PROE, CO 904/188.

25. Anderson to Bonar Law, 5 Nov. 1920, *Ibid*.

26. Wheeler-Bennett, *op. cit.* p. 73.

27. Dr Crofton and Gen Wanless-O'Gowan to Anderson, 2 Nov. 1920, PROE, CO 904/188.

(3) Collins, Cope and Archbishop Clune

28. Lloyd George to Greenwood, 2 Dec. 1920, Lloyd George Papers, F/19/2/28 quoted in Sheila Lawlor, *Britain and Ireland 1914-'23* (Dublin, 1983) p. 72; Jones, *op. cit.* pp 44, 45; Miller, *op. cit.* pp 473, 476 (His reference to Lloyd George's letter is F/19/2/26); Dermot Keogh, *The Vatican, The Bishops and Irish Politics 1919-'39* (Cambridge, 1986) pp 65, 67.

29. UCDA, Mulcahy Papers, P7a/209, p. 130; Mark Sturgis Diary, PROE, 30/59(3), p. 7 for details of the arrests.

30. J. J. O'Kelly, 'Michael Collins', p. 631.

31. Sturgis Diary, *op. cit.* pp 13, 15.

32. T. M. Healy, *Letters and Leaders of My Day, II* (London, 1928) p. 634.

33. Sturgis Diary, *op. cit.* p. 15.

34. Margery Forester, *Michael Collins – the Lost Leader* (London, 1972. First pub. 1971) p. 176.
35. Béaslaí, *op. cit.* p. 111; SPO, DE 1/3, meeting of 4 Dec. 1920 for the official formula; Gaughan, *Austin Stack*, pp 153, 154 for the personal views of Brugha and Stack.
36. *The Irish Independent*, 6 Dec. 1920.
37. M. Collins to Patrick O'Keeffe, 6 Dec. 1920, in Béaslaí, *op. cit.* p. 113.
38. *The Irish Independent*, 8 Dec. 1920.
39. M. Collins to the editor of *The Irish Independent*, 7 Dec. 1920, in Béaslaí, *op. cit.* p. 115 and p. 118.
40. Sturgis Diary, *op. cit.* pp 24, 25, Béaslaí, *op. cit.* p. 123; Jones, *op. cit.* p. 44.
41. Béaslaí, *op. cit.* pp 135, 136.
42. *Ibid.* pp 137, 138.
43. Jones, *op. cit.* p. 47.
44. Béaslaí, *op. cit.* p. 139.
45. *The Plain People*, 30 April 1922, p. 1.
46. *CB*, Jan. 1922, p. 1.
47. Béaslaí, *op. cit.* p. 138.

(4)   Collins: a price on his head?
48. Macready to Anderson, 5 March 1921, PROE, CO 904/188.
49. Anderson to Macready, 8 March 1921, *Ibid.*
50. Cope to W. Churchill, 19 March 1922, LGP, F/20/2/70.
51. Macready to Anderson, 8 April 1921, *Ibid.*
52. Anderson to Macready, 9 April 1921, *Ibid.*
53. Anderson to Chief of Police, 28 June 1921, *Ibid.*
54. Dáil Eireann, *Official Report, Debate on the Treaty between Great Britain and Ireland* (Dublin, n.d.) p. 327.
55. *The Freeman's Journal*, 5 Jan. 1922, p. 4.
56. *Ibid.*
57. Dáil Eireann, *Official Report, for the periods 16 Aug. to 26 Aug. 1921 and 28 Feb. to 8 June 1922* (Dublin, n.d.), 27 April 1922, p. 320.
58. *Ibid.* p. 321.
59. Sturgis Diary, *op. cit.* 30/59(5), for 13 Nov. 1921.
60. *Ibid.* for 15 Aug. 1921.
61. Jones, *op. cit.* p. 174.
62. Frank Pakenham, *Peace by Ordeal* (London, 1935) p. 94.
63. Ó Broin, *Revolutionary Underground*, p. 202. He takes the story from Pakenham.
64. Béaslaí, *op. cit.* p. 140.
65. UCDA, Mulcahy Papers, P7a/209, p. 131.
66. *Ibid.* p. 87.
67. David Neligan, *The Spy in the Castle* (London, 1968) p. 134 and pp 154, 155. Neligan also tells of the £10,000 reward for Collins on p. 135 and pp 181, 182.
68. Sturgis Diary, *op. cit.* 30/59(4), 13 July 1921.

69. *Ibid*. 23 June 1921.
70. Report on Release of de Valera, 25 June 1921, LGP, F/19/5/7.
71. Sturgis Diary, *op. cit*. 30/59(4), 30 June 1921.
72. Anderson to Greenwood, 30 June 1921, LGP, F/19/5/8.
73. Sturgis Diary, *op. cit*. 30 June 1921.
74. SPO, DE 2/247, pencil note of 11 July signed 'Bob'.
75. Padraic O'Farrell, *The Seán MacEoin Story* (Dublin and Cork, 1981) p. 64.
76. Sturgis Diary, *op. cit*. 30/59(4), 10 July 1921.
77. *Ibid*. 11 July 1921.
78. Macready, *op. cit*. p. 571.
79. *Ibid*. p. 493.
80. Healy, *op. cit*. p. 637.
81. Gaughan, *Austin Stack*, p. 154.

(5) Collins meets Cope
82. UCDA, Mulcahy Papers, P7a/209, p. 131.
83. PROE, Cab. 24/126 C.P. 3138. Report on Revolutionary organisations in the UK for the week ending 16 July 1921.
84. Jones, *op. cit*. p. 141.
85. *Ibid*. p. 150; Pakenham, *op. cit*. pp 176, 177.
86. Macready, *op. cit*. pp 655-659 and p. 640; Thomas Towey, 'The Reaction of the British Government to the 1922 Collins-de Valera Pact', *IHS*, XXII, 85, March 1980, pp 67-76 for Cope and the Pact.
87. Memo to L. Curtis, 27 June 1922, PROE, CO/739/5.
88. Churchill to Collins, 4 Aug. 1922, PROE, CO/739/6. Further confirmation of the importance of Cope in providing arms for the Provisional Government is hardly required but other evidence does exist. Gun-running rather than formal communiqués of the British diplomatic service provides the background to this evidence, and the central figure in the enterprise was Francis W. Fitzgerald, brother of Desmond (minister of External Affairs in the Free State Government) and uncle of Garret, the former Taoiseach. A secret report was submitted to Winston Churchill on 25 August 1922 which stated that Frank Fitzgerald had been detained in London for attempting to smuggle illegally 10,000 rifles and five Hotchkiss guns from the stores of the Disposal Board. The report was extremely critical of the manner in which the Provisional Government and Michael Collins, recently dead, were evading the proper channels for obtaining arms. Although Fitzgerald was soon released, an inquiry into the incident before a committee of Public Accounts in Ireland shed light on the role of both himself and Cope in procuring arms. It emerged that on 26 June 1922 the military authorities in Dublin had paid Fitzgerald £10,000 to buy arms, ammunition and chemicals in London which were to be used by the Northern Division of the Army in Ulster. He attempted to carry out this undertaking in cooperation with Jack White, formerly commander of the Irish Citizen Army. According to White,

Mr Fitzgerald informed me that, whereas the Free State could purchase rifles openly from Mr Cope of the British Government it was desired to obtain a large number secretly for use against Ulster, so that, in the event of any of these rifles being lost in battle, they could not be identified as having been supplied to the Free State.

The recognition of Cope as the official intermediary for the purchasing of arms further substantiates earlier evidence, while the revelation that the Provisional Government were prepared to help the IRA irregulars in the North as late as 26 June 1922, just two days before the outbreak of the Civil War, serves to underline the complexity of Irish political affairs. The affairs of Frank Fitzgerald were equally complex. He was censured by the Public Accounts Committee not for bringing guns into the country but for the impropriety of his business dealings. He was found to have made profits that were 'grossly excessive;' to have provided revolvers and chemicals that were of inferior quality to those promised; and to have engaged in practices that were misleading 'and admitted to be a trick' in order to obtain money from the Free State. The committee finally concluded in 1926 that 'almost every incident in connection with the transaction calls for adverse comment.' (Secret memo. to W. Churchill, 25 Aug. 1922, PROE, CO/739/6; *Irish Independent*, 8 and 10 May 1926; *Final Report of the Committee of Public Accounts 1922-23* (T.33), and *Final Report of the Committee of Public Accounts 1925-26* (T.40).) Possibly Frank Fitzgerald was not seeking any personal profit. It is not beyond the realms of possibility that he may have been supplying the IRA irregulars after 1922 with guns paid for by the Free State — it was noted that 10,000 rifles were unaccounted for in his dealings; but his activities make it clear why, in 1922, the British were so keen to monitor carefully all movement of arms into Ireland and did so through Andy Cope.

89. Churchill to Cope, 1 July 1922, LGP, F/10/3/136.
90. Cope to Curtis, 24 Aug. 1922, PROE, CO/739/6.

(6)   Collins, the IRA and the Catholic Church
91. L. S. Amery, *My Political Life, II* (London, 1953) p. 230 quoted in Townshend, *op. cit.* p. 192; Ó Broin, *Revolutionary Underground*, p. 194; F. S. L. Lyons, *Ireland since the Famine* (London, 1971) p. 425.
92. Interview with General Thomas Maguire, Aug. 1988. For details of Maguire see MacEoinn, *op. cit.* pp 277-303; *The Irish Times*, 29 Oct. 1986, p. 7.
93. O'Donoghue, *No Other Law*, pp 174, 175.
94. PROE, CAB 24/123, C.P. 2965, 24 May 1921. (Macready submitted two memorandums; one was written on 23 May.) Townshend, *op. cit.* pp 182, 183, Jones, *op. cit.* p. 71.
95. SPO, DE 2/251, copy of *The Irish Press*, 6 Nov. 1936.
96. PROE, CAB 24/123, C.P.2945, 16 May 1921.
97. PROE, CAB 24/125, C.P.3075, 24 June 1921; Townshend, *op. cit.* p. 190.

98. Béaslaí, *op. cit*. p. 249.
99. *Ibid*.
100. Ó Broin, *Revolutionary Underground*, p. 195.
101. Townshend, *op. cit*. p. 186 and pp 192, 193.
102. Wheeler-Bennett, *op. cit*. p. 54.
103. Sir James O'Connor, *A History of Ireland 1798-1924, II* (London, 1925) p. 337.
104. *Ibid*.
105. Interview with Fr Jack MacMahon, SJ, 17 March 1917.
106. P. A. Marrinan to Wylie, 2 July 1920, LGP, F/17/1/5.
107. Cope to Anderson, 19 July 1920, LGP, F/19/2/13.
108. Sturgis Diary, *op. cit*. 30/59(4), 3 June 1921.
109. *Ibid*.
110. De Valera to Staff Attaché, Publicity Dept., 19 June 1921, PROE, CO 904/23(7); Miller, *op. cit*. p. 483; Keogh, *op. cit*. pp 73-75.
111. Sturgis Diary, *op. cit*. 23 June 1921.
112. *Ibid*. 22 June 1921.
113. Jones, *op. cit*. p. 174.
114. *Ibid*. p. 176.
115. Interview with Fr MacMahon.
116. *Ibid*.
117. Pakenham, *op. cit*. pp 75, 76.
118. Interview with Fr MacMahon.

(7) Collins, Griffith and the Republic

119. Dáil Eireann, *Debate on the Treaty*, 7 Jan. 1922, p. 332.
120. *Ibid*. p. 340.
121. Dáil Eireann, *Official Report, 16-21 Aug. 1921* and *28 Feb. to 8 June 1922*, 8 June 1922, p. 502 and 2 March 1922, p. 202 for Griffith's remark about Plunkett.
122. *Ibid*. p. 506.
123. James Hogan, Evidence to 1924 Committee, UCDA, Mulcahy Papers, P7/C/30 in Ó Broin, *Revolutionary Underground*, p. 192.
124. O'Donoghue, *op. cit*. p. 189.
125. *Ibid*. p. 190; John O'Beirne-Ranelagh, 'The IRB from the Treaty to 1924', *IHS*, XX, 77, March 1976, p. 28.
126. O'Beirne-Ranelagh, 'The IRB', p. 27.
127. Dáil Eireann, *Official Report, Aug. '21 to June '22*, 19 May 1922, p. 467.
128. Interview with General Maguire.
129. Wheeler-Bennett, *op. cit*. p. 60 and pp 71, 72.

Chapter 6. DE VALERA AND THE REPUBLIC: THE BREAK WITH SINN FÉIN

(1) · De Valera and the creation of the Republican Second Dáil

1. J. Bowyer Bell, *The Secret Army, A History of the IRA, 1916-1970* (London, 1972. First pub. 1970) p. 451.
2. Gaughan, *Austin Stack*, p. 220.

3. *Ibid.*; M. O'K, Second Dáil Minutes, (SDM) 28 Dec. 1923, p. 1.
4. *Ibid.* p. 218 quoting Irish Catholic Directory 1923, pp 608-613.
5. *Ibid.* p. 221.
6. Seán Cronin, *op. cit.* p. 137.

(2)   De Valera and the Second Dáil after the Civil War

7. M. O'K, SDM, 15 Jan. 1924, p. 2.
8. *Ibid.* pp 2-4.
9. *Ibid.* p. 5.
10. *Ibid.* 17 Aug. 1924, p. 1; Gaughan, *Austin Stack*, pp 319-359 for the minutes of 7, 8 Aug. 1924 taken from the Mary MacSwiney Papers (UCDA).
11. *Ibid.* p. 4.
12. *Ibid.* p. 5.
13. Count Plunkett to Eamon de Valera, 29 Aug. 1924, M. O'K.
14. Peter Pyne, 'The New Irish State and the Decline of the Republican Sinn Féin Party, 1923-1926', *Eire-Ireland*, XI, 3, 1976, p. 42.
15. M. O'K, SDM, 11 Dec. 1924, p. 7.
16. Cronin, *op. cit.* p. 141; Macardle, *The Irish Republic* (Dublin, 1951) p. 881 maintains that the election results were hopeful for de Valera; Charlotte H. Fallon, *Soul of Fire: A Biography of Mary MacSwiney* (Cork and Dublin, 1986) p. 122 states that MacSwiney was disappointed with the results.

(3)   De Valera and the oath: secret negotiations

17. M. O'K, SDM, 18 March 1925, p. 3.
18. *Ibid.* p. 6.
19. *Sinn Féin*, 25 April 1925, p. 5.
20. Pyne, *op. cit.* p. 51 quoting PROI, Sinn Féin Funds Case, book 49, p. 12.
21. M. O'K, SDM, 22 June 1925, p. 6 but no explicit pagination.
22. Seán MacBride review of Dermot Keogh, *op. cit.*, in *The Irish Press*, 12 April 1986.
23. *Ibid.*
24. Keogh, *op. cit.* p. 132.
25. *Ibid.* p. 131; MacBride, *op. cit.*
26. Seán T. O'Kelly to Mary MacSwiney, 5 Sept. 1925 (additions on 7 and 12 Sept.), UCDA, Mary MacSwiney Papers, P48a/136(4); and Cáit O'Kelly to Mary MacSwiney, 14 Sept. 1925, *Ibid.*, P48a/121(20).
27. Mary MacSwiney to de Valera, 18 Sept. 1925, *Ibid.* P48a/121(24).
28. *Ibid.*
29. Mary C. Bromage, *De Valera and the March of a Nation* (London, 1956) pp 215, 216; Michael McInerney, 'Gerry Boland's Story', *The Irish Times*, 11 Oct. 1968.
30. Lemass and Aiken to Seán T. O'Kelly, 2 July 1925, contained in letter of Judge Crowley to editor of *The Irish Independent*, n.d. (c. 1936), M. O'K.

(4)   De Valera and the oath: open confrontation

31. M. O'K, SDM, 15 Nov. 1925, p. 1.
32. *Ibid.* p. 3.

33. *Ibid.* 16 Nov. 1925, p. 1.
34. *Ibid.*
35. Pyne, *op. cit.* p. 54 quoting *An Phoblacht*, 20 Nov. 1925.
36. M. O'K, SDM, 15 Nov. 1925, p. 2.
37. Bromage, *op. cit.* p. 216; Bowyer Bell, *op. cit.* pp 70, 71.
38. Fallon, *op. cit.* pp 118-124.
39. J. J. O'Kelly to de Valera, 4 Sept. 1923, M. O'K.
40. J. J. O'Kelly, *The National Outlook* (Dublin, 1936) p. 10.
41. Circular report of Augusta J. Newton of meeting held in New Haven, Connecticut, 15 June 1927, M. O'K.
42. *Ibid.*

(5)   De Valera and the split in Sinn Féin
43. *An Phoblacht*, 27 Nov. 1925, p. 3.
44. J. J. O'Kelly, *Stepping Stones* (Dublin, 1939) p. 18.
45. *Ibid.*
46. Macardle, *op. cit.* pp 895, 896; Pyne, *op. cit.* pp 55, 56.
47. Pyne, *op. cit.* p. 56 quoting *An Phoblacht*, 15 Jan. 1926.
48. *Ibid.* p. 57 quoting *An Phoblacht*, 19 Feb. 1926.
49. *An Phoblacht*, 22 Jan. 1926, p. 3.
50. *Ibid.* 29 Jan. 1926, p. 3.
51. Cronin, *op. cit.* pp 144, 145.
52. *CB*, April 1926, p. 374 quoting the *Dublin Press*, 12 Feb. 1926.
53. *Ibid.*
54. J. J. O'Kelly, *The National Outlook*, p. 11.
55. Pyne, *op. cit.* p. 56.
56. Mary MacSwiney to Seán T. O'Kelly, 26 Jan. 1926, UCDA, Mary Mac-Swiney Papers, P48a/136(7). She wrote that she was sending a copy of this letter to de Valera.
57. MacSwiney to Seán T. O'Kelly, 29/30 Dec. 1925, *Ibid.* P48a/136(6).
58. *CB*, April 1926, p. 385 for extract from *The Irish Times* and p. 387 for extract from the *Tribune*.
59. 'Gentlemen the King', a single sheet pamphlet, M. O'K.
60. *CB*, April 1926, pp 376, 377 for the official statement issued by Sinn Féin.

Chapter 7. DE VALERA AND THE REPUBLIC: THE BREAK WITH THE SECOND DÁIL

(1)   De Valera and the founding of Fianna Fáil
1. M. O'K, SDM, 28 March 1926, p. 2.
2. *Ibid.* p. 3.
3. *Ibid.* p. 8.
4. De Valera to Mary MacSwiney, 9 Aug. 1923, in Thomas P. O'Neill, 'In Search of a Political Path: Irish Republicanism, 1922-1927', *Historical Studies, X* (Galway, 1976) p. 158.
5. M. O'K, SDM, 28 March 1926, p. 8.
6. *Ibid.*

7. *Ibid*. p. 3.
8. *Ibid*. p. 16.
9. *Ibid*.
10. *Ibid*.
11. *Ibid*. p. 17.
12. *Ibid*. p. 24.
13. *Ibid*. p. 25.
14. *Ibid*. pp 25, 26.
15. *Ibid*. p. 26.
16. *Ibid*. pp 26, 27.
17. *Ibid*. 29 March 1926, p. 6.
18. Mary MacSwiney to John Hearn, 9 April 1926, NLI, Hearn Papers, 15989.
19. Longford, *op. cit*. pp 245, 246; Maurice Moynihan (ed.), *Speeches and Statements by Eamon de Valera 1917-1973* (Dublin, 1980) p. 131 and p. 133.
20. A National Policy outlined by Eamon de Valera (Dublin, n.d.) p. 10.
21. *Ibid*. p. 6.
22. *Ibid*. p. 14.
23. *Ibid*. p. 14.

(2)   De Valera and his position as President of the Republic
24. M. O'K, SDM, 22 May 1926, p. 3.
25. *Ibid*. 23 May 1926, p. 3.
26. *Ibid*. pp 3, 4.
27. *Ibid*. p. 5.
28. *Ibid*. p. 26.
29. *Ibid*. p. 27. General Maguire stated during interview that his views at this time were the same as Dr Madden's.
30. *Ibid*. 22/23 May 1926, p. 5.
31. *Ibid*. 23 May 1926, p. 40.
32. *Ibid*. p. 41.
33. *Ibid*. pp 48, 49.
34. *Ibid*. p. 41.
35. *Ibid*. pp 49, 50.

(3)   De Valera and the Second Dáil: America and matters of money, Part I
36. *Ibid*. p. 53.
37. *Ibid*. p. 55.
38. De Valera to John Hearn, 29 April 1926, NLI, Hearn Papers, 15987 (marked 1925, but from the context the date is 1926).
39. Seán T. O'Kelly to Mary MacSwiney, 26 May 1926 (additions on 5/6 April), UCDA, Mary MacSwiney Papers, P48a/136(12).
40. IRA (Headquarters USA) to Mary MacSwiney, 16 June 1926, *Ibid*. P48a/124(22).
41. Seán T. O'Kelly to Mary MacSwiney, 9 July 1926, *Ibid*. P48a/124(25).
42. 'X' to Mary MacSwiney, 2 Aug. 1926, *Ibid*. P48a/136(11). From other sources the 'X' is Art O'Connor.

43. M. O'K, SDM, 18/19 Dec. 1926, p. 88.

44. *Ibid*. pp 4, 5.

45. 'X' to Mary MacSwiney, 2 Aug. 1926, *op. cit*.

46. Art O'Connor, Presd. of Dáil Eireann, to John Hearn, 6 Oct. 1926, NLI, 15988.

(4) De Valera and the Second Dáil: America and matters of money, Part II

47. *New York Times*, 30 March 1926; Seán T. O'Kelly to H. Smithwick, 17 May 1926, M. O'K (the same letter is to be found transcribed in Augusta Newton to Mary MacSwiney, 5 June 1926, UCDA, P48a/124(21); Macardle, *op. cit*. pp 986, 987. Her figures differ slightly from O'Kelly's.

48. M. Collins to James O'Mara, 1 April 1922, Lavelle, *op. cit*. p. 286.

49. M. G. Healy to James O'Mara, 6 Sept. 1922, *Ibid*. p. 290.

50. T. Smiddy to M. Collins, 28 July 1922, M. O'K, American Bonds File (H).

51. M. Collins to T. Smiddy, 28 July 1922, *Ibid*.

52. M. G. Healy to James O'Mara, 6 Sept. 1922, Lavelle, *op. cit*. pp 290, 291.

53. Macardle, *op. cit*. p. 986; M. O'K, SDM, 18/19 Dec. 1926, pp 64-71 for statements by Seán T. O'Kelly and Mary MacSwiney on the Bond-holders Committee.

54. M. O'K, SDM, 18/19 Dec. 1926, p. 38.

55. *Ibid*. p. 93 and p. 94.

56. *Ibid*. p. 95.

57. Fr M. O'Flanagan to J. J. O'Kelly, 11 April 1927, M. O'K.

58. Art O'Connor to John Hearn, 13 April 1927, M. O'K; Art O'Connor to John Hearn, 12 May 1927, NLI, Hearn Papers, 15988.

59. Fr M. O'Flanagan to J. J. O'Kelly, 11 April 1927, M. O'K.

60. Una Ford to Daithí Ceannt (David Kent), n.d. (c. Jan. 1928), M. O'K.

61. *Ibid*.

62. M. O'K, SDM, 10 Dec. 1927, p. 2.

63. De Valera to Mary MacSwiney, 14 May 1927, UCDA, Mary MacSwiney Papers, P48a/43(50).

(5) De Valera and Fianna Fáil against the Second Dáil, Sinn Féin and the IRA

64. UCDA, Mulcahy Papers, P7/D/36, p. 12; Bromage, *op. cit*. p. 86.

65. Longford, *op. cit*. pp 254, 255; Moynihan (ed.), *op. cit*. pp 149, 150.

66. *Ibid*. p. 257.

67. Ronan Fanning, *Independent Ireland* (Dublin, 1983), p. 99.

68. Pyne, *op. cit*. p. 34.

69. PROI, Sinn Féin Funds Case, Judgement of Kingsmill Moore, 26 Oct. 1948, p. 3.

70. *Ibid*. p. 50.

71. Lemass and Aiken to Seán T. O'Kelly, 2 July 1925, transcribed in letter of Judge Crowley to the editor of *The Irish Independent*, n.d. (c.1936), M. O'K.

72. *Ibid*.; *The Public General Acts passed by the Oireachtas of Saorstát*

Eireann during the year 1925 (Dublin, 1926) p. 281 seq. for the English version of the Act.

73. Original draft copies in English and Irish written by J. J. O'Kelly, M. O'K; *Wolfe Tone Weekly*, 17 Dec. 1938.

74. Statement of Army Council of IRA, 8 Dec. 1938, M. O'K.

CONCLUSION

1. *The Westminster Gazette*, 11 March 1904.
2. Edwards, *op. cit.* p. 175.
3. John Bowman, 'Shooting down old heroes and romantic dreams', *The Sunday Times*, 23 Oct. 1988, p.B.3.
4. *Ibid.*
5. Lyons, *op. cit.* p. 153; Louis Paul Dubois, *Contemporary Ireland* (Dublin, 1911. First pub. Paris 1907).
6. Louis Paul Dubois, *Le Drame Irlandais et L'Irlande Nouvelle* (Paris, 1927) p. 17.
7. *Ibid.* p. 45.
8. *Ibid.* p. 46.
9. *The Tablet*, 1 Feb. 1913, p. 182.
10. Eoin MacNeill Memoir, UCDA, LA1/G371, p. 27.
11. Al Cohan, *The Irish Political Elite. Studies in Irish Political Culture 4* (Dublin, 1972) pp 55-69.
12. PROE, Wylie Papers, 30/89/1, pp 6, 7.
13. M. O'K, SDM, 28 March 1926, p. 6.
14. R. F. Foster, *Modern Ireland, 1600-1972* (London, 1988) p. 489.
15. Francis Stuart, *Black List, Section H* (London, 1982. First pub. 1971) p. 65.
16. *Ibid.* p. 351.

Index